CHARDONNAY and FRIENDS

VARIETAL WINES OF BRITISH COLUMBIA

JOHN SCHREINER

To Ruth,

a pleasure to share
this with a fellow wine lover

John Schreiner

ORCA BOOK PUBLISHERS

Canadian Cataloguing in Publication Data
    Schreiner, John, 1936 –
    Chardonnay and friends

    ISBN 1-55143-103-3
1. Wine and wine making; British Columbia.
2. Wineries; British Columbia; Guidebooks. I. Title.
TP559.C3S35 1998   663'.2'009711   C98-910785-X

Library of Congress Catalog Card Number: 98-85662

Orca Book Publishers gratefully acknowledges the Department of Canadian Heritage for their support for our publishing programs.

Cover design by Christine Toller
Cover photograph by Wylie Photography
Interior photographs by John Schreiner
Printed and bound in Canada

Orca Book Publishers
PO Box 5626, Station B
Victoria, BC Canada
V8R 6S4

Orca Book Publishers
PO Box 468
Custer, WA USA
98240-0468

98 99 00   5 4 3 2 1

This book is dedicated to Basil Jackson, a fellow author and an old friend who wrote the first of his ten novels a few pages at a time before breakfast and then put in a full day's work as a journalist. This admirable productivity has been an inspiration whenever I needed to find spare time to write another wine book.

TABLE OF CONTENTS

WHO HAS HEARD
OF ORANIENSTEINER?

On a world scale, the vineyard area of British Columbia is tiny. However, an unusual profusion of grape varieties is grown, many of which are varietal wines whose relatively unfamiliar names keep consumers from trying them. Everyone who enjoys wine has tasted Chardonnay and Merlot and Pinot Noir and the several other extravagantly popular varieties. But who has heard of Oraniensteiner?

There are about forty-five different varietal wines being produced in British Columbia including, occasionally, an unusual white from the German grape known as Oraniensteiner. A few varieties are being abandoned but others seem likely to make their appearance. There is considerable interest in two early-ripening German red grapes, Dunkelfelder and Dornfelder, even though these thoroughly unfamiliar names would add to the challenge of selling named varietals. (At least no one in the Okanagan has any ambition to grow another obscure German red called Deckrot!) The two northern-most wineries, Larch Hills and Recline Ridge, both have planted another early red, Agria, believed to come from the Eger region in northern Hungary. One vineyard near Oliver is experimenting with three leading Italian reds, Sangiovese, Nebbiolo and Barbera, and of those, Sangiovese—the grape of Chianti—holds considerable promise to emerge as a successful varietal in British Columbia.

Some argue strongly that, as a small wine region, British Columbia should trim down to the handful of internationally recognized varieties that are succeeding in the vineyards and with consumers. The contention is varieties such as Ehrenfelser and Madeleine Angevine, to name two, are of little international consequence. The argument is logical in theory. Alsace grows eight varieties, Bordeaux has settled on six basic varieties, Burgundy on four, Chile on eight or ten, and so forth. But these areas have been growing grapes for a very long time and have been through the trial and error needed to adapt the right varieties to the soil and the climate. Wine grapes have been grown seriously in British Columbia only since the late 1920s and the vineyards have been replanted at least three times since then as growers struggle to understand their sites and to master the varieties. The latest upheaval was the massive conversion in the 1990s to vinifera grapes, the premier wine grapes, a conversion done by a generation of growers, many of whom were coming into viticulture for the first time. There is a vast selection of vinifera available. The trial and error phase is not over. That is why there is such a riotous abundance of varieties.

There are consumers whose taste in wine runs the gamut from A to B, to borrow a phrase; basically only from Cabernet to Chardonnay. Those are estimable varieties but there are many more tastes in the vineyard than those. The wine lover in British Columbia who is the least bit adventurous can explore from Auxerrois to Vidal and only is denied an A to Z experience because no one is growing Zinfandel. At least, not yet.

This book removes the mystery from buying varietal wines in restaurants, wine stores and on winery tours. Forty-four varieties are described in detail, with information ranging from the origin of the grapes to how winemakers deal with each variety. There are clues to the taste of each variety and suggestions for food matching. The producers of each variety are listed and the winery styles are differentiated. There also are chapters on sparkling wines and on various proprietary wines, including brand names cleverly created by producers who know better than to try selling varieties with names almost as unappealing as Deckrot. Oraniensteiner is tough enough.

THE WINERY TOUR GUIDE

In October 1981, Anthony von Mandl, then the new owner of the Mission Hill winery, boldly predicted the future in a speech that many at a winery reception would have had trouble taking seriously at the time. "When I look out over this valley," he said, "I see world class vinifera vineyards winding their way down the valley, numerous estate wineries each distinctively different, charming inns and bed and breakfast cottages seducing tourists from around the world while intimate cafes and restaurants captivate the visitor in a magical setting." It is von Mandl who can smile now: his vision largely had been realized. Compared with the dozen wineries in 1981, British Columbia today has nearly fifty including those on Vancouver Island and the Gulf Islands. Where the wineries once could be toured easily in a couple of days, it now takes careful planning.

With a few exceptions, the wineries are clustered conveniently. A wine tour can be built around these clusters in such a way that more of the day is spent in the winery than in traveling from one to another. What follows are touring hints for each cluster, starting from the south end of the Okanagan Valley. Wine tourists are free to tackle the clusters in any order that suits their schedules or, indeed, free to cherry pick their favourite wineries from each cluster. Almost all of the wineries are easy to find, following directions from signs on nearby main highways. As well, most have winery brochures, including directions, which can be found in tourist information centres, hotel and motel lobbies and often in the tasting rooms at other wineries. It is a paradox, but true, that winery staff usually are happy to direct you to their nearest competitor.

First, some advice on getting the most from wine touring:

• Take along a small notebook and jot down the wines and your impressions of them. It is not uncommon to taste between twenty and fifty wines in a day. Recalling your favourite wines, especially in the weeks after the tour, is difficult without notes.

• Respect a winery's right to be private. Several are open to the public only when appointments are made in advance. This does not mean that the owners are grouchy. In family-run wineries, the extremely busy family members often are unable to drop urgent winery tasks when unexpected visitors arrive. Some winery staff prefer not to be garbed in clothing soiled by vineyard mud or splashed with spilled wine when visitors come calling. It is both wise and courteous to arrange appointments with those wineries not generally open to the public. In the off-season—generally from November to April—almost all wineries require appointments since the number of visitors is so few that even tasting rooms may not be staffed every day.

• Don't complain if there are no seats in tasting rooms. Under British Columbia regulations, seating is not permitted in tasting rooms with the exception of those that are licensed for restaurant service. The regulation is silly; some wineries ignore it and most will provide a chair on request. Of course, you could always add a shooting stick to your travel kit for wine touring.

• While tasting charges now are becoming routine in some California wineries, the practice still is rare in British Columbia (and probably is against some regulation). However, it is not unreasonable for wineries to ask modest fees for tastings of icewines. Small wineries in particular can hardly afford to give away rare and expensive wines and should not be expected to do so.

• Do not be afraid to spit. It is not necessary to swallow a wine to taste it. Tasting room staff are accustomed to providing appropriate receptacles to professional tasters who, after all, need to remain sober to evaluate wines all day long. A wine tourist needs his sobriety to drive from one winery to another during the day. Tasting rooms have containers into which one can spit or dump unwanted wine. The curmudgeonly vintner who objects to his wines being spit out is rare and the wines usually prove to be as offensive as the attitude. On the other hand, common sense dictates swallowing the wine if it is particularly fine.

• Is there an obligation to buy after tasting? No. However, tasting rooms are not free bars. One long-suffering farm winery once had regular visits from a freeloading couple who dropped in after church for a small glass of wine each before lunch. It would have been courteous to buy a bottle, even occasionally, to take home for lunch. Beyond courtesy, many interesting wines are in limited supply and can only be purchased at the winery. Never count on finding a favourite bottle in the neighbourhood liquor store when you return home. Wines purchased on a tour should be allowed to rest at home for several weeks to recover from travel shock before being served.

On with the tour!

THE SIMILKAMEEN CLUSTER

Only a handful of vineyards have been developed in the Similkameen Valley along Highway 3A between Keremeos and, so far, only two wineries have based themselves there.

ST. LAZLO

Located on Highway 3A at the eastern limit of Keremeos.
Telephone: (250) 499-5600
Open daily 9 am to 9 pm.

A visit to the most rustic winery in British Columbia is made memorable by sometimes contentious wines and by the breezy informality of the tasting room.

CROWSNEST VINEYARDS

Surprise Road at Cawston; look for the sign on Highway 3A just south of Cawston.
Telephone and Fax: (250) 499-5129
Open daily April 1 to December 24 from 10 am to 6 pm.

Expect a friendly welcome in the compact tasting room, sometimes enlivened by winemaker Andrea McDonald's energetic young family.

THE OLIVER CLUSTER

There are enough wineries around Oliver—mostly south of the community—that more than one day may be needed to visit them all. If only one day is available, start early. Highway 97 is the north-south spine of the valley, with most wineries on roads leading west off the highway. All are well-signed on the highway.

GERSIGHEL WINEBERG

29690 Highway 97.
Telephone and Fax: (250) 495-3319
Open daily from 9:30 am to 8 pm.

This small farm winery is located just at the western edge of the highway where its vineyard is wedged against the mountain. The tasting room is friendly and informal.

DOMAINE COMBRET

West on Road 13, following signs to the right.
Telephone: (250) 498-8878; Fax: (250) 498-8879
No tastings. Visits strictly by appointment.

This winery produces limited quantities of elegant wines.

GOLDEN MILE CELLARS

West on Road 13, following signs to the left.
Telephone: (250) 498-8330; Fax: (250) 498-8331
Open daily May to October from 10 am to 5 pm. By appointment during winter months.

This charming little winery is designed like a copper-roofed medieval fortress with beige stonework blending into the earth tones of the hillside behind. Excellent views of the valley from this winery, which was designed by the hard-working Serwo family, among the Okanagan's most respected grape growers.

INNISKILLIN OKANAGAN

#11 Road West.
Telephone: (250) 498-6663; Fax: (250) 498-4566; Toll free: 1-800-498-6211
Open daily 9 am to 5 pm May long weekend to mid-October; open Monday through Friday from 9 am to 3 pm in winter.

The winery is planning an attractive new winery and tasting room to showcase its well-made wines.

HESTER CREEK

West end of Road 8.
Telephone: (250) 498-4435; Fax: (250) 498-0651
E-mail: info@hestercreek.com
Open daily 10 am to 5 pm June through November. Not open weekends during winter.

Formerly the rustic Divino Estate winery, Hester Creek now has an attractive tasting room enriched by wrought iron and warm wood beams, a relaxing setting in which to taste an interesting range of wines.

GEHRINGER BROTHERS

West end of Road 8 (just across the road from Hester Creek).
Telephone: (250) 498-3537; Fax: (250) 498-3510
Tasting room open daily 10 am to 5 pm July through September. Closed Sundays and Saturday afternoons during the rest of the year. Winery tours by appointment.

Often staffed by a family member, the spacious Gehringer tasting room is relaxed and cool in summer, the samples are generous and the low price of the wines makes them an exceptional value.

TINHORN CREEK

At the west end of Road 7.
Telephone: (250) 498-3743; Fax: (250) 498-3228
Toll free: 1-888-4-846-4674; Email: winery@tinhorn.com
Open daily 10 am to 5 pm except for a December holiday closing.

Dramatically set on a promontory high above the valley, this ochre-coloured chateau would be worth the visit just for the panoramic view from the spacious tasting room. The good wines and the effortless view of the winery from a nearby mezzanine are bonuses. Wine shop is well stocked with complementary artisanal products.

CARRIAGE HOUSE
32764 Black Sage Road.
Telephone and Fax: (250) 498-8818
Open daily 10 am to 6 pm from Easter until Thanksgiving. Open in the winter by
appointment.

Vintner David Wagner is the Okanagan's most passionate advocate for the white wines made from the Kerner grape.

BURROWING OWL
Black Sage Road.

Expected to open a tasting room in 1999, this winery will have a commanding view of the valley looking toward the west. With a top flight professional as consulting winemaker, the wines are expected to be notable.

JACKSON-TRIGGS (also known as Vincor International)
Just north of Oliver, on the east side of Highway 97.
Telephone: (250) 498-4981; Fax: (250) 498-6505
Open Monday through Friday from 9 am to 4:30 pm, with tours May through
October at 10 am and 2 pm. Groups of more than ten require reservations.

A contrast to small family-run operations, this is the biggest winery in the south Okanagan, featuring a large tasting room, comfortably cool in the summer, and a wine shop with an extensive selection.

THE OKANAGAN FALLS CLUSTER

Three of these wineries can be reached by turning east off Highway 97 at Oliver Ranch Road (south of Okanagan Falls), watching for direction from the winery signs—and also watching for the mountain sheep which inhabit this part of the Okanagan. Prpich Hills is five km *north* of Okanagan Falls, on Parsons Road via Eastside Road; the latter skirts, logically, the east side of Skaha Lake and can be followed all the way into Penticton if one is in the mood for a slow scenic drive. To find Hawthorne Mountain, watch for the sign at the *west* border of Okanagan Falls. If a break is needed between tastings, Tickleberry's at the south end of Okanagan Falls is famed for ice cream and pies.

STAG'S HOLLOW WINERY & VINEYARD
Sun Valley Way.
Telephone and Fax: (250) 497-6162
E-mail: stagwine@vip.net
Open daily 10 am to 5 pm from May long weekend to Thanksgiving. Winter hours by
appointment.

Distinctive green-roofed winery with a tasting room often manned by owners Larry Gerelus and Linda Pruegger. This winery is immediately adjacent to Wild Goose, enabling wine tourists to cover two wineries easily on foot from the same parking lot.

WILD GOOSE VINEYARDS

Sun Valley Way.
Telephone: (250) 497-8919; Fax: (250) 497-6853
E-mail: wildgoose@img.net
Open daily from 10 am to 5 pm.

Members of the friendly Kruger family, who own the winery, often staff the convivial tasting room.

BLUE MOUNTAIN VINEYARDS & CELLARS

Allendale Road.
Telephone: (250) 497-8244; Fax: (250) 497-6160
By appointment with the exception of Okanagan Wine Festival weeks when the winery receives visitors who drop in.

The sought-after wines, retailed almost exclusively from the winery, are in limited supply—one reason for calling ahead to ensure the tasting room has any wine. Blue Mountain's photogenic vineyards are worth viewing even if the sales room is closed.

PRPICH HILLS

Parsons Road which is left off Eastside Road five km north of Okanagan Falls.
Telephone: (250) 497-8246
Scheduled to open in the fall of 1998, with tasting room hours to be established.

The tasting room is in the only log house in the Okanagan built specifically for a winery. It affords a dramatic 360 degree view of vineyards and Skaha Lake.

HAWTHORNE MOUNTAIN VINEYARDS

Green Lake Road, five km from the end of the bridge over the irrigation channel just west of Okanagan Falls.
Telephone: (250) 497-8267; Fax: (250) 497-8073
E-mail: hawthorn@vip.net
Open daily from 10 am to 5 pm. Groups tours arranged in advance.

The narrow, winding uphill road to the winery should be driven carefully. There are good valley views from the charming tasting room located in a well-preserved heritage house. The selection of wines is extensive. There is a comfortable shaded patio in summer. Ask to see the dog cemetery beside the winery.

THE NARAMATA CLUSTER

Naramata is a quiet village on the east side of Okanagan Lake, about twenty minutes northeast of Penticton on a busy rural road with distractingly fine views across the lake. A fit cyclist can tour all the wineries in one day, or at least until the panniers sag with purchased bottles of wine.

HILLSIDE CELLARS
1350 Naramata Road.
Telephone: (250) 493-4424; Fax: (250) 493-6294
Toll free: 1-800-923-9463
Open daily from 10 am to 6 pm. Reservations required for groups of more than twenty.

The new winery building at Hillside will startle those who recall the modest roadside cottage of former years with a tasting room the size of a large closet. The winery now is a grand three-story building with a tower. Staff in the large tasting room, attractive with its rough-hewn wood beams, give a cheery, informal welcome. Ample outdoor and indoor seating for seasonal restaurant service.

POPLAR GROVE WINERY
Foot of Poplar Grove Road, a short country lane running from Naramata Road toward the lake.
Telephone: (250) 492-2352; Fax: (250) 492-9162; E-mail: poplargrove@img.net
Appointments are recommended for this family-run winery has very limited production.

Poplar Grove owners Ian and Gitta Sutherland prudently have other jobs while they nurture their winery; they may not always be on hand for wine tourists and the winery may be out of wine. The very first wine released by Poplar Grove when it opened in 1997 won a gold medal at the Okanagan Wine Festival.

LAKE BREEZE VINEYARDS
Foot of Sammet Road, a winding country road from Naramata Road toward the lake. White winery buildings are visible from Naramata Road.
Telephone: (250) 496-5659; Fax: (250) 496-5894
Open daily from 10 am to 6 pm June through October; open weekends in March and April. Closed over winter.

Swiss-born Paul and Vereena Moser lived twenty-five years in South Africa before coming to the Okanagan where, in the midst of well-tended vineyards, they replicated a Cape winery before selling it in 1999 to Wayne and Joanne Finn, a Vancouver Island business couple. The cool tasting room is built, like the wines, with meticulous artistry. Excellent lunches are available on the shaded patio in summer.

RED ROOSTER
910 DeBeck Road, a winding road which runs from the fire hall on Naramata Road west toward the lake.

Telephone: (250) 496-4041 ; Fax: (250) 496-5674; E-mail: redrooster@img.net
Open daily May through October from 10 am to 6 pm.

Swiss-born Beat (Burt) and Prudence Mahrer preside in an attractive tasting room with views to the west over their neat vineyard. A particular affection for chickens is behind the name of this winery.

KETTLE VALLEY WINERY

2988 Hayman Road, a street which runs south from the end of DeBeck Road.
Telephone: (250) 496-5898; Fax: (250) 496-5298
Appointment required.

Partners Bob Ferguson and Tim Watts have operated successfully from a sales and tasting room in a converted three-car garage, husbanding resources for their vineyards and for production of powerful barrel-aged wines, most available only from the sales room. A new winery is planned on nearby property with a commanding lakefront view.

LANG VINEYARDS

2493 Gammon Road, with good signage directing visitors uphill from Naramata Road.
Telephone: (250) 496-5987; Fax: (250) 496-5706
E-mail: kettlevalleywinery@bc.sympatico.ca
Open daily from 10 am to 5 pm May to mid-October. Winter tastings by appointment.

Located on a terrace high above the valley, this neat and attractive winery's tasting room is generous in the selection of wines offered to visitors. The tasting room often is cheerfully staffed by owners Günther and Kristina Lang.

NICHOL VINEYARD

1285 Smethurst Road, a small country road a few hundred yards beyond Naramata, which turns uphill, or east, off Naramata Road. Signs on road direct visitors.
Telephone: (250) 496-5962; Fax: (250) 496-4275
Open from 11 am to 5 pm Tuesday through Sunday from May to October. Appointments suggested for winter hours.

The vines along the driveway to the winery are trellised in the rarely-seen double lyre system, exposing a substantial area of the plant to the sun. Kathleen and Alex Nichol staff a compact tasting room, with well-crafted, original wines. The specialty is Syrah.

THE SUMMERLAND–PEACHLAND CLUSTER

These wineries are north of Penticton and on the west side of Okanagan Lake. Summerland to Peachland is an easy half hour drive, with two wineries near each community. Agriculture Canada's research station just south of Summerland has attractive gardens for a shady picnic.

SCHERZINGER VINEYARDS

7311 Fiske Street. Good signage from Highway 97 just south of Summerland directs visitors to a winery tucked away in the hills behind the community.
Telephone and Fax: (250) 494-8815
Open daily from 10 am to 6 pm April through October. Winter visits by appointment.

The tasting room's bucolic charm is enhanced by owner Edgar Scherzinger's wood carvings. The wine patio overlooking the vineyard is available for catered lunches. Fortunate visitors may also taste Elsbeth Scherzinger's renowned butter tarts. The winery's specialty is Gewürztraminer.

SUMAC RIDGE ESTATE WINERY

Just off Highway 97 north of Summerland.
Telephone: (250) 494-0451; Fax: (250) 494-3456; E-mail: sumac@vip.net
Open daily from 9 am to 6 pm. Hourly tours April through mid-October from 10 am to 4 pm.

This winery's range of wines is extensive and the tasting room is conveniently adjacent to a restaurant. Instructive tours include the sparkling wine cellar.

HAINLE VINEYARDS ESTATE WINERY

5355 Trepanier Bench Road, uphill off Highway 97 just north of Peachland.
Telephone: (250) 767-2525; Fax: (250) 767-2543; Toll free: 1-800-767-3109
E-mail: tilman@hainle.com or sandra@hainle.com
Open from 10 am to 5 pm Tuesday through Sunday, May to October, with lunch served from noon to 5 pm. Open noon to 5 pm Thursday through Sunday, November through April (closed in January).

During the summer, the creative lunches match food and wine in this attractive tasting room, stocked with local craft products as well as Hainle wines. The room is compact but there also are tables on the spacious balcony.

FIRST ESTATE CELLARS

Top end of Trepanier Bench Road.
Telephone: (250) 767-9526; Fax: (250) 767-9528
E-mail: olitech@bc.sympatico.ca
Open daily 10 am to 5 pm during summer and daily 11 am to 4 pm in winter.

This historic winery was British Columbia's first estate winery when it opened in 1978. Gary Strachan and Nancy Johnson are redeveloping a property and a vineyard which had fallen on hard times under previous owners.

THE WESTBANK CLUSTER

The community of Westbank is roughly midway between Peachland and Kelowna. The highway signage on Highway 97 nearer to Kelowna is the easiest to follow to these wineries.

SLAMKA CELLARS

2742 Cordova Way, which can be accessed from Boucherie Road.
Telephone: (250) 769-0404; Fax: (250) 763-8168
Open daily from 11 am to 5 pm April through October. Appointments required in winter.

In this family-owned winery the compact tasting room often is staffed by one of the Slamka family. The winery also offers good views over the vineyard toward Okanagan Lake.

QUAILS' GATE ESTATE WINERY

3303 Boucherie Road.
Telephone: (250) 769-4451; Fax: (250) 769-3451
Toll free: 1-800-420-9463; E-mail: quails@direct.ca
Open daily from 10 am to 6 pm June through September and 10 am to 5 pm October through May. Tours available daily from May to September.

The heritage tasting room still reflects the spirit of the original homestead. The tour is an instructive look at a well-run winery with exciting wines, the most novel being Old Vines Foch, a robust and powerful red.

MISSION HILL WINERY

1730 Mission Hill Road, which leads uphill from Boucherie Road not far south of Quails' Gate.
Telephone: (250) 768-7611; Fax: (250) 768-2044
E-mail: kmoul@markanthony.com
Open daily from 9 am to 7 pm in July and August, with hourly tours from 10 am to 5 pm. During the other ten months of the year, the tasting room is open daily from 9 am to 5 pm. There are three tours a day at 11 am, 1 pm and 3 pm in April, May, June, September and October. From November through March, tours are available at those three times on weekends only.

This large winery has one of the Okanagan's most dramatic sites. It is perched high on a mountain with a commanding view of the valley. The tasting room is large with a comprehensive choice of wines. It also is stocked with some local crafts.

THE KELOWNA CLUSTER

Pinot Reach and Calona are in the city of Kelowna while another three wineries are close together southeast of Kelowna, convenient for a morning or afternoon of touring. Highway 97 becomes Harvey Street in the city of Kelowna. Near the south end of Harvey, turn east at Pandosy Road which becomes Lakeshore Road; just follow it and watch for winery signs after about ten km.

PINOT REACH CELLARS

1670 Dehart Road, near its intersection with Casorso. Dehart is a major street intersecting Lakeshore Road on the eastern edge of Kelowna.
Telephone: (250) 764-0078; Fax: (250) 764-0771
E-mail: pinot@direct.ca
Open noon to 6 pm Tuesday through Sunday from April to October. By appointment in winter.

This new winery's simple but functional building is perched in the middle of a hillside vineyard with a panoramic view toward the city and the lake from the tasting room. There are picnic tables under a grape arbour. The winery's attractions include spunky owner Susan Dulik and her friendly Black Labrador.

SUMMERHILL ESTATE WINERY

4870 Chute Lake Road, a paved road that forks left as Lakeshore Road swings toward the lake.
Telephone: (250) 764-8000; Fax: (250) 764-2598
Toll free: 1-800-667-3538; E-mail: summerhill@summerhill.bc.ca
Open daily from 10 pm to 6 pm except for December holidays.

Formerly housed in a converted garage, Summerhill's new winery boasts the largest tasting room in the Okanagan and offers generous samples of both sparkling and still wines. The sales room also stocks local crafts. The large covered verandah is a good place to relax with a glass of wine to enjoy the view.

ST. HUBERTUS ESTATE WINERY

5225 Lakeshore Road.
Telephone: (250) 764-7888; Fax: (250) 764-0499
Toll free: 1-800-989-9463; E-mail: st.hubertus@wkpowerlink.com
Open daily 10 am to 5:30 pm May through October and noon to 5 pm Tuesday through Saturday the rest of the year.

Visitors are warmly welcomed in this neat tasting room, often greeted by members of the two Swiss families that operate St. Hubertus. A summertime feature is the massive thirty-year-old Himrod grape vine in the farmyard, producing tasty table grapes.

CEDARCREEK ESTATE WINERY

5445 Lakeshore Road.
Telephone: (250) 764-8866; Fax: (250) 764-2603
Toll free: 1-800-730-9463
Open daily 9:30 am to 5:30 pm from April to October with tours available from 11 am to 4 pm. From November through March the winery is open 9:30 am to 5 pm Monday through Friday.

Large and attractive tasting room well-stocked with local crafts. Good selection of wines for tasting poured by a knowledgeable staff. The tours provide an instructive look at a winery with a large barrel cellar. In the vineyard, a pergola with picnic tables is a relaxing stop.

CALONA WINES
1125 Richter Street. This large winery is almost in the heart of the city. Richter is a major east-west street cutting across Harvey and the winery is toward the west end of Richter.
Telephone: (250) 762-9144; Fax: (250) 762-2999
Toll free: 1-800-663-5086; E-mail: wineboutique@cascadia.ca
Open daily from 10 am to 7 pm from the May long weekend to the September long weekend; and open 10 am to 5 pm daily during winter. Winery tours daily in summer every two hours, beginning at 11 am, and daily at 2 pm in winter.

Tours are recommended of what is the largest winery in western Canada and the oldest one in British Columbia. A wide selection of wines is available in the tasting room which also sells local crafts.

THE LATITUDE FIFTY CLUSTER

Latitude Fifty cuts through Kelowna's airport which is about half an hour north of the city on Highway 97. The Gray Monk winery uses that geographical term for its largest selling wine. The wineries north of Kelowna are relatively far apart from each other. While they can be visited in one round trip from Kelowna, a more relaxed travel plan might have the day end in the Salmon Arm region.

HOUSE OF ROSE
2270 Garner Road.
Telephone: (250) 765-0802; Fax: (250) 765-7762
Open daily from 10 am to 5:30 pm.

To find this farm winery, leave Highway 97 at the north end of Kelowna and drive east on Highway 33 for six km to Garner Road. Turn right and wind slowly along through the orchards to the winery. The totally laid-back Rose family, who operate this winery, may have to be summoned from the vineyard with the sounding of a car horn. Generous samples are offered in the modest tasting room.

GRAY MONK ESTATE WINERY
1055 Camp Road. From Highway 97 as it passes through the village of Winfield, turn west on Berry Road, proceed uphill and turn right on Okanagan Centre Road; proceed a half km and turn left onto Camp Road which winds on for another four km before the winery appears.
Telephone: (250) 766-3168; Fax: (250) 766-3390
Toll free: 1-800-663-4205; E-mail: mailbox@graymonk.com
Open daily from 10 am to 5 pm May through October and from 11 am to 5 pm Monday through Saturday from November to April. Hourly tours from 11 am in summer; one daily tour at 2 pm offered during winter.

This is one of the most splendidly situated wineries in the Okanagan, a long, low building settled in a vineyard that slopes steeply toward the lake to the west. The large tasting room, well-stocked with crafts, offers generous samples from a large wine portfolio. The huge covered deck off the tasting room, sometimes used for lunches, is pleasantly relaxing on a warm summer day.

BELLA VISTA VINEYARDS

3111 Agnew Road. In mid-Vernon turn west from Highway 97 on 30th Avenue; proceed to Bella Vista Road; right on Bella Vista and uphill to the winery on Agnew Road.
Telephone: (250) 558-0770; Fax: (250) 542-1221
Open daily from noon to 5 pm.

The winery's expansive building provides a dramatic view of the valley from the large second-floor tasting room. The welcome is friendly and informal.

LARCH HILLS

110 Timms Road, Salmon Arm.
Telephone: (250) 832-0155; Fax: (250) 832-9419
E-mail: lhwinery@shuswap.net
Open daily from noon until 5 pm May through October; by appointment in winter.

South of Salmon Arm, turn east from Highway 97B onto Black Road and follow it to Timms Road. This small winery seems almost isolated on a well-treed mountainside. There is a shaded picnic table here and a friendly welcome from vintner Hans Nevrkla. Small production limits the number of wines, primarily whites, that are available.

RECLINE RIDGE VINEYARD AND WINERY

2640 Skimikin Road.
Telephone: (250) 835-2363; Fax: (250) 835-8794
E-mail: reclineridge.bc.ca

Take the TransCanada Highway west of Salmon Arm and at 14.4 km from the Centenoka Mall, turn south on Tappen Valley Road; proceed four km to Skimikin Road. The winery, nestled in a wide and scenic valley, is expected to open in 2000.

THE LOWER MAINLAND CLUSTER

PELLER ESTATES (ANDRÉS)

2120 Vintner Street, Port Moody.
Telephone: (604) 937-3411; Fax: (604) 937-5487
Toll free: 1-800-663-6483; E-mail: info.bc@andreswines.com
Open daily from 9 am to 5 pm Monday through Friday. Tours by advance reservation with a charge of $5 per person.

The tasting room has the sober atmosphere of a men's club but this is the place to buy premium wines released in limited quantity, either under the Peller Estates or Bighorn Vineyards labels.

DOMAINE DE CHABERTON

1064 216th Street, Langley.
Telephone: (604) 530-1736; Fax: (604) 533-9687
Toll free: 1-888-332-9463; E-mail: cviolet@portal.ca
Open from 10 am to 6 pm Monday through Saturday and from noon until 5 pm Sunday from March through December; and from 10 am to 5 pm Monday through Saturday in January and February. Weekend tours from 2 pm to 4 pm April through August.

The winery, only a quarter of a mile north of the U.S. border, is about an hour from downtown Vancouver by car. Take the TransCanada Highway east to the 200th Street exit at Langley and continue south until 16th Avenue; turn left, continue to 216th Street, turn right and watch for the winery on the east side of the road. Proprietors Claude and Ingeborg Violet preside with old world gallantry at this winery, named for an ancestral Violet property in France. The wines include varietals rarely seen at other wineries.

COLUMBIA VALLEY CLASSICS

1385 Frost Road, Lindell Beach.
Telephone and Fax: (604) 858-5233
E-mail: cvcwines@dowco.com
Open daily May through September from 10:30 am to 7 pm; open October through December from Wednesday through Sunday 11 am to 5 pm; open weekends only from 11 am to 5 pm from January through April.

British Columbia's only fruit winery, Columbia Valley Classics opened in 1998. Wines are produced from raspberry, blueberry, currants, blackberry, gooseberry and rhubarb. The wine shop also sells an extensive selection of jams and jellies and other imaginative gifts.

THE VINEYARD AT BOWEN ISLAND

687 Cates Lane, Bowen Island.
Telephone: (604) 947-0028; Fax: (604) 947-0693; Toll free: 1-800-718-9463

This is an elegant bed and breakfast situated in a vineyard from which commercial wines are expected in 1999.

THE VANCOUVER ISLAND CLUSTER

Most of the wineries are in the Cowichan Valley, about an hour's drive north of Victoria or south of Nanaimo. A tourist information centre on the highway in Duncan can direct visitors to the many good bed and breakfast accommodations in the valley. Note that the TransCanada

Highway also is referred to as the Island Highway.

CHATEAU WOLFF

2534 Maxey Road, Nanaimo.
From the Island Highway in downtown Nanaimo, turn west on Townsite Road; it
becomes East Wellington; continue for two km to Maxey Road and turn north to winery.
Call ahead at this tiny winery in case the wines are out of stock.
Telephone: (250) 753-4613; Fax: (250) 753-0614
Wine shop opens every Saturday from 10 am to 5 pm.

Conventional wisdom would suggest that wine cannot be produced this far north on Vancouver Island—but then proprietor Harry von Wolff is hardly conventional. The tasting room is dominated by what looks like a huge tapestry showing the German city of Heidelberg in the Middle Ages. With aristocratic forebears, von Wolff is steeped in European history. The Pinot Noir is the flagship wine.

ALDERLEA VINEYARDS LTD

1751 Stamps Road, Duncan.
Telephone and Fax: (250) 746-7122
Hours to be established.

This winery is six km east of Duncan, reached by turning off the Island Highway north of the city at Herd Road, proceeding east to Lakes Road and right on Lakes to Stamps Road. Look for the winery on the north side of the road. Proprietors Roger and Nancy Dosman have developed a meticulous vineyard and winery.

VIGNETI ZANATTA

5039 Marshall Road, Duncan.
Telephone: (250) 748-2338; Fax: (250) 746-2347
E-mail: zanatta@seaside.net
Open from 11 am to 5 pm Tuesday and Wednesday and until 7 pm Thursday through
Sunday and holiday Mondays from May to October. Appointments required November
through April.

At the south end of the city, turn west off the Island Highway onto Allenby Road; proceed to Indian Road and turn left. As it winds through the forest, it changes to Marshall Road at the intersection of Glenora Road. The vineyard lies ahead. The tasting room is in a rambling farm house which includes a restaurant. Call ahead to find out when it is open and to reserve a table. While this winery has a range of wines, it produces a sparkling wine called Glenora Fantasia which is unique to Zanatta.

VENTURI-SCHULZE

4235 TransCanada Highway, precisely one and four-tenths of a km north of the
Cowichan Bay/Cobble Hill intersection on the highway.
Telephone: (250) 743-5630; Fax: (250) 743-5638
By appointment only.

The winery's output is so limited that the tasting room rarely is open and wines sell out within days of being released. Similarly, the winery's balsamic vinegar is rare and expensive. However, Venturi-Schulze offers occasional winemaker dinners where memorable meals and hand-crafted wines are presented with singular passion by the proprietors.

DIVINO ESTATE WINERY

1500 Freeman Road, Cobble Hill.
Telephone: (250) 743-2311; Fax: (250) 743-1087

Proprietor Joe Busnardo "retired" in 1996 when he sold his vineyard and winery south of Oliver and moved to the Cowichan Valley, taking with him enough Okanagan-produced wine to keep the Divino name in the market. On Vancouver Island, he is developing a twenty-acre vineyard just off the Island Highway and is planning a new winery.

BLUE GROUSE VINEYARDS & WINERY

4365 Blue Grouse Road, Duncan.
Telephone: (250) 743-3834; Fax: (250) 743-9305
Open from 11 am to 5 pm Wednesday through Sunday.

Turn west off the TransCanada at Lakeside Road and proceed to Blue Grouse, which winds briefly through forest before coming to the gate that protects the Blue Grouse vineyard from deer. The pleasant tasting room has a peaceful view over the vineyards and the famed Esquimalt and Nanaimo rail line at the bottom of the vineyard. Proprietor Hans Kiltz's offerings include an exotic red wine unique to the winery made from a grape called Black Muscat.

CHERRY POINT VINEYARDS

840 Cherry Point Road, Cobble Hill.
Telephone: (250) 743-1272; Fax: (250) 743-1059
Open daily from 11.30 am to 6 pm.

Turn east off the TransCanada at Fisher Road, proceed to Cherry Point, turn right and drive to the winery, landmarked by a huge wine vat beside the road. This winery also operates a comfortable bed and breakfast facility (two rooms) in a peaceful rural setting that includes a small flock of sheep and a friendly sheep dog called Pinot Noir.

SATURNA VINEYARDS

130 Payne Road, Saturna Island.
Telephone: (250) 539-2254; Fax: (250) 539-3091

Saturna Lodge is an elegant seven-room country hotel with a fine restaurant that will include wines from the vineyard that was planted on the island in 1997. The first tiny vintage is expected to be released by 2000. Saturna Island, at thirty-one square km, is the second largest of British Columbia's Gulf Islands but is one of the least populated.

AUXERROIS

WHITE TABLE WINE Sometimes also called Pinot Auxerrois, this Alsace grape variety is believed to have been imported first to British Columbia by George Heiss when, in 1972, he began planting the vineyard that surrounds the Heiss family's Gray Monk Estate Winery. Because the variety produces fruit-packed white wines in cool sites, it has been a popular choice on Vancouver Island. In Alsace, it plays an important supporting role as a grape to be blended, often with Pinot Blanc, in an affordable regional generic called Edelzwicker. In British Columbia the style of the wine continues to evolve as more winemakers tackle the grape, ranging from Gray Monk's fruit-driven style to several barrel-fermented pretenders to Chardonnay's predominance.

The Producers

Alderlea

Bella Vista

CedarCreek

Cherry Point

Crowsnest

First Estate Cellars

Gehringer

Gray Monk

Hillside

Lang

LeComte

Slamka Cellars

Vigneti Zanatta

There is no agreement whether this variety should be called just Auxerrois or Pinot Auxerrois, there being some who maintain that the variety belongs to the Pinot family. Hawthorne Mountain owner Harry McWatters, emphatic that the variety is not a Pinot, decreed only Auxerrois on the winery's LeComte-labeled offering. Also settling for the single word is the pragmatic Günther Lang, who imported his vines from France to launch his first Lang Vineyard Auxerrois in 1995. "I don't like names that are too long," he explains. Other wineries have chosen the double-barreled name, perhaps calculating that the familiar Pinot half of the name has the coattails to carry the less familiar Auxerrois in the market. Andrea McDonald at Crowsnest Vineyards launched her version as Auxerrois but then added Pinot when she saw her competitors doing it. "I went with the majority," she says. The fact is that the variety, not well known in British Columbia, is hard to sell—so hard that Crowsnest decided in 1995 to put its surplus Auxerrois into an off-dry blend with 15 percent Riesling, to be sold as *Harvest Moon*. It promptly outsold Pinot Auxerrois. There also is disagreement about the pronunciation: some prefer to say "*ux*-er-wah" while others say "*oh*-zer-wah." Such unfortunate confusion has stunted the appeal of a wine that deserves a better following. Here, Lang's dictum is followed; the variety, in the interest of brevity, is called simply Auxerrois. The pronunciation is up to the reader.

The first Auxerrois vines in British Columbia are believed to have been imported by George Heiss when he and his family developed the vineyard for Gray Monk. Walter Gehringer recalls that wines from the variety were included in the periodic tastings to assess the grapes being tried under the Becker Project (the viticultural trials between 1977 and 1985 under the guidance of German plant scientist Dr. Helmut Becker). "Auxerrois often came through as the best white wine," Gehringer recalled. However, a lack of commercial nursery stock kept the variety from being widely planted in the 1980s. Wineries like Gray Monk and Gehringer laboriously propagated it from cuttings from their own vineyards but others planted Pinot Blanc, of which vines were available in quantity and which also had scored well in the Becker tests.

In the vineyard, Auxerrois is appreciated because it is vigorous, growing in an orderly upright fashion while other varieties will sprawl all over the rows. It also ripens reliably in mid-season and is winter-hardy. "It has a lot of flavour, sometimes more flavour than a Pinot Blanc," Lang maintains, explaining why he planted Auxerrois. It also ripens before other varieties that Lang grows, allowing him to spread the rush of vintage over a longer period. But it has one quirk: as the grapes begin to mature, the acidity drops gradually—as it does in most varieties—until it reaches a point where, in the words of George Heiss Jr., "it falls off the cliff. We tend to watch the natural acidity closer than the sugar content and pick by the acidity and try to catch it just before it falls. If you lose the acidity, then you lose the fruity character." Since the Gray Monk style accentuates the fruit in all of its wines, considerable pains are taken to harvest Auxerrois before it gets too ripe. "We begin testing the grapes early in the season," says Heiss, the eldest son of Gray Monk's founding family and the winery's Geisenheim-trained winemaker. The acidity in the Auxerrois is tested weekly at first and then tracked two or three times a week as harvest approaches. At Vancouver Island's Vigneti Zanatta, winemaker Loretta Zanatta bases her picking decision on flavour. "More than other grapes, I taste it a lot more," she says. Even if the sugar level is not ideal, she picks when the acid is seven to eight grams per litre, content to make a light dry wine with what she describes as a subtle almond flavour. "That was our idea when we planted it. We felt it was more of a basic table wine, nice with pasta and light seafood." Heiss prefers to harvest his Auxerrois when the acid is around ten grams even though the grapes are likely to be mature enough to make a wine only with 10 to 11 percent alcohol. Until 1994 Heiss made all of his Auxerrois in an off-dry style, which sometimes gave the wines a lively flavour of strawberry and rhubarb. Since then he also has begun making a drier version. "Auxerrois shows its fruitiness up front and the taste confirms the aroma," he believes. "I've tasted Auxerrois, if you can believe it, with a smoked rabbit sausage in a curry sauce and it did quite well."

At Hillside Cellars, former owner and winemaker Vera Klokocka produced an Auxerrois with grassy and peach undertones in the aroma and flavour, finishing crisply. The 1995 vintage, her last, won a bronze medal at an annual Vancouver competition where consumers pair white wines with fresh oysters. "I hope I can match the richness of Vera's Auxerrois," says John Fletcher, one of Hillside's new owners. In the 1996 vintage, with its naturally high acidity, the wine, fermented slowly and at cool temperatures in stainless steel, emerged dry and austere. While the winery has introduced barrels for some other of its whites, that is not planned for Auxerrois. "We'll try to keep it as a light, fruity wine," Fletcher says.

For many years the off-dry or Germanic style has dominated British Columbia Auxerrois because that also was the style preferred by Gehringer Brothers and by CedarCreek, among the other major early exponents of the variety. Peter Slamka, the winemaker and one of the owners at Slamka Cellars, draws on Auxerrois vines planted in the early 1970s, the grapes from which were sold elsewhere until the Slamka family opened its own winery in 1996. "I like my wines, of course," Slamka says, "but of all the other Auxerrois wines, I prefer Gehringers. The flavour of peach is the last thing you feel as the [aftertaste] goes away." Walter Gehringer agrees that the wine can be made in a number of styles. "We do it, keeping the fruit off-dry and appealing to a wide section of the drinking public. Done that way, the Auxerrois is probably the perfect fit for scallops." Gehringer even pairs the wine with consommé. "The softness of the acidity of the Auxerrois allows for a very smooth pairing," he finds.

When he was at CedarCreek, winemaker Ross Mirko was inspired by the 1995 Auxerrois grapes to move in another direction as well. "In 1995 we harvested the Auxerrois at 24° Brix from the estate vineyard and with only five grams of acid per litre," he said. The grapes had become golden in colour, not unlike a mature Chardonnay. "I saw no reason not to move it toward the French style." He made his 1995 Auxerrois into a dry wine and discovered what George Heiss Jr. already knew: having dropped its acidity, the wine was not especially complex. However, Mirko in 1996 went for complexity by barrel-fermenting a quarter of his Auxerrois, later blending that with the rest which had been finished in stainless steel tanks. "It's moving in the poor man's Chardonnay direction," Mirko said with satisfaction. With its spicy, oak-matured 1995 Auxerrois under the LeComte label, Hawthorne Mountain Vineyards also moved decisively toward using oak with this variety. This is unlikely ever to be a style seen from Gehringer, where the winery philosophy generally precludes the use of barrels, even for red wines.

Which style of Auxerrois will win the day remains to be seen, for all have their fans. Gehringer added to its offering a Private Reserve Auxerrois, released first from the 1995 vintage, which represents that winery's approach to making what Walter Gehringer calls a dry "Chablis style" table wine. Lang has had success with an unoaked dry Auxerrois whose flavours, he says, remind him of Sauvignon Blanc but which he packages like Chardonnay, in elegant gold Burgundy bottles. As another example, take the experience of Peter Slamka at family-owned Slamka Cellars, where Auxerrois has been grown almost as long as it has been in the Heiss vineyard. Slamka likes his Auxerrois dry and big, something he achieved in the hot year of 1994 when he made a version with almost 13 percent alcohol. He likes it better than the charmingly fruity one he made in 1995, a slightly cooler year. But wine competition judges took a different view, giving a silver medal to Slamka's 1995 Auxerrois but only a bronze to the more muscular 1994. Slamka leans in the direction of treating the wine like a Chardonnay, at least as long as it is finished dry. "A lot of people do Auxerrois sweet but it doesn't cut it," he contends. "It does not have the acid base." As he discovered when he made a 1995 Auxerrois icewine which was so sweet that the flavour recalled cotton candy.

BACCHUS

WHITE TABLE WINE The Greeks called their god of wine Dionysus and developed cults so pervasive that his feasts became four-day revelries at which even children were given wine. The Romans appropriated the same god and the same cults but called him Bacchus. This was a most secular god indeed: his caricature in a sixteenth century book shows a round-bellied fat-thighed figure guzzling from a large pitcher. According to the *Oxford Universal Dictionary*, a Bacchanalia is both a festival in honour of Bacchus and a drunken revelry. A Bacchant is a priest or priestess of Bacchus—"*hence,* a drunken reveler." What all this has to do with an otherwise benign grape variety suitable for cool climates is obscure. The variety was classified officially in 1972 at the German research station of Geilweilerhof by crossing a Riesling-Sylvaner cross with a Müller-Thurgau cross. The grape can ripen to fairly high natural sugars even in cool climates but also loses its acidity easily. The flavour and the aroma often show an almost Muscat-like spicy fruit, also with hints of peaches and apricots. The wines are ready to drink as early as six months after harvest and are at their best during the first three years.

The Producers

Alderlea

Blue Grouse

Calona

Domaine de Chaberton

Golden Mile Cellars

Gray Monk

Pinot Reach

St. Hubertus

In plant breeding, the Riesling and Sylvaner grape varieties have been crossed many times, yielding innumerable offspring capable of producing good wine. The most incestuous example is Bacchus: the parent on one side was a Riesling-Sylvaner cross and the parent on the other side was Müller-Thurgau, itself a Riesling-Sylvaner cross. Perhaps that is why the professors at Geilweilerhof named the variety for the bibulous god of wine. The vine was created to be grown in some of the northern hemisphere's cooler sites where Bacchus yields a good wine. "It is a sipping wine, a very easy drinking wine," enthuses Cherie Jones, the winemaker at St. Hubertus Estate Vineyards. "It is wonderful as an aperitif." Pinot Reach's Susan Dulik agrees. "Bacchus is a beautiful grape," noting that the variety's tropical fruit aromas already are evident when the grapes are being crushed at harvest. "It is my personal favourite. I hope it will become my signature wine. It is an unsung grape that produces the most easy-going, drinkable wine."

The variety was one of those introduced to British Columbia during the Becker Project. Gray Monk's George Heiss Sr., one of the first growers to plant Bacchus in 1980, recounts that the researchers at Geilweilerhof were furious with Dr. Helmut Becker because the vines he sent to the Okanagan came from Becker's own research station at Geisenheim rather than from the station that originated the variety. To this day, Heiss, who got his vines from a commercial nursery, submits a report each year to Geilweilerhof on the performance of the Bacchus vines in his vineyard, keeping that research station abreast of one of its creations.

"We are winning quite a lot of international medals with Bacchus," declares Claude Violet, a proprietor with his wife, Ingeborg, of Domaine de Chaberton Estate Winery. "We are known for our Bacchus. It's a very powerful wine." Violet grows about nine acres of Bacchus at his fifty-five acre estate south of Langley, the largest vineyard in the Fraser Valley. Born in Paris and the ninth generation of his family in the wine business, Violet purchased the property, then a rundown raspberry farm, in 1980. He knew from temperature records that the cool site demanded early-ripening white grape varieties and his selections included Bacchus, with vines imported in 1982 from a German nursery in the Mosel Valley. "I chose that variety because I saw it growing well in the Mosel," Violet noted. "It's a very nice wine with a lot of perfume." In 1982 Violet also imported Riesling from the same Mosel nursery. Unhappily, the Riesling was found heavily infected with the virus that causes crown gall (the galls that develop on the trunk effectively strangle the flow of sap in the vine) and Violet uprooted and destroyed all those vines. He also destroyed the handful of Bacchus that had the same virus. Even today, extreme precautions are taken in the vineyard—including dipping pruning shears into a sterilant after *each* vine is pruned—to prevent spreading the disease, should the virus flare up again.

Bacchus is early to flower and early to mature and usually is picked about mid-September. "It was designed to have the aromatics and flavour characteristics of Riesling while being earlier to ripen," Cherie Jones notes. The vine is vigorous. "Bacchus grows very well," Gray Monk's Heiss says. "It wants to almost grow too well." He has seen the production soar to a high of eighteen tons of grapes an acre, with huge bunches weighing up to a pound and a half. In most vintages, Heiss keeps what he calls this "suicidal" vine carefully in check because Bacchus suffers winter damage when it crops too heavily. It also is important to keep production to a reasonable level, perhaps four tons an acre, to produce wine with pleasantly concentrated fruit flavours, a lively acidity and enough natural sugar to achieve an alcohol level of 10.5 percent to 11 percent. Bacchus grapes also are so tasty on the vine that, as Cherie Jones says, "you could eat them for lunch." The grapes could remain on the vine to become sweeter but that would sacrifice essential acidity while the resulting higher alcohol would leave the finished wine heavy on the tongue. "We are in a northern climate and we have a crispy, nice wine," Violet says.

What the vineyard delivers is carefully preserved in the processing at Domaine de Chaberton, which starts with picking by hand. At the winery, the grapes are crushed and left with the juice in contact with the skins for nine to fourteen hours, to extract more flavour. The free-run juice—that which drains without pressing—is fermented separately from the remaining press juice. Winemakers have found that free-run juice often produces finer, cleaner-flavoured wines than the juice extracted under pressure from the press. Violet insists on gentle pressing but even then will not combine the resulting wines if the difference in quality is significant. Press wines that fail to make the cut usually end up in the winery's proprietary blends. The products made from press wines, however, are not necessarily inferior: the difference is between better and best, not better and worse.

Unlike his ancestors in winemaking, Violet does not rely on the so-called wild yeast on the grape skins to ferment his wines; he prefers a reliable culture of Champagne yeast. "We don't use the natural yeast," he explains. "Mother Nature is always doing things 50 percent good and 50 percent bad. If it is the good yeast that takes over, you have a good wine. If it is the bad one, then you have a bad vinegar." He prefers yeast strains that do their work at cool temperatures. "I ferment my white wines at very, very low temperatures, between seven and nine degrees Celsius." At that temperature, fermentation will last as long as three weeks, a cool and gentle process that retains all the lovely aromas of Bacchus and other whites.

The wine is fermented and matured in stainless steel tanks. Bacchus is not a grape suited for aging in barrels since the oak flavours easily overpower the fruit and the delicacy that is preserved in the tanks. Violet and his consulting winemaker, Elias Phiniotis, practice a certain minimalist approach to this wine, giving it only two gentle filtrations and a chilling to drop out the wine diamonds—as harmless crystals of tartaric acid are called—before bottling. As little sulphur as possible is used because only a minimal quantity is needed to protect the wine against oxidizing prematurely in the bottle. Too much sulphur, which is the most common preservative in the wine industry, diminishes the fruitiness. In any event, Bacchus is a wine best consumed in its fresh youth and should not be cellared past its third birthday.

Traditionally, producers have made Bacchus in a so-called Germanic style, with a barely perceptible hint of natural sweetness achieved by adding unfermented juice of the same type (this is called sweet reserve). As tastes have changed, there has been more demand for a completely dry wine. Violet makes both a dry and what he likes to call his "regular" Bacchus which, with only four to five grams of sugar, has just a kiss of sweetness to round out the texture of the wine. Each style has a different place on the table. Violet describes the dry Bacchus as "fruity and very delicate," recommending it as a wine with plainly made white fish such as Dover sole, cod and even lobster. "The Bacchus regular goes very well with spicy food—with Chinese food which is spicy," he believes. He also has enjoyed it with smoked or barbecued salmon, with pork chops and with other smoked foods. Susan Dulik has paired her Bacchus with everything from Japanese food (California rolls, sushi) to coconut curries. "It's a great cocktail wine on its own," she says. "It's a real crowd pleaser."

CABERNET FRANC

RED TABLE WINE In much of France this is blended with its big brother, Cabernet Sauvignon, or with Merlot. While the variety also goes into Meritage and other proprietary blends, several Okanagan growers are exploring its varietal future, aware that Cabernet Franc makes excellent reds in the Loire Valley. Tinhorn Creek's Sandra Oldfield believes the variety will emerge as one of the Okanagan's red wine stars. Domaine Combret's Oliver Combret pleads with consumers not to drink it too young but to let it age in the bottle for several years. The variety generally matures a week or so before Cabernet Sauvignon which is why it has found a place in the Okanagan. The wines, with aromas of raspberries and violets—Sumac Ridge's Mark Wendenburg finds "strong, wet rose petals"—are lighter in body and may be more herbaceous than Cabernet Sauvignon.

The Producers

Calona
CedarCreek
Domaine Combret
Gersighel Wineberg
Hawthorne Mountain
Hester Creek
Hillside
Nichol Vineyard
Poplar Grove
Sumac Ridge
Tinhorn Creek

This is a French grape but its earliest proponents for planting it in the Okanagan had connections to Hungary. Consulting winemaker Elias Phiniotis of Kelowna, who was born in Cyprus but who has a doctorate in enology at Budapest's University of Technical Sciences, urged anyone who would listen in the late 1980s that this vinifera red was suitable for the Okanagan because it ripens earlier than Cabernet Sauvignon. "That was a really good decision," says Alex Nichol, who made it one of the two primary red varieties at Nichol Vineyard near Naramata. "The Cabernet Franc is very cold-hardy."

One of the first vineyard managers to plant the variety extensively was Hungarian-born Sandor Mayer, the mild-mannered but persistent winemaker who was in charge of replanting at Okanagan Vineyards (now Inniskillin Okanagan). That vineyard, which was a rock-strewn tangle of posts and trellis wires after undesirable varieties were removed after the 1988 harvest, has become, since 1991, a well-ordered property entirely dedicated to vinifera. "Cabernet Franc was planted originally for blending purposes, not to be bottled on its own," Mayer admitted in an interview some years later. It was decided from the beginning to devote just 10 percent, or two acres, of the vineyard to the variety, supporting the larger plantings of the heavy hitters, Cabernet Sauvignon (three acres) and Merlot (five acres). The decision has classic logic. Cabernet Franc plays a similar supporting role in Bordeaux and elsewhere, rising to solo status only in the warmer vineyards of the Loire where it is the author of excellent red wines. It has emerged as a varietal in British Columbia perhaps because more is available than is needed for blending with Cabernet Sauvignon. In the 1997 harvest, for example, 311 tons of Cabernet Franc were produced in the Okanagan compared with 150 tons of Cabernet Sauvignon.

"I had worked with Cabernet Franc in Hungary," Mayer says. "We had a little vineyard and I knew how to grow it and what kind of wine it makes." He smiles at the memory of those wines. "I can tell you that the wine is tough, especially in the first couple of vintages, sometimes disappointing for the winemaker, especially when the vineyard is still young. It can give you quite an unusual wine, in terms of acidity and tannin. The character is very difficult to describe—almost wild." The sharp acidity and hard tannins, both of which can be found in this grape if maturity is not ideal, are not harmonious in a wine.

Among the handful of other growers persuaded that Cabernet Franc should be planted was an Oliver grower named Joe Fatur, who owned a property on a bench overlooking the Okanagan Vineyards site. Fatur had only put in an acre of that variety before he sold his vineyard in 1992 to the Combret family, French vintners from Provence who moved to the Okanagan to establish the Domaine Combret winery. The vineyard then was primarily planted to Chardonnay and Riesling; Robert Combret would later add Gamay Noir as the major red but he was not displeased to find Cabernet Franc. "Why Cabernet Franc?" he asks rhetorically. "It is, among all the viniferas, the one which is the most winter-hardy. Cabernet Franc will die by freezing *only* at -28°C—which never happens here, in this vineyard." A man of vigorous opinions founded in his detailed viticultural research, Combret shrewdly had purchased one of the Okanagan's best vineyards. Many of Combret's neighbours south of Oliver planted Cabernet Sauvignon and Merlot. Combret rejected both varieties, the former because it matures too late in the season; and the latter because Merlot is not notably winter-hardy. "We have as many heat units as the Napa [in California] but we don't have that long fall season here. That is the reason we cannot grow

Cabernet Sauvignon and Merlot with consistently good quality *every* year."

Even with Cabernet Franc, Combret has hardly bet the farm, never adding to Joe Fatur's initial one acre of the variety. But by pruning and nurturing the vines personally, Combret grows grapes that yield rich and fruity wine without the "wild" flavours. Unlike the Combret whites, which receive no oak in the case of the Riesling and minimal oak with Chardonnay, the Cabernet Franc will spend six months in barrels. "At least!" Robert Combret insists.

What Mayer identifies as the wild note likely reflects the vine's natural vigour. "In the vineyard, Cabernet Franc can overcrop," Mayer has found. "You need to thin the crop to get good [sugar and acid] readings. Careful vineyard management is necessary to grow Cabernet Franc. I would say it is almost as tough to grow as Pinot Noir." He also finds it more challenging than Cabernet Sauvignon when it comes to winemaking. Often lighter and more acidic, Cabernet Franc benefits—as Combret asserts—from a long time in oak but not necessarily new oak, whose strong flavours sometimes overpower delicate wines. Mayer is inclined to mature a portion of a vintage of Cabernet Franc in older oak and another portion in stainless steel, combining them in a finished wine designed to capture the grape's fruit. "In my experience," says Mayer, "it takes at least a year of good barrel aging for Cabernet France to develop its own nice character. Mainly raspberries, cherries, blackberries. The aroma changes as it ages. At the beginning, it shows more raspberry and later on more blackberry." At Domaine Combret, winemaker Olivier Combret has employed a technique called carbonic maceration—fermenting the berries whole rather than crushing them—to achieve a wine that is softly elegant, with clean fruit flavours, beginning with the winery's first release from the 1994 vintage. In his view, this is the best way to tame the inherent vivacity—Mayer's wild taste—of grapes from young vines. Mayer admires what Combret has achieved. "I have tasted the 1995," he says. "It was a wonderful wine, with a nice fruity, strawberry character, kind of a *nouveau* Cabernet Franc."

Mayer's belief is that, as in Bordeaux, most of the Okanagan's Cabernet Franc primarily will play a supporting role in Meritage blends. "Now I know that you can grow, and release, pure Cabernet Franc from the Okanagan, no problem," continues Mayer, having done that in the 1995 vintage at Okanagan Cellars. In 1996 the winery, which became Inniskillin Okanagan that year, decided against releasing the varietal on its own, the vintage not having delivered the quality at its vineyard for a stand-alone Cabernet Franc. "My personal belief is that it is best blended with other varieties," Mayer says. In his experience, a wine based on either Cabernet Sauvignon or on Merlot is more satisfying when 10 or even 20 percent Cabernet Franc is added. But Mayer would be cautious when it comes to blending all three varieties into the same wine. "Sometimes when you do the three varieties together, with perhaps 10 percent Cabernet Franc, it can be disappointing how the Cabernet Franc can almost lower the quality. It is unbelievable. You have to be very careful in making the blend."

Sandra Oldfield

Unlike either Domaine Combret or Inniskillin Okanagan, Tinhorn Creek, Sumac Ridge and sister winery Hawthorne Mountain all have large plantings of Cabernet Franc. Tinhorn Creek general manager Kenn Oldfield decided that this variety, not Cabernet Sauvignon, would join Merlot as the two Bordeaux varieties in the winery's Oliver-area vineyards. Oldfield spent several years studying viticulture at the University of California and came to the conclusion that the earlier maturation of Cabernet Franc made it essential for the planned style of wines from Tinhorn Creek. "We almost kind of overripen our reds here," winemaker Sandra Oldfield says, explaining that the winery tries to bring in the fruit at 24° Brix or higher, sufficient for at least 13 percent alcohol. "That's what gives the flavour. We did not feel that every year we could ripen Cabernet Sauvignon to the level we would be happy with." She adds that there already is a lot of Cabernet Sauvignon in the world, another reason that swayed Tinhorn Creek in another direction. "Cabernet Franc is another variety that Washington and British Columbia will be able to call one of their own," she argues. While she has discovered she cannot achieve the meatiness of Tinhorn's Merlot with Cabernet Franc, the wine has enough weight to sit between her Merlot and her lighter Pinot Noir.

Sumac Ridge produced four thousand cases of the varietal in 1995 and also used Cabernet Franc as a 25 percent component in its Meritage blend. As well, Hawthorne Mountain Vineyards also produces both the varietal and a Meritage blend. "It's a good, honest producer," Sumac winemaker Mark Wendenburg says. "It always seems to come through." The grapes, grown in the sun-drenched Sumac Ridge vineyards on Black Sage Road, south of Oliver, ripen with consistent maturity and ruby red colours. This shows through in the 1996 Cabernet Franc from Hawthorne Mountain. Made by Eric von Krosigk—who is coincidentally Wendenburg's cousin—the wine had remarkably concentrated plum-like fruit, showing almost the intensity of Merlot and certainly none of what Mayer would have called wildness. The style has been continued by Bruce Ewert, who succeeded von Krosigk as the winemaker in 1997. At Sumac Ridge Wendenburg aims for a wine which is big, soft and mellow, with oak notes from barrels—mostly French oak, some American—framing the fruit. In the range of reds that he makes, Wendenburg views Cabernet Franc as a friendly wine for many occasions, a modest assessment more reflective of the winemaker's warm and unaffected personal style than of the wines. "For me, it's a kind of combination of a Pinot Noir and a Merlot. It can be more approachable than a Merlot but a little more tannic than Pinot Noir—kind of that in-between wine. It's a wine that you can take to a dinner party but that you can take camping as well!"

Olivier Combret insists that Cabernet Franc be cellared by consumers. The wine's natural acidity, high for a red vinifera grape, makes for a slow, steady evolution in the bottle. "My approach is to release the wine when I think it is ready to be aged by the consumer," he says, pointing out that if wineries kept the wines in their own cellars, inventory charges would drive the cost to $40 a bottle. "If people are willing to pay $40 or $50 a bottle, I will age it for them." He decries a tendency for consumers to drink domestic wines too quickly. "Why are people unfair in front of a British Columbia wine but will give a Napa or Bordeaux red a chance to express itself in the bottle? Please age it. Don't drink it young!"

CABERNET SAUVIGNON

The Producers

Burrowing Owl

Calona

Carriage House

CedarCreek

Hawthorne Mountain

Hillside

Inniskillin Okanagan

Kettle Valley

Mission Hill

Quails' Gate

Sumac Ridge

Summerhill

Wild Goose

RED TABLE WINE This grape has been described as the "undisputed potentate" because no other red variety makes agreeable wines in so many vineyards around the world. Comparatively easy to grow, this is an ancient variety. Some recent DNA research has led to the remarkable assertion that this grape's ancestors in fact are Cabernet Franc and Sauvignon Blanc. Perhaps. When Roman Legions occupied what is Bordeaux today, their scholars described a ubiquitous grape which they called *Biturica* (after the local tribe), a name still used on occasion in Italy. This geographically adaptable variety can produce medium to full wines ripe with flavours of blackberry, cassis, plums, and dark cherries; however, in a cool year or a cool vineyard, the variety also delivers vegetative flavours of asparagus and bell peppers. The wines age well if made with longevity in mind. But even a modest example will be better at five years than at two. These wines are suited to red meat, to many cheeses and, some believe, even to chocolate.

Cabernet Sauvignon yields good to exceptional wine from vineyards around the world. But prior to 1990 there was no significant planting of Cabernet Sauvignon in the Okanagan, for the very good reason that this is one of the latest-maturing of red varieties. The heat units are seldom there to produce the powerhouse Cabernets of California or Australia. "Extremes of temperature do not suit its temperament," Californian expert Bern C. Ramey has written. "Hot climates destroy its varietal character, producing wines unbalanced, and unpleasant. In the coolest areas, the variety does not ripen fully, giving a green (under-ripe), thin and very astringent wine."[1] The most consistent Cabernet Sauvignon plantings in British Columbia are those in the Oliver area which has the highest average heat units in the Okanagan. "I can tell you that I never was disappointed with that variety," says Sandor Mayer, the Hungarian-born winemaker who in 1991 supervised the planting of Inniskillin Okanagan's vineyard, including three

---

1   Ramey, Bern C.: *The Great Wine Grapes and the Wines They Make,* The Great Wine Grapes Inc., San Francisco, 1977.

acres of Cabernet Sauvignon, and who made several vintages from that sun-drenched Oliver-area vineyard before moving to the Jackson-Triggs winery nearby. "We were actually surprised at the beginning how wonderful a wine we could make from Cabernet Sauvignon." Equally surprised was Bill Dyer, the Californian vintner (a veteran of twenty years at prestigious Sterling Vineyards) who supervised his first British Columbia vintage in 1997 for Burrowing Owl. While this Oliver-area vineyard was picking its Merlot in the first week of October, the Cabernet Sauvignon was not ripe enough and Dyer advised leaving the grapes on the vines longer. They were finally picked October 25, with sugar of 22° Brix, when the weather had begun to deteriorate. "I expected the Cabernet to be quite herbaceous," Dyer says. "It wasn't. The only thing it lacks is a little bit of body." That deficiency can be repaired with judicious blending. That experience convinced Dyer that growers with the nerve to leave the fruit on the vine late into the autumn can produce Cabernet Sauvignon good enough to let the winemaker challenge the quality of Napa or Bordeaux.

Unlike Dyer, few of the valley's winemakers have had much experience with the variety or, when they have, it was gained making wine with fruit purchased in Washington State where fine Cabernet is grown. Typical of the Cabernet odyssey is Mayer's experience with the first three vintages from Okanagan Vineyards (now Inniskillin Okanagan). To capture even more heat, to which Cabernet Sauvignon responds well, Mayer trained the vines as low as sixty centimeters from the exceptionally stony ground so that radiation from the rocks could amplify the heat units. His debut Cabernet Sauvignon was from the moderately cool 1993 vintage. It was "a delicate wine with a touch of pepper and raspberry on the nose," he wrote in his tasting notes. The wine was lighter than subsequent vintages perhaps because it was made from the very first crop; the alcohol was less than 12 percent. Mayer wisely gave the wine only six months aging in Hungarian barrels, a subdued oak suited to lighter reds. In the legendary hot 1994 season, the Cabernet Sauvignon at Okanagan Vineyards produced fully mature fruit, yielding a wine with almost 13 percent alcohol and with such lush fruit that about one-fifth of the wine was aged in stronger-flavoured American oak. "This wine has a complex aged bouquet with vanilla, berry and bell pepper characteristics," his notes said. The 1995 season was not quite as hot as the year before but sunny enough that Mayer

Wines may be totally Cabernet Sauvignon but often are blended with other Bordeaux reds. Some announce the blend on the label (as in Cabernet/Merlot). Other producers call blends *Meritage,* employing a term used in California for Bordeaux blends. The term is not pronounced in the French way; it rhymes instead with *heritage.*

could make a wine with 12.5 percent alcohol. By this vintage the vines also were beginning to produce more intensely flavoured fruit. Mayer now gave 60 percent of the wine six months in American oak before blending with the remainder, which had seen six months of Hungarian oak. The winemaker's notes on this wine described it as dark red with a rich berry aroma. "This full-bodied wine reveals smooth tannins with black pepper, clove and a light herbal note. The lingering finish has a touch of coffee." His notes provide a sense of the development of the vine in the vineyard and how it has permitted the style to evolve. Bordeaux-trained Christine Leroux succeeded Mayer for the cool 1996 vintage, which was generally held to be a difficult year, especially

Christine Leroux

for the Bordeaux red varieties. "We had difficulty with some maturities but the maturity we had here, in the southern part of the valley, was really good. It could have been better but it was really good and we made some nice wines." Laughter sparkles in Leroux's expressive gunmetal eyes. "You haven't seen *tough*," she says as she recounts trying to make wine in Bordeaux in 1993 with rain falling on the vineyards, diluting and rotting the grapes. That seldom occurs during an Okanagan vintage, a fortunate thing because Leroux prefers to leave red grapes on the vine late into harvest. "Since the maturity of the skins, which will help in the extraction of the colour, usually comes after the balance of acidity and sugar we are looking for, I'll wait maybe a week more, trying to get that peak of colour extraction." The 1996 Cabernet Sauvignon from the vineyard Mayer planted (and which he continued to manage) is a dark, powerful wine, showing both that her technique works and that the vineyard has found its stride. Leroux also introduced some French oak barrels; for her style, she does not want the more pungent spicy American oak to be the dominant oak flavour. "I'd like to have the finesse of the French oak."

Her training has biased Leroux toward the Bordeaux varieties. She was born in Belleville, Ontario in 1965, and grew up in

Montreal where her father, Michel Leroux, was for many years the Canadian spokesman for the California wine industry. This exposure, along with many winery visits, led her to become a winemaker after she earned her biology degree from the Université du Quebec; in 1990 she went to Bordeaux to obtain her enology diploma. "I arrived during one of the best vintages," she notes. By 1993, one of the worst, she had her diploma and was working as a consulting winemaker in the district of Entre-Deux-Mers, with clients ranging from the largest commercial winery to very small producers still practicing traditionally primitive winemaking in outmoded cellars. An energetic and ambitious young graduate who was not only schooled in the latest ideas but apprenticed at storied Chateau Pétrus and distinguished Chateau Margaux, she describes dealing with stubbornly traditional small producers in Entre-Deux-Mers as "a lot of challenges. The French have a tendency to isolate themselves, even from the next village." She decided to take her new skills elsewhere, first to Australia during the 1994 vintage, then later the same year, working the vintage at the J. Lohr winery in California. Having heard that promising wines were emerging in Canada, she returned to work the 1995 vintage at Inniskillin's Ontario winery. Impressed, Inniskillin co-founder and winemaker Karl Kaiser sent her to the Okanagan after Inniskillin's 1996 purchase of Okanagan Vineyards.

She was excited to find a vineyard dedicated primarily to the Bordeaux varieties. "These are the grape varieties I kind of grew up with," she says, referring to her French experience. "For me, to see the quality we have in the vineyard is just amazing." Because Cabernet Sauvignon is the latest maturing of the major Bordeaux reds, there are other growers in the south Okanagan, notably Domaine Combret's Robert Combret, who decline to grow it. "You've got to be very careful with Cabernet Sauvignon," Leroux agrees. "There are some places where it will have trouble maturing. And Cabernet Sauvignon is very delicate." In the classic Bordeaux approach, Leroux draws on other varieties in the vineyard to build the varietal Cabernet Sauvignon, as much as 10 percent Merlot and perhaps 1 or 2 percent of Cabernet Franc— "just to give the Cabernet Sauvignon the softness it needs." The regulations in British Columbia (and elsewhere) allow this beneficial blending; a varietal in British Columbia can have as much as 15 percent of complementary grapes in the blend and still be called a varietal. Those wines with less than 85 percent of a single variety in the bottle are released under proprietary names or as Meritage Blends. Inniskillin Okanagan's 1995 Meritage, as an example, was 65 percent Cabernet Sauvignon, 25 percent Cabernet Franc and 10 percent Merlot. The Meritage wines which Sumac Ridge has produced since the 1993 vintage typically are 50 percent Cabernet Sauvignon and 25 percent each of Cabernet Franc and Merlot. At Kettle Valley, the Cabernet/Merlot blend usually is one third each of Cabernet Franc, Cabernet Sauvignon and Merlot. In this example, the blend is led by the composition of the winery's Naramata area vineyards, which are managed so meticulously that the varieties are matured and harvested at the same time. The grapes are crushed together at the outset and fermented together.

Winemaker John Simes, whose career began in New Zealand before coming to the Okanagan in 1992, only began getting significant quantities of Cabernet Sauvignon and other Bordeaux reds with the 1996 vintage. Like Christine Leroux and Bill Dyer, he was impressed. "They're better than what I had to play with in New Zealand," Simes says of British Columbia Cabernet Sauvignon. "We're not getting the green, stalky, bellpepper character that we typically got in New Zealand. We're getting much better balanced grapes. We're not having really, really high acids in Cabernet—from the best vineyards. It's all there in front of us. From what I've seen, we're going to make some very good quality Bordeaux reds." He handles the reds quite conventionally, leaving the fermenting juice in contact with the crushed grape skins for several weeks before racking the wine into oak barrels. "The fruit flavours we are getting, particularly in the Merlot, just astounded me—a lifted berry floral flavour." At Calona Vineyards, which made its first Cabernet Sauvignon from Okanagan grapes in the 1995 vintage, winemaker Howard Soon set up the crusher so that at least a third of the berries were still whole after the bunches had passed through the crusher. This is a winemaking trick called partial carbonic maceration in which fermentation actually begins inside the unbroken grapes. "Of course, they pop and break open in the end," he says. The technique has been found to amplify the fruitiness of the finished wine. Increasingly, winemakers go to pains to handle the grapes gently, careful not to liberate bitter tannic flavours by inept crushing and pumping. Christine Leroux has found it beneficial to insert a stainless steel tube into the fermenting tank and bubble nitrogen through the wine, gently mixing the juice with the cap of skins. "It's a gentler pump-over and you get a better extraction," she explains, adding that a "good old-fashioned" pumping of the fermenting wine over the cap is required from time to time because some exposure to oxygen also is needed to achieve stability of the wine's colour and tannin.

At Quails' Gate, Jeff Martin had extensive experience in Australia with Cabernet Sauvignon before making the first Quails' Gate example from the 1995 vintage. "That wine will last five to ten years," he asserts. The hallmark of Martin's style is that, if winemaking were music, he would sooner listen to a choir than to a soloist. "Any wine—it's always better if you can make it in portions," he insists. "If you take any batch of grapes and divide it into three wines, you will always end up with slight variations. I make three wines and do different treatments, even on Cab." The variations on the theme range from differing periods of skin contact to letting a portion complete its fermentation—or "fizzing" as Martin puts it—in oak barrels. The impact of barrel-aging on reds is complex. Going well beyond enhancing or complexing the flavours, barrel aging concentrates and softens wines and also stabilizes the colours. He counsels caution when using barrels with Okanagan Cabernet Sauvignon. "With the really nice fruit flavours you get from Cab—I have no trouble getting colour or tannins in the valley—when you get really nice varietal fruit character, it is almost criminal to swamp it with oak." The cool 1996 vintage posed a challenge with Cabernet Sauvignon, a late ripening grape at the best of times. In that vintage Martin found himself having to tame greener, flinty notes in the flavour and structure. He chose to soften that vintage by aging it fourteen to sixteen months in French oak barrels—not new ones which might have overwhelmed the wine's flavours but barrels previously used a year or two with other wines. "There's no way you are ever going to make a big warm-area Cab," Martin admits. British Columbia can never be Australia, where sunnier climates yield big juicy Cabernet Sauvignon wines. The emerging Okanagan style, Martin believes, is marked by "lighter structure, good tannins, really obvious pepper and leafy fruit characters, definitely wine with body and structure."

Almost without exception, Cabernet Sauvignon (along with the other Bordeaux red varietals) is a barrel-aged wine, sometimes boldly so, an example being Summerhill's 1995 Cabernet

Sauvignon Platinum Series, the winery's first release of that varietal. Winemaker Alan Marks had the wine spend about eighteen months in American and French oak. He favours barrels which have been used before for a year or two, a precaution against overwhelming the flavour of the wine with the stronger flavours that entirely new barrels would produce. "I think the Okanagan reds have such nice fruit characters—berry aromas and really delicate aromas," Marks says. He has a personal taste for wines even more boldly oaked than he produces at Summerhill but he has adapted his technique to what is best with the grapes. "In our region, the reds are better by letting the nice fruit come through." Of course, making reds exclusively in stainless steel tanks would deliver all that fruit but that would deprive the wines of the beneficial influences of barrel aging on the texture and other qualities. "It seems that eight to twelve months just isn't enough," Marks believes. "It seems that after more than a year in the barrel, approaching two years, something really changes. The colour changes, almost to a darker hue. I don't know exactly what's going on and I'm not sure if anybody does." His red wines are dark even before they go into barrels because Marks favours prolonged contact between the wine and the skins, including leaving the wine on the skins for up to two weeks after fermentation has finished. "People usually like their reds on the darker side," says Marks, sipping a satisfying glass of his debut vintage.

CHANCELLOR

RED TABLE WINE This is a productive red French hybrid, originally known as Seibel 7053 (from the name of the French hybridizer). Long since banned in France—along with many other hybrids—it is widely planted in eastern North America and only modestly so in British Columbia. Here it produced wines that clearly were superior to the thin sharp reds made from De Chaunac, which once was extensively planted. The wines are medium-bodied with appealing claret-like flavours, especially when given some time in American oak barrels. Both consulting winemaker Ross Mirko and Sumac Ridge's Mark Wendenburg suggest enjoying Chancellor with spaghetti or hamburgers.

The Producers

Calona
CedarCreek
Sumac Ridge
Summerhill (Icewine)

This grape's long run as a varietal may be coming to an end, to be succeeded by the Bordeaux red vinifera that are regarded as better wine grapes and whose wines fetch higher prices. Unlike Maréchal Foch, the variety has not found ardent champions among the winemakers, none of whom have any ambition for Chancellor higher than turning it into honest, affordable wine for the basic table—a modesty that perhaps should be encouraged as vinifera varietals move up the price ladder. Chancellor was among the several French hybrids that were planted in the Okanagan in the 1970s. Calona began releasing varietal Chancellor from the 1981 vintage. The wine was a revelation, compared to what had gone before; according to contemporary tasting notes, the wine was "well-balanced, lean and elegant" while the better 1982 vintage was "full-bodied, the wood well-balanced by the wine's intense brambleberry flavour."[1] The now demolished Casabello winery in Penticton and Sumac Ridge in Summerland, which was started by two Casabello alumni, both released Chancellors at this same time. Sumac Ridge's wines soon were winning awards in competition and the winery elevated its offering into a barrel-aged private reserve version, in recent years with Cabernet Franc

---

1   Schreiner, John: *The World of Canadian Wine,* Douglas & McIntyre, Vancouver, 1984.

incorporated in the blend to further enhance the fruit. Even so, Sumac Ridge winemaker Mark Wendenburg suggests that the variety's years "are numbered." The winery no longer has an abundant source of these grapes while it is getting increasing tonnages of better-bred red vinifera grapes from its Black Sage vineyards.

In a time before either Cabernet Sauvignon and Merlot were planted in the Okanagan, Chancellor arguably produced the most Bordeaux-like red. The variety does not produce wines with the bitter, smoky note in the finish found in other red hybrids. It appealed to growers here for the same reasons that it once appealed to French growers in the 1930s: it is an abundant producer and while the variety ripens late in the year, it usually achieves the maturity to produce a wine with 11 to 12 percent alcohol and with good fruit flavours. The acidity is relatively high for a red wine but not unmanageably so. The grape is not one to challenge the winemakers. "Colour is never a problem although I would like to have more tannins to work with," Wendenburg says. "We don't play with it," said Mirko, winemaker at CedarCreek at the time. "We just bring it in, ferment it, press it, settle it in barrels and then bottle it eight to ten months later. It makes a pleasant wine for us." CedarCreek has had no difficulty selling about eighteen hundred cases of Chancellor a year.

Like Wendenburg, Mirko sees Chancellor being eclipsed, perhaps to become "a proprietary blending component." It is a decent red but seldom scales the heights along with Merlot and Cabernet Franc. Unfortunately for Chancellor, it also ripens about the same time as those other reds. If a winemaker is going to be "buried with reds," as Mirko puts it, the preference is to be buried in Merlot. "We don't fuss over the Chancellor," he repeated. "It gets pumped over and treated as though we were making a proprietary or low-priced varietal. The Merlot and Pinot Noir we take the time with." To the extent than anyone has fussed over Chancellor, Gehringer Brothers, which incorporates Chancellor in its Cuvée Noir proprietary red, made a deep red icewine from the variety in the 1991 vintage. Summerhill did the same in a more recent vintage. The result reminded Summerhill winemaker Alan Marks of a Tawny Port.

CHARDONNAY

WHITE TABLE WINE Chardonnay, which surpassed Riesling in 1995 as the most widely grown white in British Columbia, is a fashionable aristocrat. "There is a hierarchy in this world with white grapes," Blue Mountain's Ian Mavety believes. "Chardonnay is at the top, just in breed alone." Chardonnay is stylish for good reason. The name rolls off the tongue as easily as the wines which, ranging from crisp and fruity to subtly rich with attractive notes of cloves, are versatile with foods from fresh oysters to fowl and fish. Almost without exception, wines made from Chardonnay are dry—that is, with almost no residual sugar remaining in the finished wine. A trace can lift the fruit but Chardonnay is naturally fruity and usually does not need the help. Edgar Scherzinger made a honeyed but dry late harvest Chardonnay from his 1995 vintage, so called *not* because it was finished sweet but because the harvest literally was late; the honey note reflected the maturity of the grapes. Kettle Valley in 1995 made a Chardonnay icewine as sweet as a slice of baklava. This definitely is the exception to the rule. Frequently, but not always, the wine is aged in barrels and often fermented in barrels, a technique that adds complexity and the richness of texture.

The Producers

Bella Vista
Bighorn Vineyards
Blue Mountain
Burrowing Owl
Calona
Carriage House
CedarCreek
Chateau Wolff
Crowsnest*
Domaine Combret
Domaine de Chaberton
First Estate Cellars
Golden Mile Cellars
Gray Monk*
Hainle
(cont'd)

* Not oaked

Many wineries in British Columbia have won awards for Chardonnay but no award had more impact than the Avery's Trophy garnered in 1994 by Mission Hill for its 1992 Grand Reserve Chardonnay. The award, given at the International Wine and Spirits Competition in London and aggressively publicized by Mission Hill, singled out the wine as the best Chardonnay in the competition that year and brought recognition to British Columbia as a competitive producer of the world's most popular white. New Zealand-born John Simes, who joined Mission Hill just before the 1992 harvest, subsequently has achieved a consistency in style and quality with his premium Chardonnay that amazes even him. "I thought there was potential when I came here [to the Okanagan] but I've been surprised at what we've been producing here. Chardonnay does brilliantly here." His was not the only British Columbia Chardonnay to win a significant award that year: Domaine Combret won a bronze medal for its debut 1993 Chardonnay at the rigorous Chardonnay du Monde competition in Burgundy in 1994, and went on to win the same award for each of its next two vintages of Chardonnay, further confirmation that Chardonnay had arrived in British Columbia.

The examples from these and, increasingly, from the other British Columbia producers have begun to define a Chardonnay style different from the mainstream examples of California or Australia. Californian Bill Dyer, the winemaker at Burrowing Owl, deliberately set out to make an individual style in his debut 1997 vintage. "There is no point in coming to British Columbia and making the same sort of Chardonnay as you could get from Chile," he says, explaining his subtle blend that showcases fruit against an oak background. Tinhorn Creek winemaker Sandra Oldfield also grew up, studied and worked in California before coming to British Columbia for the 1994 vintage. She prefers the Okanagan style with its significantly crisper acidity. "I certainly enjoy a really oily, buttery, thick, rich oaked Chardonnay from California every once in a while," she says. But she argues that Okanagan Chardonnay, with its crispness, is preferable with food. "The ones from California *are* a meal for me; I never have them with a meal," she adds. "The ones up here I don't like by them-selves—I like them with a meal."

Chardonnay is a recent arrival in the Okanagan, with less than twenty acres planted prior to 1985, requiring a learning experience both in the vineyards and in the wineries. The first Chardonnays from Sumac Ridge in the early 1980s were made from grapes grown at a vineyard near Ashcroft, then one of the most northerly in British Columbia. The wines were lean and tart and, when chilled in a refrigerator, precipitated harmless crys-tals of tartaric acid, an indicator of a high-acid wine. The Ashcroft vineyard did not survive a killing November frost in 1985. To-day, most of Sumac Ridge's Chardonnay comes from its Black Sage vineyards south of Oliver where the grapes get sufficiently mature that the winery has no difficulty producing full-flavoured, buttery private reserve wines with a muscular 13 percent alcohol and no tartaric acid crystals. When Vernon-born winemaker Eric von Krosigk returned from six years of study in Germany to be-come the first vintner at Summerhill in 1991, he had never worked with Chardonnay. He repaired that gap in his knowledge by spending time with several Chablis producers in France, including J. Moreau et Fils, noted producers of non-oaked Chardonnay. "Oak wasn't in my budget," von Krosigk says of Summerhill's underfinanced early years where he made several vintages of lean, piquant Chardonnay on the Chablis model. Subsequently in his career, he has, like many other winemakers, broadened his repertoire to include both barrel-fermented and barrel-finished wines, not just because he has learned Chardonnay techniques but also as grapes have come available from sunnier slopes than Summerhill's cool Kelowna site.

Today, the majority of Okanagan Chardonnay vines have been planted in the southern end of the valley, mostly with the high quality clones from European nurseries that became available in the 1990s. "We held off planting until we could get these French clones," says Ian Mavety, one of the owners of Blue Mountain and a veteran grape grower. Vines were available from Washington State nurseries and some growers planted them even though those clones, Mavety asserts, ripen ten days to two weeks *later* than the French vines. The Okanagan's intense but short season makes the earlier-maturing clones the better choice. At Inniskillin Okanagan, winemaker Christine Leroux uses the French clone as the backbone of the winery's barrel-fermented Chardonnay Reserve because she also finds the fruit more intense compared with Washington clone grapes.

The Combret's Oliver-area vineyard is well-suited to Chardonnay, its southern exposure making the difference between growing grapes capable of a wine with 12 percent alcohol and grapes with a potential of only 10 percent. "At 10 percent it would be a *miserable* Chardonnay because it would not express any fruit, any flavours, any aroma, nothing!" declares Robert Combret. Along with other successful Chardonnay producers, Combret limits the yield aggressively to no more than three and a half tonnes of fruit an acre, to get mature grapes, full of flavour. Equally disciplined, Blue Mountain's Mavety calculates that it costs more to thin the crop during the season than it does to pick the ripe grapes. "The key is the tonnage levels," he says. "The pruning is done very severely and everything else—watering, fertilizing—is done very minimally. You are just trying to grow the plant slowly and *just* produce enough foliage to ripen the crop. If the vineyard is over-vigorous, you can taste it in the wines." Spare cropping levels served Blue Mountain well in the cool 1996 vintage when the vineyard not only achieved ripeness but delivered fruit so sound that Mavety considered the 1996 his best white wine to that point.

After such effort in the vineyard, winemaking can be minimalist. "One hundred percent natural," is how Robert Combret characterizes the way he and winemaker son Olivier

handle Chardonnay. The grapes are handled gently in their superbly designed winery where everything moves by gravity, with no pumping of the juice. "If you pump the fruit juice, then you will lose a good part of the potential fruitiness and flavour," the elder Combret believes. "We protect this potential in that winery." The wine rests in barrels two months, "at most"— not to become oaky but to develop "finesse," according to Robert Combret—before going into

John Simes

bottle where most of its evolution is expected to take place. "After that, this fruitiness, flavours, aromas, et cetera, are developing little by little in the winery over the years," he says. "It's a very simple way but a vintner must be patient, take time and wait." With a crisp style all of its own in the Okanagan, this Chardonnay is modeled ambitiously on the Chablis Premier Cru from Moreau called *Les Vaillons*. Blue Mountain strives for a wine that combines the fresh fruit of Chablis with the subtle complexity of oak. "To me, complexity in a wine is not so much that it tastes like this, that or the other thing," says Mavety, who is not given to florid winespeak. "To me, it is the integration of all of these flavours." While half of each vintage is fermented in stainless steel tanks, the other half is fermented in French oak barrels, a high proportion of which are new, with the final result blended for either the winery's regular or striped label (reserve) wines. Because a crisp fruit flavour is essential, only about 12 percent of each vintage is permitted to go through malolactic fermentation, a process which softens a wine. This portion becomes a complexing component in the wine. "It adds a dimension to the wine," Mavety explains. At Hawthorne Mountain, Bruce Ewert, besides making a varietal entirely from Chardonnay, also makes a blend incorporating Sémillon to achieve additional layers of flavour, a technique he picked up during a winemaking year in Australia.

Unlike Domaine Combret, John Simes at first did not have the luxury of a winery-owned vineyard; that only came later once the success of his Chardonnays generated the cash and the confidence for a major investment in vineyards by Mission Hill. Thus it was that Mission Hill's contract growers learned to live with Simes's trademark habit of assessing the qualities of blocks of maturing grapes in vineyards by actually eating berries while walking among the vines. "It is important," he says. "You need to know which block you need to worry about. You don't just want to bring everything in and throw it all together in one tank. There's a lot of differences in Chardonnay. You don't want to blend away all your options." He quickly discovered that the vineyards in different parts of the Okanagan offer a range of flavours, giving him a useful palette for creating multi-layered wines. In the vintages from 1992 through 1995, Simes had available to him Chardonnay primarily from vineyards south of Oliver. In general, these vineyards—in the hottest and driest part of the Okanagan—produce grapes with a high degree of maturity, yielding big juicy wines with moderate acidity. Beginning in 1996, Mission Hill also began getting Chardonnay from the Paradise Ranch Vineyard at Naramata, a cooler site which matures its Chardonnay two to three weeks later than the Oliver vineyards and which yields fruit with more piquant acidity. "That will give more blending options," Simes says with evident satisfaction. Whatever the vineyard, Simes prefers to have grapes achieve 23° Brix (a measure of natural sugar that represents the potential of 12 to 13 percent alcohol) because—as Combret also has observed—Chardonnay's flavours intensify with greater maturity.

Even an individual vineyard, because of varying soil types and varying contours, can deliver differing qualities from the same grape variety. One example is Hester Creek, whose sixty-eight acre vineyard is just north of the Combret property but separated from it by the deep ravine through which the creek flows. Formerly the base for Joe Busnardo's Divino winery, the property was purchased by Busnardo in 1967 and turned into one of the first extensive vinifera vineyards in the Okanagan's modern era. When Hester Creek acquired the property in 1996 (Busnardo having decided to "retire" to Vancouver Island to develop a thirty-five acre vineyard), Frank Supernak, Hester Creek's winemaker, found himself with Chardonnay vines with an average age of fifteen years and some as old as twenty-five years, with root systems likely reaching far into the earth. The vineyard occupies a plateau with a variety of exposures. "Our vineyard is divided into six blocks," he says. "Our southeast exposed block we call our 'Grand Reserve' block. The soil is very tough, very hard, heavy gravel-clay. The plants are slightly stressed because of it and they limit themselves to about a tonne and a half an acre." The superior quality of fruit from that block was dedicated in 1996 to the production of the winery's Grand Reserve Chardonnay (and a comparable Pinot Blanc). The resulting wines, Supernak found, had "huge fruit, huge extract and colour." Consequently, Chardonnay from that block was barrel-fermented and aged to yield one of the biggest Chardonnays made by Supernak in his then fourteen-year career as a winemaker. "It's a 'show' wine for us for high-profile restaurants, wine tastings, wine critics, international competitions." Less intense fruit from elsewhere on the vineyard was handled differently, with the major portion fermented in stainless steel, to yield a crisply fruity and easy-drinking wine for Hester Creek's larger volume estate series Chardonnay. "If you are going make two types of Chardonnay, they *should* be different," Supernak says.

At Andrés, winemaker Tony Vlcek makes three different styles, not counting the blends produced with imported wine for the non-VQA Peller Estates Oakridge brand. One VQA version, for the top-of-the-line Peller Estates Limited Edition label with individually numbered bottles, is fermented in French oak barrels, yielding a wine with rich toffee and toasted undertones behind the fruit. The second Peller Estates Chardonnay is a blend of barrel-aged wine with tank-matured wine, which puts more accent on crispness and citrus fruit notes. The third, under the winery's Bighorn Vineyards label, is matured totally in American oak, a California style with more obvious wood. "It's nice to be able to have that variability," he says. He attributes that to the quality of the grapes that can be grown in the Okanagan; in most vintages, Chardonnay comes into the winery with specifications so good as to be the envy of vintners in hotter regions. Vlcek recounts a conversation several years ago with Californian winemakers who suggested that British Columbia is too cold to grow Chardonnay. He responded with the sugar and acid readings that are typical for the Okanagan and would not be far off the values in cooler California vineyards. "Their jaws hit the floor," Vlcek chuckles.

While many winemakers want grapes harvested gently by hand, Simes is a surprising exception. "At the moment, everything we get here is hand-harvested," he said in 1997. "Given the choice, I think I would prefer machine harvesting and the bigger vineyards that are coming into production will be machine harvested. It's much easier. You can leave the fruit until it's ready and you can get the fruit off when you want it off. You can handle it much faster in the winery. You have the option of harvesting at night or very early in the morning." The purpose of night harvesting is to pick the grapes when they are cooler and fresher that in the heat of the day. "It gives you more control over what you are doing."

In the winery, Simes employs familiar mainstream techniques in handling Chardonnay. "Typically, we'll crush the grapes, give them four to six hours of skin contact, press and then chill [the juice]." The cold juice then remains undisturbed in a stainless steel tank for about two days, during which time the solid matter settles to the bottom. Winemakers prefer to ferment clear juice, a practice yielding wines that taste as clean and fresh as the juice looks. Fermentation will start and can take place entirely in tanks when the object is to make an uncomplicated and fruity wine. Most vintners ferment Chardonnay directly in oak barrels. "I like everything that barrel fermentation does—the length, the roundness, the mouthfeel," Calona winemaker Howard Soon says. "Anyone can make it fruity." A barrel-fermented wine shows a seamless integration of the oak and the fruit, often acquiring a buttery texture that is the hallmark of barrel treatment. Most wineries prefer to use a mix of new oak (either French or American, depending on the winery's style) and one- or two-year-old barrels. "We leave as many options open as we can at the early stage," Simes says, as he taps at his computer's keyboard to bring up the information on the wine in each of the barrels in the winery—and Mission Hill ultimately will have five thousand barrels for most of its wine, not just the Chardonnay. "I've made wine with computer systems since the early 1980s."

Okanagan vineyards are delivering Chardonnay grapes with what von Krosigk calls "crisp, bright flavours" and most winemakers use oak sparingly. "It is too great to be taken over by wood," says Jackson-Triggs winemaker Bruce Nicholson, who gives barrel treatment to only 40 percent of the vintage, with the remainder matured in tanks. "Oak benefits Chardonnay nicely but not to the extent that it is overpowering. I like oak to be subtle." Simes agrees. "There's a substantial part of the Grand Reserve that is fermented in stainless steel—about 50 percent. Long, cold, slow fermentation." The barrel-fermented portion of the blend might remain on the yeast lees for a time; some will go through malolactic fermentation, which softens the acidity. "I'm trying to put complexity into the wine. So we have some [part of the blend] that has been in oak, and sat on lees and all that drama and some that has been in stainless steel and has just clean fruit. I try to put a blend together that gets you all the components when you drink the wine."

If the style at Mission Hill is singular, so is the style of many other Chardonnays, which run the gamut from crisply flinty (as at Domaine Combret) to muscular and toasty (as at Quails' Gate). "It's an extraordinary grape," Simes observes. "You can give the same grapes to another winemaker and he will produce a wine that you would swear was from a different grape or from a different region in the world. It lends itself to being manipulated in the winery and still ends up making brilliant wines that are completely different." Hillside's John Fletcher, after hearing from many consumers that too many Chardonnays are over-oaked, decided to make what he calls an "alternative style"—a very lightly oaked wine with crisp, citrus flavours. "This is simplicity," he says over a glass of his wine. Several wineries, quite consciously, keep Chardonnay away from oak entirely, producing wines that showcase the variety's clean fruit. Gray Monk came to this style from a bias against barrels (now eroding). But the non-wood Chardonnay, year in and year out, has been a lovely display of clean fruit. At tiny Crowsnest Vineyards, the cost of barrels initially deterred Andrea McDonald from making an oaked Chardonnay. By the time the winery was able to afford barrels, McDonald had a following that preferred her fresh, fruity Chardonnay. "If we change it now, there goes our style," she shrugs. "It really is different to have one with no oak at all."

A number of wineries have begun releasing so-called reserve editions of their very best Chardonnay. Typically, these are wines that have received special handling dictated by the richness of the flavours. CedarCreek, for example, released its first reserve Chardonnay from the good 1995 vintage. "There was a higher proportion that was barrel-fermented and a higher proportion of the barrels were new," said Ross Mirko who made the wine. "It is a fatter, more voluptuous wine overall." Beginning with the 1994 vintage, Quails' Gate split its wines, including Chardonnay, into three tiers, with Proprietors Reserve and Limited Release wines built to be accessible when released. The Family Reserve wines are built to be cellared. "I've seen some very attractive unoaked Chardonnays," winemaker Jeff Martin says. "But don't expect them to age for any length of time. I want a Chardonnay that can age ten years. I've got to have quality fruit—it has to have peaches and pears and all those good Chardonnay characteristics. You've got to have fully-ripened Chardonnay, like we did in 1994. You've got to have at least 13 percent potential alcohol." In a cool year like 1996, when the grapes grown at Quails' Gate's vineyard at Westbank failed to achieve that much maturity, Martin turned to grapes from Oliver-area vineyards to produce some barrels of wine with Family Reserve quality. And the wine stays in those barrels (exclusively French oak and most of them new) for some time. "To build body into the wine, it has to have over twelve months on lees," Martin continues. This is a standard practice in Burgundy. "Corton Charlemagne has eighteen months on lees—that gives you an indication of how important lees aging can be." The fermentation lees primarily are dead yeast cells and solids that have settled to the bottom of the barrel. Some winemakers go one step further, stirring the lees up from time to time to further enhance their effect. "You find that the wine develops an oatmeal character and if you leave it on the lees longer, the wine develops nuttiness. What I'm trying to do with our Family Reserve is age it a long time on lees without picking up excessive oak."

Clearly, the vineyard and the year also drive the style. During the 1996 harvest at Stag's Hollow, proprietor Larry Gerelus intended to produce a straightforward Chardonnay without any oak, a style favoured by his wife, Linda Pruegger, but changed direction because his vineyard handed him grapes that demanded the full-blown treatment, including barrel-fermentation on a portion. "You create a wine that you get from a vine," he observes. His 1996 Chardonnay, picked late in a difficult year, was made in a style he compares with "a monster Chard of the Napa Valley ... big oak, big fruit, big alcohol ... it's not one of those delicate Chardonnays by any stretch of the imagination." Mavety, whose Blue Mountain vineyard is not far away, suggests that a very fine September in an otherwise routine year can make a big difference, as happened in 1995 when perfect vintage weather resulted in yields that were 15 percent above mid-season estimates and arguably at the margin for making concentrated Chardonnay. "As much as you want to control everything that you can, you must recognize that nature is the controlling factor," he says. "You have to make wines that, hopefully, will be good expressions of the season." In 1996 the bad weather occurred in September. Paradoxically, many good Chardonnays emerged from that vintage, perhaps because most vineyards kept yields low.

Because world-class Chardonnay is a wine of the 1990s in the Okanagan, there is limited experience with the aging potential of the wines. Simes concedes that his Grand Reserve style "is not a style that has very, very long ageability." His 1992 vintage was still sound five years later, perhaps an optimum age for the style. It is probable that the densely-structured Quails' Gate Family Reserve style or the flinty Combret style, with its higher acidity—or any other wines in this style—would be better candidates for cellaring up to ten years.

When does one drink Chardonnay? It depends on the style and on the occasion. "Seventy percent of these wines are being sold in restaurants," Ian Mavety says of Blue Mountain's product, explaining why its fundamental style retains fruit and crispness. "You would have a difficult time trying to find dishes that would suit something that is big, buttery and oaky as opposed to something that is more balanced and has the acid to carry it through with the food." When it is Mission Hill's Grand Reserve, Simes says with a laugh, "we're not having it on Tuesday night with sausages ... When we do have the wine, there is some sort of occasion."

CHASSELAS

WHITE TABLE WINE Jancis Robinson, in her 1986 book *Wines, Grapes and Vines,* makes the intriguing suggestion that drawings in the burial chambers at Luxor in Egypt depict a vine resembling Chasselas. It would be remarkable if this variety has maintained a role in winemaking for all those centuries since the wines invariably are light, fresh and uncomplicated. In France it is a popular table grape. Only in Switzerland does Chasselas play a major role in the vineyards. A Swiss connection and a nursery's shipping error are the only reasons that Chasselas is produced in British Columbia. The name of the grape is pronounced "shass-la" but the sky will not fall if you utter "chass-e-lass."

The Producers

Quails' Gate
St. Hubertus

It is said of Swiss white wines that they do not travel well. Now we may discover whether British Columbia white wines from Chasselas grapes are better travelers. Swiss-born brothers Leo and Andy Geberts, proprietors of the family-owned St. Hubertus Estate Winery, began exporting Chasselas in 1997 to Switzerland! It is a logical extension of the market the Geberts brothers have developed in British Columbia's Swiss community. Because Swiss wines rarely are found here, St. Hubertus supplies most of the Chasselas required by Swiss restaurants and Swiss diplomats on the West Coast. "They love it with fondues," St. Hubertus winemaker Cherie Jones says. "Our Chasselas is very austere and delicate." Swiss-born consumers, who like wines as neutral as their diplomacy, buy nearly all of the St. Hubertus Chasselas and the winery needs do little to promote it to other consumers. However, the Geberts brothers are confident enough of their market that the acreage of Chasselas at the St. Hubertus vineyard was doubled to about three acres in 1997. "Because there is such a strong national tie here to Switzerland, it is quite neat to have wines that are traditional," Jones says.

Quite a different style is produced at Quails' Gate, whose vineyards are almost directly across Okanagan Lake from St. Hubertus. When Jones, a New Zealand native, tastes her competitor's wine, she is reminded of New Zealand Sauvignon Blanc, coincidentally the same description favoured by Jeff Martin, the winemaker at Quails' Gate. "The 1996 has a lot of herbaceous, minty peach and nectarine notes, with some grapefruit," he says. Quails' Gate recommends its Chasselas with "mild cheeses, fish and shellfish dishes, light white meat dinners, salads and seasonal fruits."

The difference in the style reflects both the site and the winemaking approach at a winery with no Swiss heritage whatsoever. Chasselas is grown at Quails' Gate only by chance. In 1963, when the original vineyard was being developed by the Stewart family, the owners of Quails' Gate, a variety called Diamond was ordered from an American nursery. Although this variety has strong Labrusca flavours that make it a poor winemaking grape, it was grown widely in eastern Canada and

Cherie Jones

New York State in the 1960s and made some inroads in the Okanagan. Fortunately for Quails' Gate, the Stewarts were shipped vines incorrectly labeled as Diamond that really were Chasselas. Richard Stewart, father of the current operators of Quails' Gate, became aware of the error several years later when a visiting French grape expert informed him that the vines which were showing red bronze leaves early in the season were Chasselas. It was Stewart's good fortune that he had been shipped an early-ripening, low-acid variety with no offensive winemaking qualities. Had he been sold what he ordered, he would have had to abandon the Diamond within a decade because, unlike Chasselas, pleasing dry table wine cannot be made from strong-flavoured Diamond. There are no plans to abandon Chasselas.

"It's a major varietal for us now," says Martin, who makes about one thousand cases a year—enough volume that the 1996 Quails' Gate Chasselas was chosen for inflight service on one of Canada's regional airlines, proving, one supposes, that Chasselas can travel. At Quails' Gate the grapes are picked during the space of a week or ten days, with the slight variances in maturity giving Martin more flavours to work with in the winery. Not wanting any bitter tannins in the wine, Martin avoids skin contact, separating the juice from the flesh immediately after crushing the grapes. The juice is then fermented in stainless steel tanks at very cool temperatures, a winemaking technique which captures fruity flavours and aromas. The fermentation is stopped (by chilling the wine) when just a hint of natural sweetness remains. Because of the natural acidity in the wine, it gives the perception of being crisply dry, with those lively fruit flavours that elicit the comparisons to Sauvignon Blanc.

Chasselas is meant to be consumed when it is young and fresh. Martin says he prefers it during its first two or three years. However, an aged Chasselas, when carefully cellared, does not necessarily disappoint. In 1995 Mission Hill, a former producer of Chasselas from the Quails' Gate grapes, released decade-old wines, among them Chasselas. Martin was pleasantly surprised to find that the wine still had the life of, perhaps, a four-year-old wine.

CHELOIS

The Producer

LeComte Estate Winery
(Hawthorne Mountain
Vineyards)

RED TABLE WINE One of the many red hybrids developed by Albert Seibel, a nineteenth century French plant breeder, Chelois was planted extensively in Ontario and New York state in the 1950s where it impressed some critics with its wine. "Very good, deeply coloured wine, resembling a French Burgundy," Ontario wine writer Georges Masson wrote in his 1979 book, *Wine from Ontario Grapes, A Guide to Winemaking from the New Hybrids.* Apparently because the variety is susceptible to winter damage, Chelois ultimately took a distant second place to De Chaunac in Ontario and to Foch in British Columbia. Most of it now has been removed from Okanagan vineyards in favour of vinifera even though the Beaujolais-like freshness gives the wine an easy appeal.

A red hybrid variety originally identified as Seibel 10878, this was planted in British Columbia in the 1960s because it had already proved itself in Ontario as an early-ripening vine. Most of it was pulled out after the 1988 vintage, but Albert LeComte, who founded this winery, was such a fan that he not only retained his mature vines at the LeComte Okanagan Falls vineyard but planted more at a property on Black Sage Road, south of Oliver. LeComte was a self-taught winemaker who, amid a lot of strikeouts and singles, occasionally had home runs with his wines. One of those was Chelois. The winery's 1986 Chelois Private Reserve won a gold medal and the chairman's grand prize at the 1989 Pacific National Exhibition wine competition. With that kind of encouragement, LeComte kept the variety in his portfolio. The investors who bought LeComte in 1994 and renamed it Hawthorne Mountain have kept LeComte's favourite red in production, under the LeComte label. Between three and four hundred cases are made each year.

"It's nice to have an approachable, entry-level wine," says Michael Bartier, an assistant winemaker at Hawthorne Mountain Vineyards. "This is a red wine with training wheels." He is not meaning to put down the winery's Chelois but rather to define its quaffability. Indeed, the wine does sell itself when he pours a soft, spicy glass of the 1996 Chelois which, only nine months old at the time of this tasting, is bursting with appealing berry flavours. "It's a nice variety," Bartier says. "It bears a remarkable resemblance to Gamay Noir when it is young. And if you macerate it [prolonged skin contact], you can come up with a very good Bordeaux lookalike." In the 1994 vintage, the winery even released a Grand Reserve edition of its Chelois, the pretentious equivalent of adding a motor to the training wheels.

The winemaking is as straightforward as the wine. The grapes usually come in from the vineyard with the ripeness sufficient for about 12 percent alcohol and with moderate acidity, somewhat unusual among the red hybrids, many of which retain high acidity because they crop so vigorously. Perhaps the Hawthorne Mountain grapes are less productive because the vines are more than thirty years old. Because the style is Beaujolais-like, the Hawthorne Mountain winemakers limit the skin contact, wanting no tannic astringency to show up in the wine. The 1996 vintage benefited from several months aging in older barrels which softened and concentrated the wine. By the following summer it was ready to be bottled and released.

With its fresh blackberry flavours, Chelois is a good summer wine. But for all its charm, it is unlikely to command the aggressive retail price needed to make a red variety a good business proposition when grown on the Okanagan's high-priced vineyard land. Bartier doubts that more will be planted for that economic reason. "You'd have to question the sanity of anyone doing that," he says. Indeed, the old vines on the Hawthorne Mountain vineyard have a tenuous hold because of their low productivity. "It's a waste of good vineyard land," Bartier grumbles. Chelois fans should enjoy it while it is still around.

CHENIN BLANC

The Producers

Gersighel Wineberg
Inniskillin Okanagan
(as Icewine)
Mission Hill
Quails' Gate

WHITE TABLE WINE An ancient white variety important in the Loire, Chenin Blanc only has a precarious foothold in British Columbia. It got a reputation as a tender variety when a government test plot, based on vines imported from Washington State, was devastated by the deepfreeze winter of 1978-79. Former Oliver grower Terry Wells championed the variety, even after being denied crop insurance. His four and one half acres of Chenin Blanc were pulled out during the 1988 eradication of grape varieties, generally hybrids, no longer wanted by wineries. This unfortunate example of a good vinifera being pulled out occurred because no winery was prepared to contract the grapes at that time.

Quite unfairly, this variety does not command much respect. "Chenin Blanc typically internationally is a cheap grape," says Mission Hill's John Simes, who gets a small quantity of the grapes from various Okanagan vineyards, imports additional tonnages from California and generally puts the variety into proprietary blends. "You can make wonderful, wonderful wine with the grape but you can grow ten to twelve tons to the acre in the Central Valley of California or in South Africa." As a result, many varietal Chenin Blancs on the market are simple jug wines. "Nothing wrong with it. Drink it as a Tuesday-night-with-sausages wine, which is all that it is intended to be. How can you make a $10 or $12 wine when there is that sort of wine sitting there? We're not planting any Chenin Blanc."

The colourful Dirk DeGussem, the Flemish-born owner of Gersighel Wineberg, a small winery north of Osoyoos, produced an initial forty cases of Chenin Blanc in 1997 from his modest planting. Like Mission Hill, he is unlikely to plant more. He also does not think the variety has a future; in his experience, it ripens much too late. The El Niño-affected autumn of 1997 was long and mild, enabling DeGussem to pick the grapes on November 15—and even then, the acidity was bracing enough that DeGussem thinks the wine should be allowed to mature in the bottle for three years so that the acidity mellows somewhat. When the normal weather pattern applies, growers are picking frozen grapes for icewine around mid-November. "The Chenin Blanc will not be a high flyer here because you have the early frost," DeGussem asserts.

In the 1990s, Quails' Gate is the only winery to make the varietal regularly, beginning with the 1994 when Australian-born winemaker Jeff Martin took over the vintage and began expanding the winery's range of varietals. "I asked myself what wines can I make from the fruit that's out there [in the vineyard] and how can I mold them into styles that are unique to us," he explains. "That's how we ended up with Chenin Blanc and Foch and so on." Quails' Gate only has about an acre and a half of Chenin Blanc but had been buying grapes from a vineyard in Oliver. Previously, Quails' Gate simply

blended the juice with its Chasselas, a good idea that broadened the flavours in the Chasselas blend and used up the Chenin Blanc. The Oliver fruit subsequently was contracted by Vincor and turned into icewine by Inniskillin Okanagan. Quails' Gate, however, has expanded its own planting modestly and has supplemented that with plantings of Sémillon and Sauvignon Blanc with the intention of blending some of these varieties with the Chenin Blanc. "I want to make a really high-end Fumé Blanc style based on those three varietals," Martin says. "You have Sémillon for body and some straw characters and you have Sauvignon Blanc for aroma." The resulting wine, of course, will not be a Chenin Blanc varietal since it would not have the required 85 percent of Chenin Blanc. But given the economics as pointed out by Simes, a well-made proprietary wine likely can command a higher price.

The Quails' Gate Chenin Blanc itself is an attractive white with aromas of freshly cut grass and, when young, is a wine with lively citrus fruit flavours that finishes quite crisply dry. The juice is fermented at cool temperatures and matured in stainless steel to retain its fresh-picked flavours. "I think it's perfect as a summer salad wine, a salad with a really good vinaigrette, and barbecued salmon," Martin recommends. "But you put that wine in front of someone who talks dry but really drinks sweet, and they will think it is far too dry for them, too austere." The winery only makes a small quantity of Chenin Blanc and it sells quickly each year.

EHRENFELSER

WHITE TABLE WINE This variety was created in 1929 by the plant breeders at Geisenheim, who named the variety after Schloss Ehrenfels, a ruined castle on the Rhine not far from Geisenheim. The parent grapes are Riesling and Silvaner. The result is a variety that ripens more readily than Riesling, one reason why it has been almost as widely planted in the Okanagan as Gewürztraminer. Able to produce wines with savoury tropical characters, the flavours of Ehrenfelser include pineapple and lime. Late harvest wines from this grape can be lush. Winemaker Tilman Hainle writes: "Its Riesling heritage shines through in a flint/apricot/apple character which makes it a lively companion for many foods."

The Producers

Calona
CedarCreek
Gehringer
Gray Monk
Hainle
Hillside
Inniskillin Okanagan
(as Icewine)
Jackson-Triggs
Nichol Vineyard
Peller Estates
Poplar Grove
Summerhill

Because of the trend away from Germanic varieties once seen as the salvation of British Columbia wine, Ehrenfelser struggles to maintain its franchise. Major wineries, chasing the consumer interest in mainstream varieties like Chardonnay, largely have turned away from such lesser-known and hard to pronounce varieties. The author recalls a telling conversation about the variety with a product consultant for the Liquor Control Board of Ontario (Ehrenfelser is not significant in Ontario viticulture) who could not even pronounce the variety but kept calling it the "eph" grape. One of the Okanagan's most original wineries, Nichol Vineyard at Naramata, gave up on Ehrenfelser after the 1996 vintage, grafting the 380 plants in the vineyard to Syrah, the winery's acclaimed red. "I've always liked it," winemaker Alex Nichol says of Ehrenfelser. "But it was always the last variety that we sold out. We got the very clear message that this is not a hot item." The last straw for Nichol was the small yield he was able to harvest from winter-damaged vines in 1996. He made a dry white wine, with 10 percent Pinot Gris in the blend, that he described as Chardonnay-like in its finish. The wine, a mere twenty-four cases, was released with the proprietary name *Maxine's*, a tribute to his mother-in-law who in 1973 had fired his winemaking ambition by showing Nichol how to make plum wine.

While *Maxine's* bid Ehrenfelser adieu at Nichol Vineyards,

the variety survives elsewhere. It was a favourite with the late Dr. Helmut Becker, the renowned German plant scientist from Geisenheim whose advice guided new wine-growing areas from Canada to New Zealand. Ehrenfelser came to the Okanagan partly on his advice and partly at the recommendation of a Becker protégé, Walter Gehringer, now one of the proprietors of the Gehringer Brothers winery. In 1977 the Inkameep Vineyard near Oliver decided, in conjunction with the Andrés winery, to convert the vineyard from hybrids to quality European vinifera grapes. Gehringer, the first Canadian-born winemaker to graduate from Geisenheim, was then still studying there but had begun to work with Andrés. The manager of Inkameep at the time, Ted Brouwer, asked for recommendations from the young winemaker and Gehringer, after consulting Dr. Becker, suggested Riesling and two varieties that had been developed by German plant breeders, Scheurebe and Ehrenfelser. Inkameep boldly planted one hundred acres, divided equally among the three varieties. Only Scheurebe failed to gain a significant foothold in British Columbia.

Ehrenfelser appealed to Gehringer because it was a variety created to rival the great Riesling in quality while ripening better in difficult vintages. "If you want to have your cake and eat it, too," Gehringer argues, "you want to have all the positive aspects of a ripe Riesling in an unripe year." It certainly proved itself in the challenging year of 1996. While it ripens almost as late as Riesling, it achieves better sugar levels with its only significant disadvantage being a somewhat low acidity in warm years. The 1996 growing season, however, was cool and grapes ripened late, especially at some of the more northern vineyards. One of the cooler growing sites is the Rainer Mannhardt vineyard near Westbank, which grows Ehrenfelser for the CedarCreek Estate Winery. The winery's Ehrenfelser that year was excellent, ripening so well that winemaker Ross Mirko was able to make a table wine achieving the normal alcohol of 11.5 percent while balancing the prickly acidity typical of the year with fourteen grams of residual sugar per litre. The wine scored a top-ranked gold seal from the Vintners' Quality Alliance (VQA) tasting panel.

In Germany, Gehringer found, the attributes of wine from Ehrenfelser were strikingly similar to Riesling. "In our region, it is different," he notes. "That is something that we are really proud of, that the Ehrenfelser has adapted to our region with its own distinctive development of flavours." He reaches for a musical simile to distinguish wines from the two grapes grown in the Okanagan: Riesling delivers the high notes while Ehrenfelser, with a softer acidity, delivers the mid-range. Somewhat unusually for a white grape, Ehrenfelser can develop a fair degree of tannin in its skins when fully mature, lending an additional structural element to the wine. "It does give the wine a longer, lingering presence on your palate," Gehringer suggests. "People who like red wine will sometimes quite enjoy the Ehrenfelser, not knowing why, but it is basically this similarity of tannin finish." This character, he believes, makes Ehrenfelser a wine to pair with spicy foods. Gehringer today produces both a dry and an off-dry Ehrenfelser and finds that the latter is most popular among his clientele. "It's a great aperitif wine on its own because it is quite rich," he says.

Because of its historic link with Inkameep, Andrés has been a major Ehrenfelser producer for nearly two decades, with styles that include icewine. Winemaker Tony Vlcek leans to a table wine Ehrenfelser that is fruity and off-dry, bringing out flavours that remind him of a ripe peach. "That's one of the wines that we have done here for years and it has done well that way," he says. Another large producer of Ehrenfelser as a table wine is Summerhill, perhaps because the involvement that winery owner Stephen Cipes had with the Nordique Blanc project. The name refers to a concept wine launched in 1989 by Inkameep Vineyards, which wanted to test the American market's acceptance of a white table wine made from the vineyard's Ehrenfelser grapes. Cipes was involved in distributing the wine in New York and Chicago, where the 1988 Nordique Blanc, impeccably made by Walter Gehringer, was a critical success. After Cipes launched his own winery, Summerhill made a number of wines under the Nordique label, including Ehrenfelser, before phasing out the label. But with a contract for Inkameep's Ehrenfelser and with Ehrenfelser in Summerhill's own vineyard, the variety has remained in the winery's arsenal. One version is the Ehrenfelser Dry, made in the crisp Nordique Blanc style. An off-dry Summerhill version, made since 1992, has captured its own fan club. "For some reason," winemaker Alan Marks laughs, "it got the nickname as the hot tub wine. They pumped it in the sales room as something to sip around the hot tub. A lot of times, people still come in and simply ask for the hot tub wine."

"Ehrenfelser is like a chameleon," Ross Mirko suggests. "In

1995 it got extremely ripe and heavily botrytized and made a really oily, fat wine." The wine evolved quickly in the bottle to show intriguing complexity, including a bouquet that Mirko likened to beeswax. Dessert-style wines from Ehrenfelser have been produced occasionally when the vintage justifies those wines. Andrés won a series of awards at wine competitions for its late harvest Ehrenfelsers from the 1980s, including a remarkable botrytis-affected wine in 1989. Now, the winery also incorporates the variety in its three-grape icewine, called, aptly enough, *Trinity*. As a table wine, Ehrenfelser may be at its best when it is youthful, perhaps to its third birthday, especially from hot vintages. In 1996, because the season was dramatically cool and late, Mirko made what he calls a Germanic style wine, crisply fresh with lemon and lime flavours, with the potential for developing in the bottle four or five years before peaking. "It is really interesting to work with," Mirko says of Ehrenfelser. "It always has a lot of character."

Marks believes it is important to maintain the aromas and flavours which set the variety apart. "Ours seems to have nice tropical flavours," he says. "It definitely has apricots and peaches. Some citrus characters are usually there, especially in the cooler years. It's a very floral wine, very perfumed. That floral character seems to hold up well in the bottle. I have tasted some of the older ones here and they still have a nice floral aroma. Our aromatics in British Columbia are longer lived than in some other regions."

Marks, a self-described serious amateur chef and the son of a professional chef, recommends Ehrenfelser with Asian foods, with the so-called hot tub version being well-suited to spiced cuisine. "Curried chick peas is really nice with a sweet Ehrenfelser," he says. "We like to say that our wines go well with everyday food, too. You don't have to make a roast pheasant or something. You can enjoy a bottle of Ehrenfelser with a simple meal, maybe even a burger on the grill and a fresh garden salad. You don't have to make a six-course dinner for guests to enjoy a bottle of our wine."

FRUIT WINES

SOCIAL AND FOOD WINES It is a conceit of wine tasters to describe wines from grapes in terms of supposed fruit and berry tastes, such as plum, cherry and black currant. The paradox is that commercially available wines rarely are made from the fruits themselves. There is a healthy tradition of amateur fruit wine production and, in British Columbia, a history of fruit wines. For the most part, fruit wines do not compete with grape wines as beverages for the table with food. More typically, they are consumed socially or as dessert wines. This is not a hard and fast rule. Creative chefs are finding interesting pairings of fruit wines with salads or as marinades for game.

The Producers

Calona Vineyards
Columbia Valley Classics

The first Okanagan vineyard to be contracted to a winery in British Columbia was established in the late 1920s. However, wine production had begun earlier using loganberries, a sweet, juicy berry developed by an Oregon plant scientist named Logan who crossed the cultivated raspberry with the blackberry native to the west coast. Farmers on the Saanich Peninsula and in the Vancouver suburb of Richmond planted loganberries with such enthusiasm that surpluses overwhelmed the fresh market. There are anecdotal reports that an entrepreneurial Vancouver Island resident named Steve Slinger began making and selling loganberry wine even before British Columbia emerged, in mid-1921, from five unhappy years of Prohibition. The Slinger operation and brands later were acquired by the Growers' Wine Company which had been set up in 1923, and which flourished with its fruit wines. Even though Growers' contracted the first grapes from the Okanagan, the fruit wines remained in its portfolio for almost half a century.

"The [loganberry] wine," Growers' explained in a 1927 brochure, "which is made mainly from the juice of freshly picked, ripe Loganberries and cane sugar only, is of the Port Class, having a proof percentage of 28. It is delicious in flavour and bouquet and of wonderful colour." Wines of this style were popular through the 1960s. Indeed, Calona Wines in 1968 launched its Jack wines, a line of fruit wines fortified to 20 percent alcohol. The wines were modeled on successful fruit wines made by California wineries and the name was taken from Applejack, a distilled apple brandy. Calona's apple wine was called *Double Jack*. It was joined by *Berry Jack* (from loganberries), *Cherry Jack* and *Grape Jack*. The winery recommended serving these wines chilled "for entertaining or after dinner." More likely, the aficionados of these enormously popular beverages were the drive-in movie theatre crowd. Jack wines were still being produced in the late 1990s and have been joined from time to time by other fruit-based pop beverages such as alcoholic lemonade and fruit-flavoured coolers.

The fruit wines now emerging are modeled after conventionally-made wines and not the alcohol-laced beverages of the 1960s. Columbia Valley Classics, which opened its winery in 1998 at Cultus Lake in the Fraser Valley, is the first exclusively fruit winery in British Columbia since the loganberry wineries almost seventy years earlier.

The winery is the brainchild of a horticulturist named John Stuyt. Born in north Holland in 1930 into a family that has been farming for at least 350 years, Stuyt emigrated to Canada and the Fraser Valley in 1956 and naturally continued farming, raising everything from raspberries to chickens at his property near Aldergrove. He discovered the Columbia Valley (which includes Cultus Lake) on a Sunday afternoon drive in 1989 and was so seized with its agricultural potential that he purchased a farm within five days. "All of a sudden, I got these little childhood dreams," booms the craggy-visaged Stuyt, an ambitious freethinker who does things his own way. "I believe in functioning according to John."

Functioning according to John meant planting twenty acres of hazelnut, along with an array of fruits on the remaining twenty acres, including raspberries, blueberries, red, white and black currants, gooseberries, saskatoon berries and kiwi. If he can get the plants, he will add chokecherries, a staple of amateur fruit winemaking across the Prairies. He also added two grape varieties suited to the Fraser Valley, Ortega and Madeleine Angevine. Stuyt intends to explore the fruit producing potential of the Columbia Valley. "You should see the quality," he enthuses about his red currants. "It is totally different from Aldergrove. The colour is deep and rich and full."

The intensive agriculture practiced elsewhere in the Fraser Valley had bypassed the Columbia and Stuyt soon found out why.

The Columbia is off the beaten track for consumers motoring out from the city to buy fresh fruit, and Stuyt's so-called Bertrand Creek farm, which is on a hillside overlooking the south end of Cultus Lake, is even further from the casual buyers. That is what prompted Stuyt to add fruit wines to the farm's portfolio. He had earlier begun making and selling jams and preserves from his farm, including a hazelnut spread. Having a food processing license from the federal government smoothed the way when he applied for a winery licence from the province. "There wasn't too much encouragement," he admits, "but there weren't too many excuses for anyone to deny me a licence." The winery opened in the spring of 1998, sharing premises with the jam production facility.

Dominic Rivard

After making small experimental lots of fruit wines, Stuyt concluded he needed a winemaker with experience and he recruited Dominic Rivard. Born in Quebec's Gaspé region in 1971, Rivard is schooled in business and science with a passion for wine and a diploma from a rigorous British wine course. "I've basically been making wine since *before* I was legally able to drink it," he confesses. Largely self-taught, he acquired basic skills while working in the laboratory of Spagnol's Enterprises Ltd., a large Vancouver supplier of grapes to amateur vintners across western Canada.

Fruit wines arguably are more difficult to make than grape wines. Properly grown grapes are the complete package for wine when they are harvested, containing the required flavours, acids, sugar and liquid to yield wine with only the addition of yeast. Fruits seldom comprise the complete package; sugar and water need to be added, while acidity generally needs to be reduced, except for blueberries which often are too low in acid. Rivard and Stuyt, sensing what they were getting themselves into, sought advice from Todd Moore, the winemaker at Cherry Point Vineyards on Vancouver Island, and the only young vintner in British Columbia with significant fruit wine experience. He provided some of the initial recipes for the Columbia Valley Classics products.

Born in Vancouver in 1966, Moore is a lithe, tall young

man with two driving interests. One is bicycle racing: he has ridden in international level road races and was the British Columbia champion road racer in 1997. The other is wine, surprising because he claims he was not even a wine drinker in December, 1987 when he became an assistant to winemaker Frank Bandelow at the Lewis Brothers fruit winery in Grande Prairie, Alberta. Moore quips that he got the job because he was dating the daughter of one of the owners. By the time Bandelow left suddenly eighteen months later, Moore had acquired the necessary skills. The Lewis operation had opened in 1986 with wine made from saskatoon berries, including *Nouveau Saskatoon*, a drinkable parody of France's over-promoted *Beaujolais Nouveau*. This was followed with a honey wine called *Wild Rose Mead*. A variety of fruit-flavoured honey wines was

Todd Moore

produced, including a raspberry honey wine that made the list of domestic wines the Canadian government recommended its embassies order for entertaining. In 1990, the winery added a dry rhubarb wine called *White Swan* which enjoyed surprising, if short-lived, success in Japan. The wines sold well in all markets on novelty appeal and on the remarkable nose for publicity possessed by Cledwyn and Michael Lewis (respectively, a doctor and a dentist). But when the novelty wore off in the mid-1990s, the winery closed. Moore had left Grande Prairie by 1993. After a vintage at a grape winery in Australia, he came back to British Columbia to work first at Quails' Gate and then at Blue Mountain. In 1996, he reinforced his technical abilities with chemistry and biology courses at Okanagan College before joining Cherry Point for the vintage that fall. Here, Moore has found time to train for competitive cycling on the back roads of Vancouver Island while making wine from one of island's most carefully-grown vineyards.

When Stuyt and Rivard needed advice, Moore had the experience with the idiosyncrasies of fruits for wine. For example, he knew that rhubarb wine tends to throw an unsightly sediment (flakes of oxalic acid) and he had learned to prevent it by precipitating that acid out in the first place, replacing it with the more stable tartaric acid found in grape wines. Raspberry wines, he had discovered, may lose their brilliantly attractive colour, another problem than can be corrected with acid adjustment. Every fruit has its own challenge and Moore had met most of them.

In contrast to grape wines, those made from fruit generally are produced in relatively small batches (five hundred to three thousand liters at Columbia Valley Classics) throughout the year. This is because fruit wines are ready to drink much earlier after fermentation and seldom benefit from prolonged aging. Fruit wines, with the exception of red currants, seldom have the structure or the acid that support significant aging. At Columbia Classics, the fruit is frozen after being picked and stored in buckets, either as whole berries or as purée. Freezing and then thawing is beneficial because it extracts more juice and character from the fruit. The elapsed time from bucket to bottle can be as short as three months. "You make them, you bottle them and you drink them," Rivard says. Because the wines are made throughout the year, none are vintage dated. Besides, Rivard questions whether vintage dates would be appropriate with fruit wines. "There is no point in pretending we are what we are not," he says.

While mead and the loganberry wines invariably were sweet, Rivard makes fruit wines that are comparatively dry. The wine made from white currants, in fact, is easily mistaken for white grape wine, with its golden hue and flavours vaguely recalling Riesling. "It is a very food-friendly type," the winemaker says, having enjoyed it with chicken pot pie. The red currant wine is a medium-bodied beverage, attractively ruby in the glass with an off-dry finish. The black currant wine, dark in colour and almost port-like in texture and flavour, has been served with chocolate desserts. Rivard's blackberry wine is light and delicate, while his raspberry wine has fresh, zesty aromas and flavours vividly expressing the berry's character. The hard-to-make blueberry wine has a deep colour and is abundantly fruity, reflecting the quality that John Stuyt gets from his Columbia Valley site. While blueberry wines generally are social beverages, consultant Todd Moore believes that this, and perhaps other fruit wines, have the potential for more daring winemaking. "One of the best 'Cabernets' I ever had was a blueberry wine," Moore laughs, recalling a barrel-aged blueberry wine from an eastern United States producer. "But they couldn't sell it. With fruit wine, it is such an uphill battle."

John Stuyt knows that, but it does not discourage him. "There is a niche market, a specialty market, for this type of wine. We have to make an above average product and if we don't, we'll have a tough time."

GAMAY NOIR

RED TABLE WINE The French use this grape to make mostly easy-drinking reds of Beaujolais and once grew the vine throughout Burgundy until Philip the Bold, one of the dukes of Burgundy, ordered it banished in favour of the more aristocratic Pinot Noir. For consumers not expecting a profound experience with every glass, Gamay is an affordable alternative to Pinot Noir. In general wines from Gamay are light, lively and quaffable. Gray Monk's George Heiss Jr. finds a raspberry note is typical to the wines. Several producers, led by Blue Mountain, make a more substantial style comparable to the well-known classified "Cru" wines of Beaujolais. Hester Creek winemaker Frank Supernak believes that, whatever Philip the Bold thought a few centuries ago, Gamay today is a variety "on its way up."

The Producers

Blue Mountain
Domaine Combret
Gray Monk
Hawthorne Mountain
Hester Creek
Hillside Cellars
Larch Hills
Oak Bay
St. Hubertus

Without a doubt, no one claims to have taken more care with vineyard site selection than Robert Combret when he and his family, after ten generations of winegrowing in the south of France, moved to the Okanagan in 1992. His research ultimately drew him to a property south of Oliver, on the west side of the valley, and among a stretch of vineyards called the Golden Mile. Combret analyzed everything from heat units to the composition of the soil before settling on varieties to plant. Remarkably, his major red (three and a half hectares) is Gamay—surprising because it has been planted the length of the valley, mostly by growers in search of an early-maturing, easy drinking red. The awesomely-researched Combret compares his relatively warm site with vineyards at the north end of Beaujolais where the wineries produce not the everyday Beaujolais but the fine-textured Beaujolais Cru. "Chénas," Combret begins to tick them off. "Moulin-à-Vent … Morgon … Brouilly, et cetera." Clearly, he has laid high expectations on the shoulders of his winemaker son, Olivier.

The first basket of Gamay from the Combret vineyard was harvested in 1996. Hardly enough to make a wine, the fruit nevertheless was "fabulously excellent," Robert Combret recalls. "Gamay is 100 percent adapted to this country. What kind of soil does Gamay love? Gamay will reach a full expression in the glass if grown on granitic soils." It so happens that there is an element of that composition in the soils of the Combret property. The vines only began producing enough for wine with the 1997 harvest. The Combret family grow three clones of Gamay. One is suited to making a nouveau style, a second is designed for a full-bodied, barrel-aged red and the third clone is the switch-hitter, able to support either the nouveau wine or the full-blown one, depending on the vintage and the market. It is no surprise to learn that the intense Robert Combret is not a great admirer of young reds. "Personally, I have never been favourable to young red wines," he admits. "But it is a fad all over the world." The Combrets will allow their grapes to lead them. "If by nature the grape is very, very fruity, then it [the Gamay clone suited for young wine] will produce a super excellent young red wine. We will know immediately when the grapes arrive at the winery." The winery also has developed a lower-priced second label, Domaine de Bellac, for its lighter, more approachable wines— such as the 1997 Bellac Gamay *Noir Eclipse One*, very much a fresh Beaujolais Nouveau style. In part, the strategy is aimed at capturing consumers that might otherwise be deterred by the prices which some wineries put on premium varietals. "Over 70 percent of the wine drinkers in the world are not wealthy people," Olivier Combret suggests. "It is not by increasing prices that we will get more people appreciating more wines."

Advice from a visiting French winegrower (not Combret) led Blue Mountain proprietor Ian Mavety to include Gamay early in the 1990s in his immaculate vineyard near Okanagan Falls. "I took him outside and said, 'Look around, what variety do you think would be adapted to this area,' " recalls Mavety. "Without hesitation, he said Gamay Noir." The reasons, as at the Combret estate, included the quality of the soil and the climate. "We only planted a very little bit," says Mavety, who typically avoids reckless decisions at a vineyard where he has grown both hybrids and vinifera successfully since 1971. He only began expanding the Gamay planting in 1998 after the grape had indeed proven itself in the vineyard. "Our experience to date has been it is a more difficult variety to deal with than Pinot Noir, on our site," he found. "One of the reasons is that it is a very prolific variety and it takes longer to get established." This is overcome with careful viticulture, keeping the production comparatively low, although not as low as Pinot Noir. In warm years, the Gamay has ripened enough to produce full-bodied wine with a strapping 13 percent alcohol. However, in 1996 the vines struggled to get ripe enough to yield naturally just over 11 percent alcohol and Blue Mountain was required to chaptalize (add sugar) to the juice before fermentation to raise the alcohol to 12.5 percent, necessary to achieve the structure desired in the robust Blue Mountain style.

A common winemaking practice in Europe, where it is officially sanctioned, chaptalization is named for a French chemist, Jean-Antoine Chaptal, who was Napoleon's Minister of the Interior. In a winemaking text he wrote in 1807 and in several essays on the topic, Chaptal advised winegrowers that alcohol levels in table wines could be raised easily—if nature had not done the job—by adding either grape concentrate or sugar to the must before fermentation. Along with the sugar already in the grapes, the added sweetener is turned into alcohol as fermentation proceeds. There are other ways of boosting alcohol, such as adding spirits, but the marriage is not as seamless. Prior to 1990 in British Columbia the addition of sugar or spirits was widespread because wineries frequently received inadequately-ripened grapes, usually the result of poor viticulture, not poor weather. The wine standards of 1990 sought to curb abuses by prohibiting the addition of sugar to any wine that was to be eligible for the Vintners' Quality Alliance, or VQA, designation. "It was an absolutely stupid rule," Mavety says. The prohibition was an over-reaction to past excesses and flew in the face of widespread chaptalization wherever wine is grown in cool climates, including Oregon, which has some of the world's most rigorous wine standards. The rule was dropped in British Columbia in 1996, a year when many vineyards were unable to achieve optimum sugars naturally. Paradoxically, the grapes often stayed on the vine so late that season that they developed other attributes of ripeness—good colour, intense flavours. Chaptalization was the only way to achieve the alcohol needed for a balanced, well-structured wine. "The key is that you don't chaptalize in excess," Mavety says. "I wouldn't take it to the limit. If you were forced into it year after year in this climate, I think you would have to assess your vineyards pretty carefully."

Like Combret, Blue Mountain's model is the mouth-filling style of northern Beaujolais. The comparatively full-bodied Blue Mountain Gamay shows hints of raspberry and black pepper, enough character that Mavety recommends it with full-flavoured foods, even including wild boar steaks from a nearby wild boar farm. "Gamay as North Americans know it is very much a light and fruity wine," Mavety observes. "But as Europeans know it from the Grand Crus and Premiers Crus, it's a *real* red wine." When the grapes arrive at the winery, they are destemmed totally at crush and are fermented on the skins until total dryness, with frequent punching down of the "cap" to extract colour and flavour. The cap is the layer of skins and grape flesh that is buoyed to the top of a fermentation tank by the carbon dioxide released during ferment. In making red wines, it is routine to re-immerse the cap several times a day, either by pumping the juice over it or by punching it down manually. "I prefer always to punch by hand," Mavety says, "but if the fermentation is sluggish or if you are trying to extract more for climatic reasons, you would want to pump more than you plunge." When fermentation is done, the wine is pressed off the skins, going immediately into barrels (a mix of one- to four-year-old barrels) to finish malolactic fermentation. It is bottled in May or June following the vintage and released in the fall. Blue Mountain's first vintage of Gamay was 1994 and, with production of only about three hundred cases a year, the variety has been a bit player at a winery more noted for Pinot Noir. However, Mavety was sufficiently pleased with successive vintages, even including the challenge of 1996, to plan an eventual doubling of production. "I like the wine," he smiles. "It doesn't have the inherent qualities of Pinot Noir. No matter what you do with it, it doesn't have the complexities and subtleties. But what it does have that Pinot doesn't, is that it's more forward." Which means it is ready to drink sooner. Even so, he is confident that Blue Mountain's Gamay, like a Beaujolais Cru, readily will age five years.

Hester Creek, whose vineyard is across a gully to the north of Combret, planted a modest half acre of Gamay in 1997 and a further acre in 1998, with vines imported from France. The research here was perhaps more commercial. "With all the Merlot plantings in the ground [in the Okanagan], we need something new," winemaker Frank Supernak maintains. "From what I understand is happening in California and Washington, Gamay is on its way up. We wanted to jump on the bandwagon before everyone else did." While the winemaking also will be dictated by the grapes, Supernak believes the wines can be shaped through the use of several different types of oak and fermentation treatments. "I just want something that is fun to play with."

Searching for a red variety suitable for growing in the north Okanagan, George Heiss Jr. put a trial plot of Gamay in his vineyard, not far from the Gray Monk winery at Okanagan Centre. The first vintage, made in 1994, was sufficiently pleasing that he planted more Gamay and convinced one of Gray Monk's growers to plant five acres. "It's just a little bit earlier than Pinot Noir," Heiss has found. "And it can handle the winters here." At St. Hubertus, owners Leo and Andy Geberts and their vintner Cherie Jones like the variety so much so that the winery produces two styles, a fruity Beaujolais style under the St. Hubertus label and a more complex oak-aged version under the Oak Bay label. "One thing about a cool climate is that you get such intense flavours and aromas from the varieties," Jones believes. "There is so much life to them."

The variety even produces attractive blush wines. In 1996 Hillside Cellars released such a wine, a light-bodied, fruity wine with an attractive bronze pink hue. "This was a wine we hadn't planned on doing," winemaker John Fletcher says. "It was a creature of necessity." The harvest was late in that notoriously cool vintage and the Gamay grapes delivered insufficient colour or flavour for a full-blown red. In order to concentrate what colour and flavour there was, Fletcher drained off, or bled, about 20 percent of the juice from a tank of Gamay that had been two days on the skins. The procedure concentrated the winery's standard Gamay, which completed its fermentation on the skins, while the juice was fermented into a fresh, off-dry rosé that was ready for market four months after it had been made and played a role, Fletcher says, as a "summertime refreshment." For its standard Gamay, Hillside also falls into the light, fresh, serve-it-cool style, an entry wine for many consumers. "The Gamay consumer seems to be more the novice," Fletcher has found.

GEWÜRZTRAMINER

WHITE TABLE WINE This European variety has found a good home in British Columbia where it performs well in all but the hottest vineyards and where most consumers are seduced by its lush perfume and exotic flavours. The parent of the variety is the Traminer grape, a green-skinned variety that evolved perhaps around 1000 AD in vineyards around the northern Italian town of Tramin (pronounced *Tra-meen*). That variety, which mutates readily, gave rise in Germany to a vine whose berries at maturity are dark pink and whose wines are somewhat more spicy. Since *gewürz* is a German word for spicy, the mutation was called Gewürztraminer. The variety was introduced to Alsace after 1870 when that territory on the west side of the Rhine came under one of its occasional periods of German governance. Many argue that Alsace Gewürztraminer is the finest expression of this variety in the world. The wines complement full flavoured cooking such as Chinese dishes. The wine also flatters humble cuisine, like sauerkraut in Alsace. Helena Ulrich at Cherry Point Vineyards has served the winery's dry style successfully with herbed pastrami on rye bread. One debatable recommendation is to serve Gewürztraminer with East Indian food—debatable because of the sparring match that is created among conflicting spice flavours.

This is a true story. In the 1980s the Casabello winery at Penticton —which was demolished after its closure in 1995—had a winemaker called Tom Seaver whose cousin of the same name was a renowned major league pitcher. One year the Gewürztraminer grapes arrived at Casabello during the World Series, beautifully mature grapes with the classic pink skin of ripe Gewürztraminer. They were crushed but before the juice could be pressed from the skins, a tense, extra-innings baseball game intervened, temporarily distracting winemaker Seaver— also a baseball fan—from the winery. Many hours later the juice, when pressed from the skins, had a darker hue than is considered desirable for Gewürztraminer.

With that story in mind, a casual question is put to Edgar Scherzinger about his philosophy on skin contact with Gewürztraminer. If there is anyone who should have a point of view on making wine with this grape, it is Scherzinger. The six and a half acres that constitute picturesque Scherzinger Vineyards at Summerland is given over almost totally to this variety, with only minor plantings of Pinot Noir and Chardonnay. Scherzinger's reply, a recital of the trials of Job, tops the Tom Seaver story.

Prior to the 1996 vintage, Scherzinger, who leans to un-complicated fruit-driven wines, was not in the habit of giving his Gewürztraminer juice much skin contact at all. But that year, after the grapes had been picked and crushed, the rubber bladder on his Italian press failed, splitting dramatically under pressure. Since the press was then only two years old and the bladder should have a life span of four to five years, Scherzinger had no spare. But neither did the supplier in Toronto, who said it would take three months to get a new one from Italy (it did!). Scherzinger began calling wineries and suppliers all over North America with similar presses: no one had a spare bladder. Then in an apparent stroke of luck, a winemaking supplier in Vancouver had one with the same serial number as Scherzinger's broken bladder. He drove all night to Vancouver—the Gewürztraminer after all was steeping on its skins all this time—only to discover that the bladder, even though the number was the same, was for a smaller model Italian press. On the long drive back home, Scherzinger remembered that Crowsnest Vineyards at Cawston had a small German bladder press. On inquiry, he found the press was available. He hauled it back to his Summerland winery and resumed pressing the grapes, which now had spent several days on the skins. Half-way through the job, the borrowed press also broke its bladder. This time Scherzinger was able to get a spare locally and completed the pressing without more delay. "I think it did the wine a favour," Scherzinger recounted later, having found that the grapes with prolonged skin contact delivered the most flavour in the wine. "I think I'll try it again."

Scherzinger was lucky that his presses chose the 1996 vintage to fail. In a much warmer year, his Gewürztraminer would have emerged from that experience a fat, rose-coloured wine without any finesse—at best. Wild Goose's Adolf Kruger on occasion has given the variety as much as thirty hours of skin contact but believes that twelve to eighteen hours is quite long enough. Bruce Ewert at Hawthorne Mountain, whose vineyard includes thirty acres of Gewürztraminer, has learned from research that skin contract longer than forty-eight hours can impart minor notes of harshness to the wine. In a really ripe year, there is far too much tannin in the skins of this variety to let a winemaker get away with prolonged skin contact. "If you get Gewürz too ripe," Quails' Gate winemaker Jeff Martin believes, "you end up with really broad, greasy Muscat characteristics." Sumac Ridge's Mark Wendenburg takes a somewhat different view: to assemble the winery's lushly-flavoured Private Reserve Gewürztraminer, he is able to draw fruit from different parts of the Okanagan, including the Black Sage vineyard south of Oliver. "I like to get that Gewürz really ripe, *killer ripe*, just to accent the Muscat and the Gewürztraminer flavour," he says. "Most of our Gewürz comes from north of Okanagan Falls." He prefers the grapes to arrive with what he calls "rosa" skin colours and he does not hesitate to give skin contact to the best quality grapes. On occasion, Wendenburg also includes aromatic Perle of Csaba or Schönburger as fruit highlights in a blend whose style is distinctive and so well-received that, when there is sufficient fruit, production will be nine thousand cases a year.

However, 1996 was one of the coolest years in the memory of many winemakers, lacking the sunshine to put a great deal of blush in the cheeks of Gewürztraminer. It was precisely the year to reward skin contact, as Scherzinger discovered when he compared the two lots of wine he made in 1996. The initial pressing, with little skin contact, produced a much lighter wine than the subsequent pressings after prolonged skin contact. A gentle man with a sweet personality, Scherzinger, a wood carver by trade, is a self-taught winemaker with something of a love affair with Gewürztraminer. It began shortly after he decided to convert the Summerland cherry orchard he had purchased in 1974 to a vineyard. Most people, including a neighbour, advised him to plant winter-hardy hybrids. Scherzinger hesitated to commit his entire vineyard although he did plant some Bath and some De Chaunac. "You couldn't make wine out of them," he discovered. "You couldn't even make vinegar. I tried to combine it with 7 UP and you still could not drink it." One day his neighbour discarded some Pinot Noir and some Gewürztraminer vines, dismissing them as "some stuff from Europe that hardly bears anything." Scherzinger planted them and, busy with building a house, ignored the vines until the autumn when he picked the few grapes and was pleased with their winemaking quality. When these vines survived the winter, he gradually planted almost the entire six and a half acre vineyard to vinifera, most of it Gewürztraminer. There was some Johannisberg Riesling after a vine nursery had mixed those together with the Gewürztraminer plants, saddling Scherzinger with a nightmare of vineyard management until he replaced the Riesling with Gewürztraminer. He even had planted an acre of Okanagan Riesling, his neighbour having advised him to do so to be "on the safe side." Those vines were pulled out in the 1988 eradication of unwanted varieties in the Okanagan.

"It's not hard to grow," Scherzinger has discovered of Gewürztraminer. "It wants warm days but cool nights." Wayne Ulrich of Vancouver Island's Cherry Point Vineyards is the only grower in the Cowichan Valley with a significant planting of the variety. "You swear at it all summer because it's such a miserable vine to look after," he laments. "It grows fast and tangly." But he is quick to add that the variety comes through every year with sound, healthy fruit. The vine is somewhat susceptible to winter damage but is otherwise well-suited to cooler vineyard sites in British Columbia. "We seem to get wine that is a little more fruity and less spicy than the Okanagan gets," Ulrich has found. Sumac Ridge's Wendenburg, who makes more of the variety than any other vintner, takes a contrary view that arises from his experience at blending the winery's spicy and slightly off-dry Private Reserve style each year. "A lot of people say that the Gewürz is better in the cooler areas. I don't know if I agree with that in the Okanagan. We buy Gewürztraminer from a whole bunch of different areas. I think there's a real place for Gewürztraminer to be grown in the south. I don't think there is any lesser quality, whether it is grown in Oliver or Kelowna." Similarly, Bruce Ewert at Hawthorne Mountain draws the variety from four sources, including one in the Similkameen Valley, and carefully assembles the winery's rich, off-dry style from these four different wines. Tinhorn Creek boldly planted seventeen acres of the variety near the winery south of Oliver but located those vines on the coolest and most elevated part of the vineyard on the west side of the valley. Initially, the winery had planned to focus exclusively on Chardonnay, Pinot Gris and Pinot Blanc as its whites until the owners decided one evening in 1994, over a bottle of wine, that those three varieties are not sufficiently well differentiated in style and flavour from each other to offer enough choice to its customers. Gewürztraminer, recalls winemaker Sandra Oldfield, seemed an obvious alternative. "We could have gone to Chenin Blanc or Sauvignon Blanc, but Gewürztraminer stands out," she says.

Arguably, the variety is best suited to cooler sites. Alan Marks, the winemaker at Summerhill, explains that "Gewürz is prone to losing its acid in warmer regions. In a matter of days it can get really flabby and the acid will drop out and then we have to do more manipulations." The addition of fruit acids during fermentation is allowed if required—but it usually is not needed because the nights usually are cool in the Okanagan, especially at Summerhill and the other Kelowna-area vineyards. "The Gewürztraminer just keeps it acids beautifully and, along with that, its aromas," Marks says. "Our style is to preserve the beautiful fruit aromas in the Gewürz." The unusually cool 1996 vintage resulted in Gewürztraminer grapes quite atypically retaining lively acidity while still delivering the natural sugars needed for good wines. "Gewürz we can get ripe every year," assures Günther Lang of Lang Vineyards at Naramata. "Even though 1996 was a challenging year—it was our most complicated year in seventeen years of grape growing—we got all the grapes ripe. It was not a high producer. With a low yield philosophy, you always get the grapes ripe."

"I really love Alsace Gewürztraminer," admits winemaker Ross Mirko. "I don't know how they do it. I wouldn't draw parallels between those wines and our wines [in the Okanagan] just yet." CedarCreek, where he was winemaker for four years, is one of the larger volume producers of Gewürztraminer, about 2,600 cases a year. The Gewürztraminer in Alsace almost always makes bold wines with rich fruit flavours and aromas of spice and lichees, all of it neatly supported on a strapping structure of 12 percent or more alcohol. These are big wines, capable of taking on such tasty local Alsace dishes as *choucrout garni* (sauerkraut) and can be paired easily with holiday fare such as roast turkey. With a very few exceptions, Gewürztraminer in the Okanagan is a different wine: not as big, more floral in its spice, usually finished off-dry. "A lot of people say they like it dry," Jackson-Triggs winemaker Bruce Nicholson says. "I do a lot of tastings and I always find that people like it a little bit sweeter than they say." Most of the Gewürztraminer vines in British Columbia come from nurseries in the United States and are the so-called Washington clone, arguably more appropriate for the off-dry style than those from the French clone. Gray Monk winemaker George Heiss Jr.

says of the Washington clone that it is "more flowery, almost a wild rose character." The Alsace clone, which Gray Monk grows in its own vineyard, makes an elegantly dry wine with a spicy perfume. Lang Vineyards also imported vines from France for its vineyard at Naramata, launching a wine in 1995 that is made dry, with restaurants and food in mind. "With a meal, with East Indian food, it's a wonderful wine," Günther Lang says. Heiss believes the Alsace clone "tends to be more earthy; at times it goes almost into a grapefruit character. It does not seem as intense on the nose but more intense on the palate." It is the other way around with the Washington State clone, Heiss adds. Gray Monk's non-reserve Gewürztraminer is made from the latter clone, the grapes purchased from vineyards elsewhere in the Okanagan. Much more attention has been paid in the 1990s to clonal selection. At Hawthorne Mountain, a replanting program deliberately has brought a mixture of clones to the vineyard. However, the mainstream Gewürztraminer style in British Columbia is not to be disdained just because it is different from much-admired Alsace; it only needs to be matched with different cuisine and served a little cooler. "If a wine has any residual sugar at all, it almost needs a little extra chilling," suggests Bruce Nicholson of Jackson-Triggs.

Several winemakers, including Jeff Martin at Quails' Gate, have no intention of making Alsace-style wines. Practically all of his white wines showcase fruit and freshness. Going the Alsace route would require picking the grapes when they are quite ripe and processing the juice differently to achieve that robust dry style. "A lot of those wines can take three to four years to come around," Martin believes. "Alsace Gewürz is very good with bottle development. What are we trying to make, a style that is pleasant and drinkable now or one that we've got to sit on for five years to come around?" The Quails' Gate style is an off-dry, drink-now Gewürztraminer. The Scherzinger Gewürztraminer comes in three styles—dry and off-dry table wines and a sweeter late harvest wine—in part because of what Scherzinger's consumers request when they come to the tasting room. "The males usually prefer the dry wines and the women like it a little sweeter," Edgar Scherzinger observes. "I cannot go by my taste. I have to go by what the public wants."

KERNER

The Producers

Carriage House

Crowsnest

Golden Mile Cellars

Gray Monk

Hainle

Hillside

Tinhorn Creek

Venturi-Schulze

WHITE TABLE WINE In 1969 Germany's Weinsberg Institute in Württemberg classified a new white grape created by crossing Trollinger, a red variety, with the great Riesling. Vine breeder August Herold called the variety Kerner—for nineteenth century German poet Justinus Kerner who had been one of Weinsberg's leading citizens. It is one of the most successful new varieties to emerge from German plant breeding. The vine is vigorous, ripening reliably while maintaining the essential acidity in the grapes. The variety now has a toehold in vineyards beyond Germany, including both the Okanagan and Vancouver Island. Exceptionally versatile, Kerner's wines cover the field from dry table wines to icewines. The wines are comparable to Riesling while perhaps slightly fleshier on the palate. The wines are attractive when fresh and young but also age well. Gray Monk's George Heiss recommends dry Kerner with pasta with cream sauce or clam sauce.

In her otherwise excellent 1986 book *Vines, Grapes and Wines*, Jancis Robinson dismisses Justinus Kerner (1786–1862) as a mere librettist of drinking songs. In fact, he was one of the most distinguished citizens of Weinsberg where he lived most of his adult life and where he is buried beside his wife, a clairvoyant about whom Kerner once wrote a book. He had a medical degree from the University of Tübingen and ultimately settled his practice in Weinsberg, becoming district health officer. He also was an accomplished writer of both popular medical books and of poetry which blended romance, melancholy and the supernatural. In 1840 composer Robert Schumann set fifteen of Kerner's poems to music, including *Wanderlied* (Travel-song), which opens with the line *Wohlauf, noch getrunken den funkelnden Wein* (Come, one more glass of shimmering wine). The poem, however, is not a drinking song but a nostalgic memorial to a friend with whom he had shared wine. Weinsberg was so proud of its literary doctor that the city gave him a house (now a museum) just outside a historic medieval castle. Public buildings and city squares have been named for him; in 1895 a monument to Kerner was erected in Stuttgart, the state capital of Württemberg. The vintners who work with the Kerner, Weinsberg's most successful wine grape, have quite some reputation to live up to.

Yet in Canada, Kerner remains an unfamiliar variety among consumers. Perhaps the Okanagan's leading proponent of the variety, Carriage House's Dave Wagner, sounds an evangelical note—it matches his Biblical beard—to convert people to the appreciation of Kerner. At Crowsnest Vineyards, Andrea McDonald has one hundred and fifty Kerner vines for late-harvest style wines. "The first thing customers say is 'what is Kerner?'" she has found. "But then they would taste the wine and they really liked the taste. They don't know the name, that's what holds it back, but it's a great variety if you can do a late harvest with it." It is a comment on Kerner's flexibility that almost every British Columbia winemaker

Dave Wagner

sees a different role for the variety. Wagner makes a dry version and an off-dry wine (he prefers the dry and his wife, Barbara, prefers the off-dry).

At Gray Monk, George Heiss Jr. makes a dry Kerner, a late harvest Kerner and, in years that permit exceptional ripening, a select late harvest from grapes left on the vines almost into the icewine-making season. Kerner, which grows in triangular, big-berried bunches, has a thick skin and usually remains healthy late into the season. His father, also named George, was the first to import Kerner vines to the Okanagan in 1975. "We didn't know much about the variety," the senior Heiss says. "The idea was to plant a variety that would have more flavour than Riesling in a bad year." He has found the reliable variety has several advantages, including considerable hardiness. The vine's tough leaves can withstand mild frost, remaining on the vine to continue the grape's maturing process after other varieties have lost their leaves. Kerner's ability to build sugar levels and more intense flavours than Riesling explains why the variety often is chosen to produce sweet late harvest wines.

Sandra Oldfield at Tinhorn Creek only makes icewine from the Kerner grown in the winery's Fischer vineyard (named for vineyard manager Hans Fischer who owned the property before selling it to Tinhorn Creek). The California-born Oldfield, who had never encountered the variety before coming to the Okanagan, enjoys the flavours of dry Kerner table wine but dedicates Fischer vineyard grapes to icewine because this gives Tinhorn Creek a product of appealing uniqueness amid a sea of Riesling icewines. Thick-skinned Kerner is well suited for icewine. "It likes to cling to the vines and does a good job of hanging on the vines when the weather gets quite cold," Oldfield discovered. "It holds its acid really well and the fruit remains healthy." There are only two acres of Kerner in the vineyard, arranged in twenty-four rows, only eight of which are reserved for icewine in any year (the remaining grapes are sold to other wineries for table wine). The stress of retaining icewine grapes is rotated each year to a different eight rows. "There is a theory that you will kill them if you use the same vines for icewine year after year after year," Oldfield says. Tinhorn Creek limits its production to a maximum of 2,500 half-bottles of Kerner icewine each year, all of it sold from Tinhorn Creek's wine shop, where Oldfield cheerily takes her turn explaining the variety to visitors.

Another twist on Kerner originates with Vancouver Island's Venturi-Schulze winery, whose approach is anything but mainstream. The winery's first release was barrel-aged in French oak to yield what is described as an Alsace-style white—big in structure, dry and with racy acidity. "Kerner just screams for a barrel," Giordano Venturi asserts. "It's just one of those grapes." He did not hesitate to price the wine around $40 a bottle, believing that Kerner, unlike the more obscure and difficult to pronounce German crosses, can attract consumers prepared to pay Burgundy prices. He may be alone in the view but then he usually marches to his own drummer.

Wagner's infatuation with Kerner began in the mid-1980s when, as a member of the Bacchus Alumni amateur winemaking club in Abbotsford, he made his first wine from grapes, joining other members of the club in sharing Kerner purchased from a Similkameen vineyard. Previously, he only had made fruit wines. "For my first attempt at a grape wine, I thought it was excellent. After that, we started buying different varieties—Ehrenfelser,

Chardonnay, Riesling, Pinot Blanc, Pinot Noir, Merlot and Chancellor. The Kerner was one that we kept coming back to because of the flavours and bouquet of it. It had citrus and tropical fruits on the nose. When came time to get this winery started, we [referring to his wife, Barbara, as well as to himself] decided that Kerner was such a good grape and not many people were making it, so it would be a good one to have in lieu of a Riesling. We decided we would make it our flagship wine." Wagner settled on producing it only in the two table wine styles and avoided the dessert styles to which other wineries already were committed.

Carriage House, whose eight and a half acre vineyard south of Oliver inclines slightly toward the west to capture the abundant sun, has devoted two acres of that to Kerner, with Wagner sourcing cuttings from a nearby grower's nursery. He buys more Kerner from Tinhorn Creek since that winery uses only a third of its Kerner grapes for its icewine. In time there will be additional Kerner from another south Okanagan vineyard being developed by one of Wagner's friends. Because Kerner can drop its acidity quickly if it gets too ripe—a possibility at his sunny vineyard—Wagner's ability to draw fruit from different vineyards provides a better natural blend of acidity, the Tinhorn Creek block being a little cooler than the Carriage House site. Piquant acidity is needed both to enliven the fruit flavours of the wine and its longevity. The winemaking with Kerner is straightforward. "I haven't strayed too far from the techniques I've learned over the years," Wagner says. The juice is usually left in contact with the skins for a short period, then fermented at a cool temperature. For the off-dry version of the Carriage House Kerner, Wagner adds sweet reserve, being careful to add only Kerner grape juice from the same vintage. "It is important to be true to the vintage," he believes.

In time Wagner expects to be making enough wine so that he can age some of the Kerner rather than selling all of it soon after it is bottled. A young Kerner, Wagner jokes, is "a little tart of a wine," referring to its lively grapefruit zest, as he lines up a three-year-old example beside a nine-month-old wine. The older wine has mellowed in texture and the aroma shows a hint of truffles, not unusual when a white wine begins to evolve in the bottle. "Being a Riesling, it ages very well in the bottle," he says. "Kerner is probably the wine that I enjoy drinking the most," Wagner confesses. "I like the freshness. It's a very fruity, very satisfying wine. It never seems to have any bitter flavours. It's just always something new in the glass for me. It goes well with pretty well any food, especially spicy food. As a sipping wine, on a nice, hot summer afternoon, it is very refreshing." And with a knowing chuckle, he adds: "Too refreshing!"

LEMBERGER

RED TABLE WINE This juicy red variety has won a devoted following among the wineries of Washington State. Its introduction to British Columbia was stalled by plant quarantine restrictions and it is only in the 1990s that enough vines have been propagated from existing plantings to expand the Lemberger base. Hainle Estate Winery pioneered Lemberger wine, with grapes from various small plantings. The grape is grown in southern Germany where it is called Limberger and makes a light fruity wine. While that name on a label always inspires lame jokes about delectably odourous cheese (called Limburger), at least that is more digestible than Blaufränkisch, as the Austrians call the grape. "In our warmer growing conditions," winemaker Tilman Hainle writes, "Lemberger ripens beautifully to produce wines of Merlot-like intensity, with good deep colour and a lovely raspberry/cracked black pepper character."

The Producers

Hainle
Hawthorne Mountain
Prpich Hills

As much as any variety, Lemberger symbolizes the Okanagan's conundrum. "Why are there so many grape varieties grown here?" Tilman Hainle asks rhetorically. "Is it wise for the Okanagan to squander itself on this huge array of grape varieties—probably a wider assortment than most wine regions have." The term "probably" is an understatement. Until the expansion of the late 1990s, the wine industry in British Columbia had a total vineyard area no bigger than Vancouver's Stanley Park growing so many varieties that the number would be a respectable football score. Some have argued vigorously that winegrowers in British Columbia should narrow their focus to the nine or ten classic European varieties. It is hardly a surprise to those who know him that contrarian Hainle does not agree, even while admitting the economic rationale for zeroing in on only a few varieties, as Oregon has done. "There's merit in that but for me it is too much of the conformist attitude, that if people don't know how to pronounce it right away, you should forget about it," Hainle responds. "I love being able to do a little bit of Lemberger each year. It's a marketing nightmare because you've got to spend more time explaining about it. But if it does well and makes good wine, I don't see that the name of the grape will be as much of a problem."

"There is a big segment of the market that is looking for something different, that isn't just on the 'give me Chardonnay or Cabernet or Merlot and that's just about it,'" Hainle says, warming to the subject. He refers to a Washington winery which uses all of its Lemberger in brand name blends because the marketing department there declines trying to sell it as a varietal. "For me that is just an abomination," Hainle insists. "To me it seems completely wrong that the [name of the grape] should determine what you do with the product." He is willing to concede that a large winery with a full range of familiar varietals should avoid the arduous chore of selling an unfamiliar varietal. "There are different dynamics in a large company. You have to listen to the market a lot more." Hainle Vineyards, on the other hand, is a small, family-owned estate winery. "We have the luxury of being able to ignore the mainstream market. There is so much that you can do without having to sell so and so many hundreds of thousand cases of it a year."

Hainle prides himself that his winery was the first in British Columbia, beginning in 1987, to make Lemberger, using purchased grapes from a vineyard in the Similkameen Valley. Perhaps because only small quantities were available, Hainle blended it for several vintages with Trollinger, a complementary red variety also from Southern Germany. While significant plantings of Lemberger have been made in Washington State, most growers in British Columbia seriously interested in the variety in the 1980s were unable to have the plant material cleared for import into Canada. The irony is that the first Lemberger in the Pacific Northwest appears to have been grown by the long-vanished Tunbridge Nursery at Vernon, which is believed to have obtained the variety from Hungary. Lemberger cuttings from Tunbridge were used to start the variety in Washington State in 1941.[1] In the 1970s when some British Columbia growers sought to buy Lemberger vines from American nurseries, the Canada Department of Agriculture stopped them. The reason: the variety was found to host several vine diseases then thought not to be present in Canadian vineyards. Canadian growers argued in vain that Lemberger's diseases were infectious only to Lemberger. Only in the 1990s was a serious effort made to develop an indigenous

---

1   Clore, Walter J. and Irvine, Ronald: *The Wine Project: Washington State's Winemaking History*, Sketch Publications, Vashon, Washington, 1997.

source by propagating cuttings that, presumably, traced their parentage to the Tunbridge vines. The growers now include the Heller family, whose Adelheid's Vineyard at Okanagan Falls supplies Hainle with premium grapes and the Gidda brothers, now operators of the Similkameen Vineyard which provided the fruit from which Hawthorne Mountain made a debut 1996 Lemberger. Okanagan Falls grower Dan Prpich, who is developing the Prpich Hills winery, has laboriously been creating his own block of Lemberger from twenty cuttings obtained several years ago at the Summerland Research Station. Prpich is a native of Croatia and can make the same claim for the grape, said to have taken its name from a Croatian community called Lemberg. Prpich points out that in his homeland the variety is called Frankovka. Whatever the name, he has had high ambitions to make a reserve-quality red wine ever since reading of the wine being served at official functions there.

"It's a bit touchy in the vineyard," Hainle says of Lemberger. "It is similar in some ways to Merlot, except it is a bit fragile. It has huge leaves and flops around and is quite demanding of heat units and sunshine. You really need to plant it in a good site. It is fairly late ripening." The vine will produce vigorously and growers need to keep the yield in check if the fruit is to be matured adequately. In the winery, Hainle handles Lemberger much as he would Merlot. "I do fairly intensive maceration with it," referring to the practice of leaving the juice in contact with the skins for an extended period to extract both flavour and colour. The wine then gets modest barrel-aging, modest because Lemberger is somewhat lighter than Merlot. He finds the wine is similar to Merlot in flavour as well. "Maybe more fruit, a bit more pepperiness and spice and less cassis and blackberry." Hawthorne Mountain assigned its Lemberger project in 1996 to Glen Fukuyama, a winemaker who had previous experience with it in Washington State (and who subsequently left to work at Washington's Kiona Vineyards, a premier Lemberger producer). On its own and without barrel-aging, Lemberger can be a one-note wine. Fukuyama filled in the harmonies by adding 10 percent Merlot and five percent Pinot Noir to the blend and then aging it in American oak. The outcome was a bright lively wine with flavours of cherries and raspberries. Less than two hundred cases of Hawthorne Mountain's 1996 Lemberger were produced. With not much more being made by Hainle, Lemberger wines are destined to be hard to find.

MADELEINE ANGEVINE

The Producers

Domaine de Chaberton
Recline Ridge
Venturi-Schulze

WHITE TABLE WINE   This white vinifera was developed in 1857 by a Loire nurseryman named Moreau-Robert. He sought to create new varieties simply by planting grape seeds and selecting the chance varieties that came, since the grape seed is genetically unpredictable in the progeny that results from this method. Three varieties emerged that are still grown, often for table grapes rather than wine grapes: the other two are Madeleine Sylvaner and Madeleine Royale. Other sources maintain that Madeleine Angevine—the Moreau-Robert nursery was at the city of Angers—resulted from a cross in which Madeleine Royale (bred in 1845) was one parent. "Why do they call it Madeleine?" Domaine de Chaberton's Claude Violet asks rhetorically. "Because they are very, very early plants and they are blooming on the feast of Saint Madeleine [in early May]." This vine has the rare attribute of being almost totally "female" which means that, unlike other vines, it is not self-pollinating but must be planted near to other varieties in order to be fruitful. Madeleine Angevine is a mainstay for English wine production. In British Columbia, it produces an aromatic and floral table wine excellent as an aperitif and with many Asian cuisines. Venturi-Schulze has recommended its dry version with grilled salmon or steamed mussels or clams.

Madeleine Angevine is grown for cool-climate winemaking because the grapes ripen early. That was the reason that Claude Violet planted the variety in 1983 when he was developing his Domaine de Chaberton vineyard in Langley. A native of France and from a family with generations in winegrowing, Violet knew the Madeleine family of grapes from the Loire. It is a family that also includes Madeleine Royale, primarily a table grape and now out of favour because it has seeds, Madeleine Sylvaner and Madeleine Noir. The latter is an early-ripening red which Violet has considered importing one day, adding it to the six or seven acres each of Madeleine Angevine and Madeleine Sylvaner in his vineyard.

When Violet was developing his vineyard, the Madeleine Angevine cuttings were imported from Mount Baker Vineyards in Washington State, a small winery just south of the Canadian border, not far from Sumas and half an hour's drive from Domaine de Chaberton. "I said, 'It must grow here as well,'" Violet reasoned. A tasting of Mount Baker's Madeleine Angevine reassured him that the variety could produce a good table wine.

A naturally productive vine, it requires disciplined cutting back during the season to prevent a heavy yield of low-quality, thin-flavoured wine grapes. The variety also has found its way into vineyards on Vancouver Island. "It produces beautiful medium-sized bunches of early-ripening grapes that are the first to be picked in our vineyard," explained Venturi-Schulze Vineyards in the tiny but informative booklet often accompanying each bottle sold by this Cowichan Valley winery. "It requires perfect weather at the end of August; if it rains during this period, as it did in 1991, the grapes split and the crop is lost."

It has proven to be a versatile grape. Claude Violet, who picks the grapes by hand and ferments them at a cool temperature to preserve the fruity aromas and flavours, describes Madeleine Angevine as "a very nice wine. It goes with a lot of different food. It goes very well with a salad, which is normally a difficult pairing." Violet describes his wine as "very smooth and very delicate but not very powerful." It also is a wine to be consumed when it is young and fresh and Violet recommends cellaring the wine a maximum of three years. This is not a hard and fast rule, as he discovered one evening in 1997 at a Chinese restaurant near the winery when the bottle of Madeleine Angevine he ordered turned out to be the 1993 vintage, long since sold out at the winery. In the glass, the wine had taken on a lovely golden colour, indicating maturity, and the flavours had become richer but no less satisfying. Worried that his wine was selling very slowly at the restaurant, Violet asked the proprietor why the old wine still was available. To his relief, he learned that the restaurant had neglected to rotate its stock: newer vintages of the wine just kept being stacked on the few remaining older bottles whenever a new shipment arrived. The winery's sales staff now checks regularly to make sure the stock is rotated.

At the tiny Venturi-Schulze winery, there is a love-hate relationship with Madeleine Angevine. Giordano Venturi and Marilyn Schulze decided to plant their Vancouver Island vineyard in 1987 when there was an extreme shortage of available vinifera vines. After some searching, they located a vineyard in the Fraser Valley that was about to rip out all of its vines because the owner, for health reasons, was leaving viticulture. Venturi and Schulze acquired about twenty varieties, including Madeleine Angevine. "It was four years old," Venturi recalled. "We had to hand dig every plant over several weekends." The second volume of winery's newsletter, in August 1994, included a profile of the variety that began this way: "Picture this: a wonderfully vigorous vine with large, light-green leaves and a staggering number of good sized, just forming bunches. It is the image of the perfect vine, the one that everybody should plant. But, a few days later, these same florid bunches seem to go through a moulting process and begin to look like a mass of dried up brown flakes. This is only the beginning of the troubles that Madeleine Angevine seems to experience every season: its obsession for wide spaces that openly defies the strict rules of the trellis; its canes, like hockey sticks, that produce tendrils with internal steel wires—where they grab, they stay—committing vegetal suicide in many parts of the vine, choking to death the tenderest parts of their own canes." Venturi went on to write that he vowed to replace the vines every year, only to relent when the grapes yielded a satisfactory wine. Typically, the variety is included in one of the winery's highly original proprietary blends. The first release of *Millefiori*—Italian for one thousand flowers—that emerged from the winery in 1994 was a blend of Madeleine Angevine and Siegerrebe. The latter variety, Venturi notes, is the "daughter" of Madeleine Angevine since Siegerrebe is a crossing of that variety with Gewürztraminer.

MADELEINE SYLVANER

WHITE TABLE WINE This is one of the early-ripening varieties developed in the last century at the Robert-Moreau nursery in the Loire, one of a series whose first name, Madeleine, recalled a Catholic saint whose feast day is early in spring when these vines are in flower. With this variety, Sylvaner became the second half of the name because the plant breeder believed the wine reminded him of a Sylvaner from Alsace. The wines, usually dry, are fruity, with tropical aromas sometimes suggesting pears and lichees and a cut-grass freshness in the flavour. Marilyn Schulze recommends her winery's wine with asparagus, salads and, in some vintages, even with Stilton cheese. "The food matching qualities of this wine are incredible," she believes.

The Producers

Domaine de Chaberton
Venturi-Schulze
Vigneti Zanatta

"If you take care even of a humble variety, you can make some incredible things," insists winemaker Giordano Venturi. He refers to the winery's one acre of Madeleine Sylvaner, a grape which he has pressed into service not only for white wine but for the production of balsamic vinegar. The winery released its first Madeleine Sylvaner from the 1990 vintage and has, on occasion, done vertical tastings with knowledgeable wine people who thought they were tasting the presumably more distinguished Pinot Gris.

The lengths to which Venturi-Schulze goes with the variety begins in the vineyard where the vine's production is limited to four and a half tonnes an acre; like all varieties, Madeleine Sylvaner's "humble" personality is diluted if the vine is over-cropped. "You don't want fifteen tonnes to the acre, which the Madeleine would be happy to supply, no problem." A man of detail, Giordano Venturi consults his vintage log and announces that, in 1996, the winery harvested precisely 9,005 pounds from that acre. But it took eight careful pickings over twenty days to assemble that quantity because, in that cool year, the grapes had ripened unevenly. Marilyn Schulze, Giordano's wife, and her daughter Michelle, did all those pickings themselves, doubting that any picker from outside the family would understand, or have the patience to understand, their obsessive quest for only perfectly mature grapes. "They have to be perfect," the uncompromising Giordano Venturi insists. "We can't afford to put out middling wines."

In a large winery each lot of grapes would have been processed and fermented separately. But, in 1996, Venturi had such small quantities that several lots of juice were pressed and then combined before fermentation started. This somewhat unconventional winemaking worked because the cool harvest weather on Vancouver Island, especially the nights, kept the juice as fresh as if it had been refrigerated. In previous years Venturi-Schulze used commercial cultured yeasts. Beginning in 1996, the winery began isolating its own native yeast strains (Marilyn Schulze, a skilled microbiologist, took advantage of a National Research Council grant to work on a project for culturing strains native to the winery). Some vintners worry that wild yeasts are risky, because they can create off-flavours or cause fermentation problems. "With wild yeast, during the first part of the fermentation, you can get some wild aromas," says Schulze, confident she knows what she is doing. "But they blow off and you are left with a symphony of flavours."

During several previous years, the ever-curious Giordano Venturi had made several experimental small lots in twenty-litre carboys, allowing wild yeasts to produce the fermentation. The wines were not acceptable. "It was disgusting," he recalls. "But in 1995 we have an incredibly good production with the Madeleine. We had too much and we said, 'Well, maybe it's the year to try it again.' So I made one more carboy, set it in the corner of the winery and I totally forgot about it until we needed the space. I saw that carboy there and thought, oh, another driveway candidate!" He got a surprise when he tasted the wine and discovered an aroma and flavour that he characterized as essence of pears. So in 1996 the winery prepared cultures of native yeast from the lees of that carboy and used that to ferment about three-quarters of that year's Madeleine Sylvaner. "I have to be honest," Venturi says, reflecting on what he has learned from his brief experience with wild yeasts. "I think the answer lies in a combination of native yeast wine [with] selected yeast. I think it is the best of both worlds." Another element of the Venturi-Schulze style is that the wines remain in contact with the lees (dead yeast cells and other fruit proteins) which settle to the bottom of the fermentation container. The wines are bottled directly from this tank, often without even any filtration. This is called "sur lies" winemaking, using the French phrase for "on the lees," and is not uncommon in white wine production when the winemaker aims at making wines with added complexity and a slightly richer texture.

Slow and cool fermentation is as critical with Madeleine Sylvaner as it is with any white variety. In the early years at Venturi-Schulze, the wines were made in a comparatively warm room which, during fermentation, was alive with grape aromas. Now the wines are made in temperature-controlled tanks and the air no longer is heavy with aromas. "I want those smells to stay in the wine, not escape into the air," Venturi says. The wines are bottled at quite cool temperatures as well, retaining some of the carbon dioxide still trapped in the wine from fermentation. This "spritz," as it is called, may appear as no more than a few fine bubbles on the inside of the wine glass but it contributes to the freshness of the wine.

At Venturi-Schulze, the Madeleine Sylvaner is versatile in the extreme. About half the grapes each year are dedicated to the production of the winery's balsamic vinegar, a process that begins with simmering the grape juice over a wood fire for several hours to reduce the volume before beginning the long, slow process of barrel-fermenting this concentrated juice into vinegar. The technique is based on a very old tradition of fine vinegar production in Modena, the community in northern Italy where Venturi grew up. Because vinegar bacteria are unwelcome in a winery, the vinegar is made and aged in a completely separate building. The vinegar remains in small barrels for many years, becoming further concentrated through natural evaporation, until the product has the intensity of a pungent cologne. A mere drop on the back of the hand—the usual method for "tasting" vinegar—is enough to liberate the savoury aroma. Not surprisingly, balsamic vinegar of this quality is bottled in tiny bottles and sells for the price of fine cologne.

RED TABLE WINE French plant breeder Eugene Kuhlmann (1858–1932) was the creator of this and of several other hybrid varieties, most of which now have been phased out of vineyards in France and North America. The variety is named for a French hero of World War One, Marshall Ferdinand Foch, commander in chief of the Allied armies in 1918. (An apparent admirer of French leaders, Kuhlmann also created another blood-red variety that was named Léon Millot after a prime minister.) Like the other hybridizers of his day, Kuhlmann created new varieties by crossing native American vines with European vines in a search for productive and disease-resistant varieties. Georges Masson, an Ontario wine writer in the 1970s, wrote that Foch "makes a good wine resembling a French Burgundy." The comparison to Burgundy, which is made with Pinot Noir, may have been inspired by the vaguely similar earthy aromas and smoky note in the finish of a Maréchal Foch wine. Other flavours include plums and spice. Masson thought the wine aged well. It depends on the style: most are made to be enjoyed when released with only a rare one crafted for long-term cellaring. St. Hubertus winemaker Cherie Jones advises drinking it by its fifth birthday.

Most of the French hybrid grape varieties have been disparaged and torn from vineyards. Maréchal Foch is a survivor. It is the best-selling red at Lang, St. Hubertus and Wild Goose and is used in generic blends at several other wineries. St. Hubertus has a sales agent who argues that Foch is the Zinfandel of British Columbia and urges decanting the wine before serving to allow it to express itself in the glass. At Alderlea Vineyards near Duncan, proprietor Roger Dosman consciously included Maréchal Foch among his selections when planting for the new winery because the variety matures early to mid-season, a benefit for the cool growing conditions of Vancouver Island. "It's a wine that people either hate or love," Dosman believes. Michael Bartier, assistant winemaker at Hawthorne Mountain Vineyards (which includes the LeComte label), admits to "tipping back quite a few bottles myself. It's a very juicy wine, very approachable and easy to drink when it is young. It's a red wine with training wheels."

Arguably, the winemaker who lifted Foch beyond its work-horse image was Australian Jeff Martin at Quails' Gate. When he arrived at the winery in 1994, he discovered that the vineyard included twenty-five-year-old Foch vines, one of the few really mature blocks of this variety left in the Okanagan. In Australia there are Shiraz vineyards more than one hundred years old that still produce wine. The vines are not very productive but the wines are dense and concentrated. Martin set out to make a comparable red from the old Foch at Quails' Gate, deliberately reducing the crop level of the vines to concentrate the wine as much as possible. The result was a stunningly powerful red called *Old Vines Foch* that won critical acclaim, so much so that each

premium-priced vintage is on limited allocation to the cult of admirers of this singular Maréchal Foch.

Foch was among the French hybrids that were imported to Ontario and New York State just after World War Two by wineries and growers searching for hardy, productive and disease resistant varieties that could make better wine than the North American varieties then being grown. (Almost no one then believed that the classic vinifera would survive in eastern North America.) While Foch had already been named in France, most varieties generally arrived bearing only the hybridizer's number, such as Seibel 9549, and had names assigned to them by the wine industry in the early 1970s. The significant red hybrids besides Foch were De Chaunac, Chelois, Baco Noir, Chancellor and Rougeon. De Chaunac and Chelois largely have been dropped because the wines are light and uninteresting. The others, while less important than they once were, are hanging on or, in the case of Foch, making a comeback. As recently as 1985 Foch had accounted for a quarter of British Columbia's grape harvest. But most of the vines were pulled out after the 1988 vintage, leaving Foch at less than two percent of the crop. "To my way of thinking, that is just ridiculous," Jeff Martin states. "I looked at the records for the hybrids we purchased in the 1980s. The grapes were immature. The problem was not the variety—it was grape-growing and winemaking." In the early 1980s yields of ten to twelve tons an acre were common, three times the yield now demanded of those vines in the Quails' Gate vineyard. In the 1990s the variety generally is grown more carefully.

A reliable and productive early ripener, Foch can be a winery's bread-and-butter red, as at Wild Goose. Adolf Kruger describes his soft, youthful easy-drinking version as an "unpretentious" wine that has been a consistent seller to the winery's Foch fans, except in 1997. Kruger could get no Foch grapes for the 1996 vintage when an informal supply arrangement with another winery's contract grower fell apart. The resourceful Kruger was able to convince Okanagan Falls grower Roland Heller to regenerate some Foch from old trunks with the result that Wild Goose put this variety back in its offerings with the 1997 vintage. At Lang Vineyards, Günther Lang at one time used a part of his Foch vineyard as the host on which to graft Pinot Meunier when he was in a hurry to increase production of that variety. But after he secured enough plants for three acres of Pinot Meunier, the Foch vines were allowed to revert to growing Foch grapes. Lang's style is to finish his non-oaked Foch (he uses no oak at all in his winery) with a hint of residual sugar to produce a soft, jammy red that has a large following—so large, in fact, that Lang in recent years has expanded his Foch plantings. "The medium dry Foch is the most popular red we produce," Lang has found. "If we allowed it to ferment fully dry, it would take much longer to fully develop the flavour. A medium-dry Foch—a fruity one with a little bit of sweetness—you can drink it younger." In this style, the wine already is being sold at Lang Vineyards nine months after it is made.

"One of the reasons we're growing it is because it is an earlier-release type of red," concurs Dosman, who has a different view of barrels than Lang. "We're trying to get deeper colours, richer flavours. We're aging it in American oak and aiming for a large wine." Quails' Gate also matures its Foch in American oak barrels; the sweet spice of the oak integrates well with the big fruit flavours of the wine. "I'm looking for that big, toasty, cedary character," winemaker Jeff Martin explains. "By getting Foch ripe, you end up with plummy characters, so I look for good quality, intense, pungent American oak that will lift the aroma. I'll even throw a bit of VA in there if I can." The reference is to volatile acidity, the vinegary note in some wines that, when kept under control by the winemaker, lifts the aroma of a wine. It is an old Australian trick perfected in the making of Penfolds' Grange, Australia's finest Shiraz. "I'm trying to make a Penfolds' red," Martin admits. "Oak is really the key with Foch," believes Cherie Jones, the winemaker for St. Hubertus and for that winery's premium Oak Bay label. She believes that Foch without oak can be overbearing and she argues that the intense aromatics of the variety—"raspberries and cherries and a chocolaty aroma"—are tamed by careful, but not excessive, barrel-aging. The one and a half acres of Foch at St. Hubertus also is a mature planting. "It comes off here so intense in body, flavour and colour. It is black as the ace of spades ... wine that would stand up on its own and shout and scream. Oak helps." The 1995 Oak Bay Foch, which spent five months in American oak barrels, was further "tamed" by the addition of 15 percent Merlot to the blend. The result, according to her tasting notes, was "a rich, luscious nose of ripe currants, toasty, smoky oak and a subtle herbaceous earthiness." Because it is often a big wine with gamy tastes, Foch is a good choice when the cuisine itself is powerful. "Foch goes wonderfully with stronger-flavoured dishes," Jones believes. "Like game sausage or venison, duck or strong New Zealand lamb."

MERLOT

RED TABLE WINE In a local Bordeaux dialect, Merlot also is the word for "blackbird." Whether the grape is so named because of its dark colour or just because the birds like it is unclear. However, the variety has flown all over the world this century, thriving in both hemispheres and producing friendly wines everywhere that account for the current popularity. Merlot yields wines which have been called "plump" and "lush" or, as Jackson-Triggs winemaker Bruce Nicholson puts it, Cabernet Sauvignon without tannins, which makes it a very popular red. "Consumers like everything about Merlot, even its name," he says. "I even know people who have named their pets after it." Inniskillin Okanagan's notes for its 1995 vintage spoke of "green pepper, candied cherry, blackberry, plum and wild berry aromas." Winemaker Ross Mirko speaks of "big jammy wines with plum and tar flavours." Some of the oldest Merlot vines in the Okanagan were planted at the CedarCreek vineyard at Kelowna in the late 1970s, a cool site not ideal for the variety. Most of the plantings in the 1990s have been farther south, with more reliable results at the vintage. Merlot is capable of medium-term aging (four to ten years) but the amiably-flavoured wines seldom get a chance to last that long.

Merlot's star emerged in British Columbia when CedarCreek Estate Winery's 1992 vintage won an unprecedented Platinum award from the judges at the 1993 Okanagan Wine Festival. The judges created the award on the spot, swept away by the wine which, ironically, CedarCreek had not even intended to make. The Merlot plot at CedarCreek's home vineyard at the Kelowna winery, planted in the late 1970s and likely the oldest producing Merlot in the Okanagan, is a mere half acre in size. In 1992, the winery, preoccupied with larger volumes of other varieties, arranged to sell the Merlot to another estate winery. When the intended purchaser failed to take the grapes, Anne Sperling, CedarCreek's winemaker at the time, had to vinify the Merlot and make a classic wine. Only seventy cases could be produced, much of it dedicated to the prestige gifts which winery owner Ross Fitzpatrick proudly gave his friends. The platinum award's powerful message encouraged many producers to plant substantial acreages of Merlot. CedarCreek is planning a lot of its future around Merlot, with output of this varietal to reach about three thousand cases a year. However, no one rushed into Merlot like Sumac Ridge, which planted so much of this variety in 1993 at its Black Sage vineyard that in the vintage of 1997, it made thirteen thousand cases. The winery was rewarded for its boldness when its 1995 Merlot, competing against 445 other wines, walked away with the trophy for the best wine in the contest at 1998's All-Canada Wine Competition. The sister winery, Hawthorne Mountain Vineyards, also draws grapes from Black Sage Road and also produced a 1995 Merlot that was highly rated by the critics. "With that Merlot, you can go anywhere in the world," suggests Eric von Krosigk, the winemaker who made it. "I think Merlot is fantastically suited to the Okanagan. The fruit flavours are very intense."

With its comparatively soft texture and rich fruit flavour, Merlot has played primarily a critical supporting role in lends with leaner, harder Cabernet Sauvignon in its home turf of Bordeaux and in California. In the 1990s, it has become as a consumer favourite on its own, making reds ranging from light Italian Merlot to spicy, jammy Chilean Merlot. When yields are controlled carefully to four or five tons an acre, the resulting wines are big and supple, with concentrated berry flavours that benefit from oak and have aging potential. CedarCreek's 1992 Merlot is expected to improve in the bottle for ten years or more. "After that," laughs winemaker Ross Mirko, "it becomes stylistic whether you like your wines brown and dried out like the British like them, or fruity and oaky like the Americans like them."

Accessible as the wine is, the grape can be difficult to grow in the more northern parts of the Okanagan. Tilman Hainle in the September 1996 newsletter for Hainle Vineyards wrote: "Its winter tenderness and susceptibility to disease can be challenging, and in our vineyards, our plantings of Merlot have been battered time and time again by low winter temperatures." The same problem faces CedarCreek Estate Winery whose vineyard on the far side of Okanagan Lake from Hainle is slightly more northerly. Both of these wineries sought to resolve the issue by sourcing Merlot from vineyards farther to the south. In Hainle's case, the winery contracts from a grower near Okanagan Falls. CedarCreek not only contracted grapes from the Naramata area but planted Merlot at Greata Ranch, a vineyard south of Peachland

The Producers (cont'd)

and close to the lake where winter temperatures are more moderate than at Hainle's mountainside vineyard only a dozen kilometers away but much higher. The major Merlot acreages, such as the Sumac Ridge, Burrowing Owl and Tinhorn Creek vineyards, are at Oliver and south of there, in the warmest part of the Okanagan, producing ripe "blackbird" grapes that yield big, chewy wines with alcohol readings in some vintages approaching 14 percent, the result of grapes approaching super ripeness.

The variety has rivaled Pinot Noir as the most widely planted of the new vinifera reds in British Columbia. The variety already is a proven producer of excellent reds in Washington State, where the warm days but cool nights suit Merlot. Since the southern Okanagan has a comparable climate and soils, the variety also should succeed north of the 49th Parallel. Merlot flowers earlier and ripens earlier than Cabernet Sauvignon which means that—unless a late spring frost occurs—vineyards can expect to produce mature fruit almost every year. Winemaker Ross Mirko believes that the ideal maturity is achieved when the grape has between 23° and 24° Brix (a measure of natural sugar which will produce 12 to 13 percent alcohol). "You are not going to get fruit maturity [flavour] at 20° Brix," Mirko asserts. In a hot year like 1994 most British Columbia Merlots were brawny blockbusters. Tinhorn Creek, an exponent of big reds, harvested its Merlot on September 21, 1994 when the grapes already were ripe enough to make a wine with a muscular 14 percent alcohol. In the following year, when growing conditions were not quite so hot, Tinhorn Creek waited until October 16 to harvest. The extra few weeks allowed the winery once again to make another big red with just under 14 percent alcohol.

"More is not better," Mirko cautions. "I found that out from the 1994 vintage. We didn't bottle a 1994 Merlot [from Cedar-Creek grapes in its Kelowna area vineyard] because it was picked at 26° Brix." That translates into 15 percent alcohol, almost invariably too high to produce a pleasing table wine. "It was just stewed, totally cooked fruit," Mirko says of that 1994 Merlot which was not a patch on the stellar 1992. "It had leathery, dry tannins. I blended it away. Merlot has beautiful berry, plummy fruit and you lose that somewhere around 24° Brix." CedarCreek did in fact release a 1994 Merlot, made from grapes grown at King Vineyards at Naramata. The grapes had been harvested just a little earlier than those at the estate vineyard and the resulting alcohol was 14 percent.

The popularity of Merlot has a lot to do with its obliging accessibility, both to the winemaker and to the consumer. "I think that Merlot has got to be absolutely my favourite red grape," Peller Estates winemaker Tony Vlcek admits. "It just has such a broad base of flavours—the fruit is so incredible." He first worked with the variety in the 1993 vintage, when the winery produced fifty cases. The wine won a bronze medal at the 1994 Okanagan Wine Festival and Vlcek improved on that the following year, winning a silver for the 1994 Peller Estate Merlot and a gold medal at a competition for wines of the Pacific Northwest. "It got us off on the right foot," he smiles. Subsequently, Vlcek has expanded the winery's Merlot arsenal, making the Peller Estates line in French oak and the more recently launched Bighorn Vineyards line in American oak. The grape, with its rich plum flavours and its abundant but soft tannins, has the depth to yield at least two styles of wine. "I love the combination of plum with vanilla and the soft round palate and the tannins that linger," he says.

"My feeling is that Merlot," believes Tilman Hainle, "[is] if you've got good quality fruit, then it is almost a no-brainer. The wine will make itself." He has found that the variety, aside from its notorious tenderness to winter frosts, is a straightforward vine to grow, tolerant of a wide range of sites. "There isn't as much differentiation [among sites] as there is with Pinot Noir." As a result, cooperative Merlot, which almost always yields satisfying wines, lacks the mystique of fickle, challenging Pinot Noir. "I guess I find it more rewarding to work with grape varieties like Pinot Noir," says Hainle.

Perhaps Merlot is not quite as easy as Hainle suggests. Before the 1992 vintage at CedarCreek, the Merlots from that winery and from its predecessor, Uniacke Estate Winery, were light, mediocre reds with little varietal character. While some of the cause may have been in the vineyard, a lot was in how the wines were made. Prior to 1991, all of the red wines at CedarCreek were made by a technique called thermal vinification, in which the must (a term describing crushed grapes) was heated to extract colour and tannins quickly; it was then pressed so that the now dark juice was fermented in tanks, with no skin contact, much the same as a white wine. That is not good red winemaking. The result appeared dark at first but the unstable colour dropped out, leaving a pallid, simple wine. In 1991, with a change of winemakers, CedarCreek ditched the thermal vinification unit. "We began to make red wines like the rest of the world," said Mirko, who was then an assistant winemaker there. "After that, you will have seen a quality lift in every red we made, from Chancellor to Pinot Noir and Merlot." Many reds, and Merlot in particular, benefit from skin contact. Burrowing Owl's consulting winemaker, Bill Dyer, did research for his master's degree on extended maceration, the technical term for prolonged skin contact. In the 1997 vintage, his first in British Columbia, the California-born Dyer gave the Merlot twenty-one days of maceration; and he will consider longer skin contact when that is warranted. After all, Dyer notes, extended maceration is employed in some vintages by Bordeaux's Chateau Pétrus, whose wines are the world's most expensive Merlots.

Merlot adapts readily to the preferred style of a winemaker, with some of the biggest having come from Tinhorn Creek and Peller Estates. "The 1994 just beats you on the head," Tinhorn Creek winemaker Sandra Oldfield said later of her debut dark robust red, which was unfiltered, unfined, aged boldly in new American oak and had strapping alcohol. Peller Estates is the premium varietal brand for wines made by Andrés, whose president, John Peller, is the third generation of his family to run the winery. He graphically described that winery's equally intense 1994 Merlot as a "balls buster." Big swaggering Merlots to a degree reflected the hot 1994 vintage. In subsequent vintages the Tinhorn Creek Merlots, while only slightly less alcoholic, are more refined, with more fruit and, because not all the barrels were new, less oak. "Our Merlot will always be our big, heavy, rich red wine," Oldfield promises. "We don't grow a Cabernet Sauvignon at Tinhorn Creek. The Merlot *is* our biggest, beefiest red wine. We make it that way. We do extended maceration on it, sometimes for three or four weeks, and we make the Merlot up here to be our equivalent of California's Cabernet Sauvignon."

"What I am looking for is elegant wine versus the balls buster," Ross Mirko says. When he determined the style at CedarCreek, the fruit rather than the oak was forward. His barrel regime was a conservative mix of new and used barrels, most of them American oak that have been used for other wines for a year to eighteen months. In this way, the wine got the benefit of barrel treatment (a softening of the texture and a hint of oak flavour) without being overpowered by oak.

Some winemakers found Merlot something of a challenge in the cool 1996 vintage. At Hester Creek, a comparatively warm site, the wines showed intense fruit and deep colour but the tannins were surprisingly hard. "In the years that I had been making Merlot, I had never faced that," winemaker Frank Supernak says. "I had a visit from an Oregon winemaker who said they deal with that problem all the time." On that winemaker's advice, Supernak reduced the astringent effect of the tannins by fining (clarifying) the wine with both gelatin and egg white, natural substances that cause tannins to precipitate, thus softening the wine. "It's just amazing," Supernak said of the result. Ten months later a sample of the Merlot, drawn from the French oak barrels in which the vintage was maturing, was still firm in texture but also showed the attractive fruitiness of the vintage. The Hester Creek Merlot also has a hint of pepper among the flavours, a complex characteristic unique to the vineyard. It was evident for years in reds that were made from the property when it was operated by Joe Busnardo as Divino Estate Winery. This distinctive quality likely is the result of the mineral composition of the soils and perhaps of the perennial stress to which the vines were subjected by Busnardo's viticultural techniques. Busnardo once suggested that a blush-coloured apéritif wine he made showed the same pepperiness because a portion had been aged in a barrel he believed had previously been used for shipping a spicy Italian apéritif. That barrel, if it ever existed, is long gone but the pinch of pepper remains in some of the site's wines. It also showed in and added a refreshing lift to Hester Creek's 1996 Blanc de Noir rosé, a wine made with a blend of Baco Noir, Pinot Gris and some juice which had been drained, or "bled" from both the winery's Cabernet Franc and its Merlot. "I believe 100 percent in bleeding," Supernak says. This is a technique of draining juice from the must before fermentation on the skins is started, the objective being to concentrate the fruitiness and the colour of the remaining juice. It needs to be done carefully since it also concentrates other elements, including the tannins. Bruce Nicholson, the winemaker at the Jackson-Triggs winery near Oliver, believes that 15 percent is the maximum volume of juice that should be drained off. Supernak, who preceded Nicholson at Jackson-Triggs, says that the deep colour of that winery's Merlots in the 1993, 1994 and 1995 vintages was increased by his decision to bleed away an average of 9 percent of the juice, which also went into rosés. At

Hester Creek, Supernak continued the practice, bleeding between 9 and 10 percent of the juice from the Hester Creek reds in 1996. Changes in viticultural practices for the 1997 vintage appear to have enabled the Hester Creek vineyard to deliver deep coloured grapes, eliminating the need for bleeding.

At Sumac Ridge the quest for mouth-filling red wines, including Merlot, led the winery to stop filtering its major red wines, beginning with the 1995 vintage. A growing number of premium wine producers believe that filtration strips flavour along with the fine solids which remain in suspension in young wines for several years before beginning to settle. Those solids are the by-product of winemaking that includes extended skin contact before, during and after fermentation in order to achieve deep colours and rich flavours. The coarser particles, usually tannins and pigments, settle readily as the wines rest in barrels and most of the finer solids can be precipitated by fining. In this process, either an inert clay or a substance such as egg whites is stirred into the wine, binding with the remaining solids and settling out in a matter of days to leave the wines brilliantly translucent. For reasons of efficiency, most wineries buy commercial egg white preparations, although Sumac Ridge winemaker Mark Wendenburg vividly recalls cracking farm-fresh eggs and carefully separating the yolks in order to fine the winery's prize-winning 1995 Merlot (the whites of two to three eggs will do a barrel). "We learned that that is inefficient, tedious and not altogether effective," he chuckles. "You end up with a lot of shells and a lot of yolks. You end up with yolks in some of your whites and that won't do." The solids that remain after fining, not visible to the eye, stay in suspension for several years, only settling out if the premium red wines are stored quietly in wine cellars. Very gradually, a pencil-like feather of solids will settle at the lowest point in each bottle. This is why aged red wines should be decanted carefully before being served, with the harmless sediment left behind in the bottle. There always is a concern that the novice consumers just discovering British Columbia's premium reds will reject unfiltered wines that have thrown a sediment. "I tried to explain the risks to the management," Wendenburg says. "It used to be that if you were spending $15 on a bottle of Merlot, you knew [how to deal with sediment]. But we don't think that's the case anymore," he says, remarking on the rapid growth of wine enthusiasts who still are inexperienced. "Where is the threshold now? $20? $25?"

MÜLLER-THURGAU

WHITE TABLE WINE   The father, so to speak, of this grape was one Dr. Hermann Müller, who was born in the Swiss canton of Thurgau but was working in Germany when he made the cross that resulted in Müller-Thurgau. Depending on the reference, this variety was created either in 1891 or 1892 when Riesling was crossed with Sylvaner. Pierre Galet, the eminent French ampelographer, said the grape may have sprung from a self-pollinated Riesling seed. More recent genetic research suggests the cross was Chasselas and Riesling. Whatever the origin, the variety came to rival Riesling as the most widely grown German white in the 1980s; it also was New Zealand's most extensively planted white. It came to British Columbia because the vine is vigorous and matures early, often producing an agreeable but occasionally bland table wine. The vine is notoriously susceptible to mildew, making it especially unsuitable to Vancouver Island even though several vineyards there have tried to grow it.

The Producers

Blue Grouse
Cherry Point
Gray Monk
LeComte
Peller Estates
Venturi-Shulze

Giordano Venturi makes a point by opening one of his last bottles of Venturi-Schulze 1994 Müller-Thurgau Sur Lie, pouring into the glass a light golden liquid with the aroma of baked pears and with a silky, rich texture. "What a wine!" he exclaims, adding that he hopes one day to be able to pour a similar sample for Jancis Robinson, the renowned British wine writer who panned the variety in her 1994 book, *The Oxford Companion to Wine*. "She hates it," Venturi says. He pulls his copy of *The Companion* from the bookshelf and reads the Robinson description of this grape as being "the bane of German wine production" and of being "mediocre." Venturi believes that his wine could cause her to revisit her views. No one else in British Columbia is quite so impassioned for the variety but then no one else takes the trouble to leave the wine on the lees ("Sur Lie"). That treatment is reserved usually for varieties that fetch a considerably higher price to justify the work, such as Chardonnay or Pinot Gris.

   At Gehringer Brothers, Pinot Gris was planted first in the vineyard but when disease (crown gall) struck those plants, they were replaced with Müller-Thurgau, a vinifera to which the brothers had immediate access at the time. "We made some the first year with grapes from many different sites," Walter Gehringer says, recalling that wine from the 1988 vintage. "Near the end of fermentation, I was telling myself 'This is a *great* glass of wine!'

Hans Kiltz

We were just impressed." So were the judges at the Pacific National Exhibition's wine competition in 1989 who awarded the wine a gold medal and "best of class" honors. "Every vintage thereafter," he says with a note of frustration, "we've been trying to come close."

Walter Gehringer is a skilled vintner, especially with white varieties, but he admits to finding Müller-Thurgau a constant winemaking challenge. "It has extremely slow fermentation," he has found. "That's okay when it starts but when you get towards dryness, you start getting to wondering if it is stuck or if it will make it all the way." Many Gehringer whites either are stopped before all of the natural sugar has fermented or have sweet reserve (unfermented grape juice) added to give the wine a perception of fruitiness. Müller-Thurgau, because of its naturally low acidity, is one white the winery consistently intends to be fully dry. And each year Gehringer can count on the variety giving him the fright that it will not achieve desired dryness. "It's been hair-raising in some vintages," he says with exasperation. How absurdly slow the fermentation can be is evident from notes from Venturi-Schulze for that winery's 1992 vintage, which was harvested on October 1. "We fermented it at 10°C for twelve months without any interference ... Fermentation stopped around the end of October, 1993, with a natural residual sugar of five grams per litre ..." (which is below the threshold of perceptible sweetness). The Venturi-Schulze vintners believed that the long, cool fermentation preserved "floral aromas reminiscent of roses and wild flowers" while the prolonged time on yeast lees contributed nutty flavours and "a buttery, full-bodied mouthfeel." The generally cool growing conditions in Vancouver Island's Cowichan

Valley may suit the variety better than warmer sites in the Okanagan, except for the significantly higher rainfall on the island. Harry von Wolff, the proprietor of Naniamo's Chateau Wolff, gave up the battle of spraying the vines against mildew and replaced the variety with one more suited to the climate.

Walter Gehringer questions whether Müller-Thurgau is suitable in the south Okanagan as well, saying frankly: "When I look at the merits of other varieties in our climate, I think the Müller-Thurgau falls short from being a real quality wine. Müller-Thurgau in Germany, where it is cooler than here, has more Muscat and more fruit flavours. Ours tends to be a more Southern-style food wine. And since I am a proponent of the fruitiness that our climate and location brings out, [Müller-Thurgau] is almost an anomaly of what I am trying to incorporate in my portfolio." And thus it is that Gehringer, a decade after replacing Pinot Gris with Müller-Thurgau, has begun to reverse that process. "I see Pinot Gris replacing it." He pours his 1995 Müller-Thurgau, sharing a wine that is pleasantly fresh and clean but carrying the humble price of $8.95 a bottle. Overly critical, he dismisses it: "It's nothing terrific."

In fact, it is much better than that—an honest, uncomplicated wine, appealing for its simplicity, never threatening to upstage food it is paired with. Perhaps Giordano Venturi should forget about hosting Jancis Robinson and invite Walter Gehringer instead.

MUSCAT

The Producers

Blue Grouse
Gersighel
Hawthorne Mountain
Hillside Cellars
Wild Goose

WHITE TABLE AND DESSERT WINES Grapes of the Muscat family or with apparent Muscat blood lines all have intensely aromatic aromas and flavours. These lush qualities often steer the varieties toward the production of dessert wines although one variety, Muscat Ottonel, also yields dry white wines whose dramatic perfume can fill the room. There are a number of Muscat cousins, such as Perle of Csaba and Perle of Zala, rarely seen any longer as varietals. Examples of those varieties can still be found in vineyards but the quantities are small and the juice often disappears into tanks of Gewürztraminer. An intriguing addition is Blue Grouse's Black Muscat, a rich dry red with layers of spice flavours. Hillside's John Fletcher recommends Muscat wines with Asian-style fusion cooking.

Before its dramatic 1997 expansion, Hillside Cellars was a bucolic little operation in a tiny roadside cottage winery on the Naramata Road. It backed onto a tough, rock-strewn vineyard, about seven and a half acres in size, on a slope bordered at the top by the roadbed for the abandoned Kettle Valley Railroad and on the bottom by the road. It is a warm southwest-facing site which the founders of Hillside, Vera and Bohumir Klokocka converted from orchard to vineyard, beginning in 1984. They knew little about vinifera grapes at the time; nor did many others in the Okanagan. With the blind leading the blind, the Muscat that became the winery's flagship wine appeared initially with the wrong varietal name on the label.

They secured some of their first cuttings for the Hillside vineyard from a hobby grower in Penticton and some were inaccurately identified as Pinot Blanc. Vera Klokocka (pronounced klo-kotch-ka) knew that was wrong when the wine was much more aromatic than Pinot Blanc ever can be. Unsure what she had, she decided to call it Klevner because in Alsace and Germany, the name is applied, rather loosely, to a number of varieties, including Pinot Blanc. Hillside's first release of Klevner was from the 1989 vintage. The misidentification continued to be used for the next two vintages until 1992 when a visiting French nurseryman informed the Klokockas that their Klevner really was Muscat Ottonel. This variety was developed in the last century by the Loire breeder Robert-Moreau (also responsible for Madeleine Angevine and Madeleine Sylvaner) and has come to be grown in Alsace, Austria and eastern Europe, no doubt coming to the

Okanagan because it is reputed to be a reliable cool-climate variety. After the winery was sold in 1996, the new owners, including winemaker John Fletcher, immediately set out to increase production of this dry, fragrant wine. "I have five thousand more cuttings," Fletcher said in the summer of 1997. Included among those plants are cuttings of Morio-Muskat. Named for a European plant grower called Peter Morio, the grapes produce even more intensely flavoured grapes than Muscat Ottonel, which can be a bit vapid at times.

John Fletcher

Fletcher plans to blend the two varieties into one wine. (Muscat is commonly spelled Muskat in Germany.)

Muscat Ottonel is a grape with its own challenges, as Fletcher discovered during his debut 1996 vintage at the newly acquired Hillside. The winery then still lacked devices to control the temperature of fermentation. Muscat varieties should be fermented slowly and at cool temperatures to preserve their alluring orange blossom aromas. "The temperature got away on me one night," recalls Fletcher, who was sleeping at the winery during this critical period, checking fermentation temperatures every three hours. He had two tanks of Muscat, each one thousand liters in size, and the temperature spiked significantly above the desired 15°C, resulting in a rapidly frothing ferment. At midnight Fletcher rushed to a nearby convenience store to buy blocks of ice which, suitably bagged in watertight plastic, were lowered into the two tanks. "And I ran water over the outside of the tank," he says. "I was panicking. It took me until morning to get the temperature back down to fifteen." He believes the wine bubbled away some flavour and aroma during this episode. "We laughed about it later," he says. The winery now is equipped to control temperatures and safeguard the quality of one of its flagship wines.

At Wild Goose Vineyards, the Morio-Muskat variety was added to the winery's Okanagan Falls vineyard in 1997 when cuttings from this variety were grafted onto two hundred and thirty Riesling vines. This remains an uncertain technique for accelerating the introduction of a new variety as Wild Goose discovered when only 30 percent of the grafts were successful. However, the Kruger family, owners of the winery, have pushed ahead, planting the remaining area with plants that were nurtured in a greenhouse. The variety is popular in Germany. Kruger has a cousin there who prefers Morio-Muskat above other wines and Kruger himself admits to being very partial to it even if, he adds, wine writer Jancis Robinson panned the variety in her widely-consulted *Oxford Companion to Wine*. As Robinson notes, the variety is not a true Muscat but a cross of Silvaner and Pinot Blanc which, paradoxically, shows the intense grapey characteristics of a Muscat family grape. "The main reason that I've planted it is that it is tremendously aromatic," Kruger explains. "I've had wines whose flavours were enhanced by adding a bit of Morio-Muskat." Kruger, who specializes in Riesling and Gewürztraminer, will decide in the future whether to use it in a supporting role or to produce a varietal on its own.

The family of Muscat grape varieties is large and old, with a popularity based on the distinctive spicy aromas and flavours of both the grapes and the wines. Plant breeders often have used various Muscat varieties to breed others, seeking to retain some of the variety's flavour qualities while correcting its deficiencies (such as a tendency to low acidity). Muscat varieties long have been grown as table grapes and as cooking grapes. Anyone who enjoys ripe-flavoured raisin pie knows the richly exotic taste of Muscat. The wines invariably mirror the taste of the grapes, whether made in the dry style preferred by Hillside or in the many dessert styles made elsewhere in the world. In greater or lesser degree, the same spicy characteristics are found in such varieties as Gewürztraminer and Perle of Csaba, which perhaps evolved from Muscat. The great Riesling grape sometimes shows a trace of Muscat character in its flavour. Indeed, the rarely seen Chardonnay Musqué clone, from which Ontario's Cave Springs Cellars produces award-winning whites, has fruity overtones of

Muscat that set it apart from any other Chardonnay.

Perle of Csaba has had a spotty career as a varietal. For a number of years in the 1980s Sumac Ridge released a dessert-style wine in half bottles while Divino produced an off-dry table wine. The variety is believed to have originated in Hungary. Canadian growers began planting it in the 1930s, often using it as a parent in crosses because the variety is an unusually early ripening grape. That also is a disadvantage because the variety's aromas and flavours appeal to birds and wasps alike, attracting them to vineyards in early August, thus ensuring they will then stay to devour other varieties as they ripen. The wine itself is luscious and drinkable by the time it is nine months old but does not age well. For these reasons and for the commercial reason that the variety was hard to sell in quantity, Sumac Ridge ultimately discontinued its Perle of Csaba. The remaining grapes usually are blended into Gewürztraminer wines. At Blue Grouse on Vancouver Island, Hans Kiltz blends Perle of Csaba with an equal quantity of Chasselas and releases the resulting wine as a Dry Muscat; as well, he has a varietal Perle of Csaba in his line. Kiltz also has a unique and exotic red grape called Black Muscat, perhaps an American-developed variety with several Muscat grapes in its parentage. Kiltz purchased the Blue Grouse vineyard in 1989 from John Harper, a veteran British Columbia vineyardist whose insatiable curiosity had him growing a vast array of obscure grape varieties. Kiltz found a dozen Black Muscat vines on the property and decided to propagate them. The resulting wine is a sensation: brilliantly deep purple in colour, it has a powerful aroma of cherries, blackberries and even lichees, with concentrated flavours to match and a dry finish. It is a wine best paired with cheese, when the wine can be found. The production at Blue Grouse unfortunately is very small.

OKANAGAN RIESLING

The Producer

House of Rose

WHITE TABLE WINE   A grape whose origin is unclear, Okanagan Riesling once was the most widely-planted white grape variety in the Okanagan and the backbone of a host of wines from varietals to Calona's original Schloss Laderheim. Since the 1988 vine pull-out, the variety has almost been eradicated. It was further ostracized when the British Columbia Wine Institute removed it from the list of varieties eligible for VQA status. House of Rose is the only winery still producing this wine but not even this winery puts the variety's name on the label. It never was a variety for finesse wines; badly made Okanagan Riesling was pungent and dull. House of Rose mutes that pungent aroma to achieve a dry and somewhat spicy wine.

Asked to pose for a photograph, winery owner Vern Rose neglects to tuck in a shirt whose tail worked itself loose while he was in the vineyard. Only after a dozen pictures have been taken does Rose notice he is a bit disheveled. A man happily untroubled by ego, Rose does not ask that the photographs be redone. Rose takes life as it comes, which perhaps explains why he is still making wine from Okanagan Riesling. The variety was in the vineyard north of Kelowna that he purchased early in the 1980s. This is one of the colder vineyard sites in the Okanagan but the variety grows vigorously and reliably there. Rose reduced its acreage and planted several of the classical European varieties but, unlike almost all other growers, he never abandoned Okanagan Riesling and included it in his portfolio when he established the House of Rose farm winery in 1993. He recognized that Okanagan Riesling has its fans; now they all have to find his little off-the-beaten-track winery if they want the wine. Apparently they do. Okanagan Riesling—which Rose calls Riesling Trocken (German for dry)—outsells his Johannisberg Riesling.

Okanagan Riesling's fall from its eminence is the perhaps most astonishing collapse of any variety in the history of Canadian viticulture. Even the reviled Concord has hung on in some parts of Canada, no doubt because that variety still makes jellies and juices with some wide market appeal. As recently as 1986

Okanagan Riesling, with 986 acres planted in the Okanagan, accounted for a quarter of the total vineyards. A decade later, perhaps five acres still survived, some at the Rose vineyard and some in a small vineyard south of Oliver.

One theory has it that this variety evolved from a Hungarian grape called Excellent, brought to the Okanagan by a grower in the 1930s who was himself Hungarian. Another theory is that it is a labrusca hybrid developed by chance in the Okanagan and propagated widely because it grew vigorously and easily. Russell Rose, Vern Rose's son and assistant, says that no variety in their vineyard has trunks and stalks as sturdy as Okanagan Riesling and no variety comes through the cold winters as unscathed as the grape. The variety appealed to growers because it is capable of prodigious tonnages while still producing mature fruit with good sugar levels and usually good acidity.

Vern Rose

However, the wines made from the variety often were coarse and unappealing, perhaps with the exception of the early Okanagan Rieslings from Sumac Ridge which were commendably clean and fresh. Sumac Ridge dropped this variety, even from its blended wines, as soon as it had sufficient vinifera grapes. Most winemakers loathed the variety and often complained that this grape gave a bad name to the better whites made from Johannisberg Riesling. No doubt that was true. It was equally true that few winemakers bothered giving Okanagan Riesling their best efforts.

But then there is the unpretentious Vern Rose. A former Alberta schoolteacher, he only took up grapegrowing when he moved to the Okanagan after retiring in 1982. Some teachers never stop learning and Rose fits that mold. Once he had mastered being a grower, he then began to learn winemaking, largely by trial and error. A man with insatiable curiosity, he will (and has) made wine from almost anything that will ferment, including fruits from his orchard. Those wines were not successful, except as a learning experience. What he learned there was applied later when his amateur skills grew to the point that he could open a winery where his most successful wines—all from grapes—have included Chardonnay and Maréchal Foch.

Of course, he would include Okanagan Riesling among those successes. Like all of his wines, Rose approaches this with a minimalist hand—no barrels, no chips, just simple clean fermentation and, when it is done, into the bottle. "It needs aging," Rose believes. "Once it ages it really gets good." The current release at the winery typically is three to four years old.

Rose makes just a few hundred cases of Okanagan Riesling each year, since he only has about half an acre of the variety remaining in his vineyard. Once the King of the Okanagan, the variety only retains a tiny niche, largely thanks to Vern Rose.

OPTIMA

WHITE TABLE AND DESSERT WINE This grape was developed in 1970 at Germany's Geilweilerhof research station from a Silvaner/Riesling cross as one parent and Müller-Thurgau as the other. The variety ripens to a high natural sugar content with the unfortunate disadvantage of low acidity. But when grown primarily on cool sites in British Columbia, Optima achieves better balance, one reason why award-winning dessert wines have been made by several wineries. Both Quails' Gate and Domaine de Chaberton have had the good fortune in some vintages to have botrytis or so-called noble rot among their Optima grapes. This contributes honey and tobacco flavours, adding richness to the aroma and taste of the wines.

The Producers

Calona
CedarCreek
Domaine de Chaberton
Gray Monk
Mission Hill
Pinot Reach
Quails' Gate
Recline Ridge

Dessert wines made from Optima have been overshadowed in that category by the icewine deluge but, especially when the grapes have been touched by botrytis—also called noble rot because the fungus looks like rot—the resulting wines show a complexity seldom matched by the far more costly icewines. From Optima in its own vineyard, Quails' Gate has made such an exceptional dessert wine almost every year for more than a decade. "It used to be made into a table wine," laments winemaker Jeff Martin. "We are trying to make wines that are exclusive, or almost exclusive, to us." Susan Dulik at Pinot Reach quickly speaks up for Optima as an off-dry table wine after her debut 1996 Optima won a bronze medal (the new winery's first award) at the 1998 All-Canada wine competition.

Bone dry is probably not in the cards for Optima, a variety well suited for sweet wines because of its happy susceptibility to botrytis, a fungus which, by dehydrating the grapes, concentrates the flavours and sugars to the point where a sweet wine is the obvious choice. The Pinot Reach winery is within the Dulik family vineyard near Kelowna and botrytis appears to be a reliable visitor each autumn. In the 1997 vintage, consulting winemaker Eric von Krosigk was able to produce a barrel-aged late harvest dessert wine from fully botrytised Optima grapes in the Pinot Reach vineyard; he planned to move even closer to a Sauternes style in 1998 by fermenting the grapes in barrels as well. The Dulik vineyard also has been the source of Optima grapes for Domaine de Chaberton although it is probable that Pinot Reach ultimately will take all of the grapes itself. Susan Dulik likely will consider producing some table wine Optima as well as the dessert style, depending on vintage conditions.

Susan Dulik

The dessert version is a challenging wine to make, even for someone with Martin's self-confidence, because nature cannot be relied on to deliver noble rot every year. Botrytis cinerea is a fungus that grows on the skins of the grapes on misty mornings late in the season, dehydrating the grapes without breaking the skin. The Optima block at Quails' Gate is just below the winery, facing east toward Lake Okanagan. "In this climate," Martin says of the generally dry Okanagan, "you get spasmodic botrytis infection and you also get a lot of raisining. You can get botrytis infection on 10 percent of the bunches and then it will dry out. Then you get more botrytis on another 10 percent. The final result is that you end up with a high percentage of raisin fruit character." Whether or not that is desirable is a matter of taste. Some like raisin flavours in dessert wines. Martin, who learned to make botrytis-affected wines in Australia from Sémillon, the classic variety, does not care for the raisin character. "If I'm trying to make a Sauternes-like late harvest wine, raisin characters are great in Muscats and Tokays but not in Sauternes-like wines." The Quails' Gate 1994 Optima, a wine with plenty of raisining, won a gold medal in one major competition. "The judges liked it," Martin explains sheepishly. He was much happier with the wine he made in 1995, when the season was not as hot as it had been the year before and when botrytis infected the Optima vines evenly. "It was more Sauternes-like and it had the peachy, apricots, pure botrytis character." By the 1997 vintage he had refined his technique to achieve a late harvest wine with the aroma of pears and anise and rich melon flavours—and not a hint of raisins.

No Optima could be made at all at Quails' Gate in the 1996 vintage. "It was a super-wet year," Martin recalls. "Not only did we have botrytis infection but we also had mildew developing in that block of Optima. Mildew and botrytis do not mix. All you end up with is an unpleasant mustiness like an old damp basement somewhere. We went through and hand-picked the clean bunches, which ended up going into Gewürztraminer." After that experience, Quails' Gate re-arranged the way the vines grow their canopy of leaves, better exposing the bunches to the breeze in an effort to thwart mildew. In the same vintage the Dulik vineyard, only a few miles away as the crow flies but on the other side of the lake, had a more reliable onset of botrytis. Because Susan Dulik's winery is within the Dulik vineyard, she is able to select choice grapes for Pinot Reach. "Botrytis affects little blocks of plants within the row and I grabbed my bins [of grapes] from within those areas with the most raisined grapes in them that I could find," she says of the 1996 vintage.

Whether one prefers Martin's racy, fruit-driven style or Dulik and Von Krosigk's raisined style is entirely a matter of taste. The Optima grape is happy to produce either.

ORANIENSTEINER

The Producers

Hawthorne Mountain
LeComte

WHITE TABLE WINE A variety handicapped by its unwieldy name, this is one of many experimental grape varieties developed in Germany in the 1960s and 1970s at Geisenheim. The parent varieties are Riesling and Sylvaner, prolific parents because, in the hands of various plant breeders, they also spawned Müller-Thurgau, Ehrenfelser, Osteiner and others. The object always was to produce better varieties than Riesling, an old cultivar that evolved naturally. Like many Geisenheim varieties, Oraniensteiner is named for a castle, Schloss Oranienstein. Few of the "castle" varieties have succeeded in winning consumer acceptance; none quite matches the natural elegance of Riesling although most make wines of character. Oraniensteiner is notable for vivid flavours and bracing acidity.

Treasure this wine if it can be found, for it is extremely rare in the Okanagan, where the only significant planting of the variety is at the Naramata vineyard owned by Wolfgang Zeller and his family. In 1995 LeComte Estate Winery (now Hawthorne Mountain Vineyards) bought the grapes and produced eighty cases (less than one thousand bottles) of table wine. "This wine was so different that I had to make a varietal of it," says Eric von Krosigk, then the winemaker at Hawthorne Mountain. "It has very strong spicy characters like good Pinot Gris and then a most unusual note of ripe oranges or tangerines." In 1996, the notorious cool vintage, the same late-ripening grapes from the Zeller vineyard were made into icewine. Von Krosigk found that the grapes, while mature, had retained unusually high acidity, making for a racy and long-lived dessert wine. "I filed the teeth down but I didn't take its bite away," the winemaker told the Zellers.

No growers are more ardent supporters of the variety than Karl Zeller, the winemaker in the Zeller family, and his father, Wolfgang. "I am really confident," Wolfgang insists during an early morning walk in his vineyard. "They will have their place among the top varieties." The family's Naramata vineyard has about two thousand Oraniensteiner vines; the only other planting of any consequence, a few hundred vines, is in Lanny Martiniuk's vineyard near Oliver. The variety arrived in the Okanagan in 1978 among the many to be tested in the Becker project, directed by the late Dr. Helmut Becker, the renowned director of plant breeding at Geisenheim and an advisor to British Columbia grapegrowers in the 1970s. The first vintage from the test plots was made in 1982 by the Brights winery (now Jackson-Triggs) at Oliver, which released a modest 384 bottles for tastings and for sale only at the winery's own shop. One contemporary tasting note described the wine as "different!—a peppery flavour." In 1984, the Zellers agreed to plant the variety for Brights on a small commercial scale. As it happened, Oraniensteiner was one of the first varieties that Brights dropped from the long list of experimental grapes it had under trial, a list that included even Russian grapes such as Sereksia Chornaya and Rkatsiteli. Aside from their variable winemaking qualities, these trial grapes had obscure and unpronounceable names that made them commercially nonviable.

Wolfgang Zeller

Late-ripening Oraniensteiner's tendency to retain high acidity at maturity is its most serious drawback. The 1982 Oraniensteiner ripened to a quite acceptable 23° Brix—but still had 1.3 grams of acid per litre, or almost double the acidity winemakers prefer in a balanced table wine. In 1984, Brights winemakers had to deal with an acid reading of 1.7 grams, more appropriate for making lemonade than wine. Perhaps the vines in the experimental plots were being overcropped. Karl Zeller was much happier with the grapes he began growing. "In my own winemaking I soon discovered that the Oraniensteiner is easy to make and constantly turns out well, with a lot of fans who love it," he says. "So we decided to take cuttings [from their original small block] and plant another block, to have a large enough block to give this grape a chance as a varietal." He was even more convinced the variety had a future when his home-produced wine swept a competition among the growers who were gearing up in 1989 to apply for farmgate licenses. The Zellers subsequently decided not to open their own winery, preferring to concentrate on their business as dealers in imported winery and vineyard equipment. But they continued to grow grapes and Karl Zeller continued to make wines, including Oraniensteiner, for the family's personal consumption. Even though the Oraniensteiner vines have bushy, almost unmanageable growth, the block has pride of place in the Zeller vineyard where the light green foliage sets it off from the surrounding varieties.

The Zellers have been so determined that Oraniensteiner should have recognition that they have moved their grape sales contract from winery to winery, looking for a patron. After Brights lost interest, the Zellers began selling to Mission Hill, pressing the winery to release it as a varietal. Mission Hill generally blended the juice with Riesling. "I knew the potential that this variety has, that it will create for itself a customer base," Karl Zeller believes. "From a marketing point of view, I considered it an absolute plus for a winery. Only one winery would have this varietal, so that anybody who learned to appreciate it had to buy it from that winery." Mission Hill, which was building its future around mainstream French varietals, was no more interested in making a hard-to-pronounce Oraniensteiner varietal than Brights had been. The Zellers, who had emigrated to Canada in 1981 from southern Germany, chafed at being told that the variety's name was too difficult to be marketable on its own.

When the Zellers in 1983 developed their Naramata area vineyard on what had been horse pasture, they rejected advice to plant hybrid grapes, putting in only vinifera. Consequently, they had no vines to eradicate and no compensation to collect during the industry vine pull-out after the 1988 harvest. After the pull-out, the wineries signed seven-year contracts with the remaining growers with the prices for each variety being established with a complex formula that took into account the previous five-year average price and quality parameters for each variety. The Zeller vineyard had been the sole commercial source of Oraniensteiner and the Zellers believed they had been delivering grapes that were exceeding the quality standards then in place. The surprising result was that Oraniensteiner emerged from this formula with a base price of $1,175, making it among the most valuable of the white vinifera. Lynn Bremmer, who had been the winemaker at Brights, disputes that the Zellers achieved such a high price because the grapes were so excellent. "The variety NEVER reached ideal settings to make a balanced wine," she says. "Because the acidity was always out of balance with the sugar and it never matured fully in the areas it was grown, the price was set unrealistically high as it was assumed that the grower would never be paid more than 70 percent of the price for ideal grapes." Whatever motivated the Marketing Board, the Zellers were delighted with the high price. "It was pay-off time for us to have stepped into the uncertainty of this variety and we were very happy that we had taken the risk," Karl Zeller says. "But now I needed to ensure that the value of the Oraniensteiner grapes would stay at that level. This could only be done by a winery picking up on its potential as a varietal."

Mission Hill could not be talked into doing so and when it offered to renew contracts with the Zeller vineyard in 1995, its offered price for Oraniensteiner was significantly lower. The unhappy Zellers began selling their grapes to LeComte after von Krosigk agreed to produce a varietal wine. "The grapes did take a bit of a devaluation but with the provision for reconsideration of pricing if the wine did establish itself positively in the market," Zeller recounts. But von Krosigk left Hawthorne Mountain in the summer of 1997, having made only two vintages of varietal Oraniensteiner. When incoming winemaker Bruce Ewert dropped it as a varietal, the Zellers sought to sell the grapes to one of the smaller wineries near Naramata where Oraniensteiner fan von Krosigk now was consulting and were prevented from doing so only by the terms of their contract. In the end the grapes were delivered to Hawthorne Mountain, which passed them on to sister winery Sumac Ridge where they disappeared into a white blend. Once again the grapes had challenging numbers. Despite being harvested in early November, the vines struggled to achieve 20° Brix and the acidity, in the words of assistant vintner Michael Bartier, was "in the teens." He adds: "Although time may prove me wrong, I don't foresee much of a future for the variety. I've worked with six separate lots of Oraniensteiner in the last three vintages and I have only seen one of them ripen up [1995 from the Martiniuk vineyard in Oliver]. A grape that can't ripen in Oliver is a tough nut indeed." It is inevitable that the Zellers will deliver the grapes to von Krosigk when they have the opportunity to do so since he is the only winemaker who truly shares their enthusiasm for the variety.

Oraniensteiner has a penchant to make wines that behave like a Mosel. There could be worse outcomes. The Zellers have bottles of Oraniensteiner in the family cellar which are quite sound with eight to ten years of maturity—just like a good Mosel. "They are fabulous," Wolfgang Zeller insists. "It is not a wine for quick releasing." He looks across his vines in the morning sun and confesses that he is considering even extending his plantings of Oraniensteiner. As son Karl says: "No other variety had so much influence in the decisions made for our vineyard than Oraniensteiner."

ORTEGA

WHITE TABLE WINE This German-developed grape is a cross of Müller-Thurgau and Siegerrebe. Its major advantage is its ability to mature readily to adequate to high sugar levels early and in less than ideal growing conditions. For this reason the variety has become a staple to wineries on Vancouver Island and in the most northerly extensions of the Okanagan Valley. The somewhat exotic flavours of the wine—Muscat and apricots— make it both a good aperitif and a favourite with Asian foods. Cherry Point's Wayne Ulrich likes it with his wife's home-made bread and peanut butter. "I've had it with Cajun chicken," vintner Loretta Zanatta says. "It takes a lot to wipe out Ortega."

The Producers

Blue Grouse
Cherry Point
Domaine de Chaberton
Larch Hills
Recline Ridge
Vigneti Zanatta

When immigrant Dionisio Zanatta established a dairy farm south of Duncan on Vancouver Island in 1959, it was not too long before he—being Italian—also planted a few grape vines to make wines for his own table. That small decision had momentous results. The vineyard he started became the foundation for government-sponsored grapegrowing trials in the 1980s and ultimately, when Vigneti Zanatta opened in 1992, was the basis for the first modern winery on Vancouver Island. Ortega was one of the varieties in that trial. While the variety was proving itself in Zanatta's rolling Glenora Road vineyard, his petite, dark-haired daughter went to Italy to study winemaking. As a result, Loretta Zanatta has the most mature vineyard of Ortega in British Columbia and has one of the most assured touches with the variety, having made wine with it since 1990.

The vine has been planted in numerous other vineyards where early-ripening varieties are required. It grows at both Larch Hills and Recline Ridge, the two Salmon Arm wineries that are the most northerly in British Columbia. Larch Hills proprietor Hans Nevrkla, a ruddy-cheeked Austrian from Vienna who became a capable amateur vintner after coming to Canada in 1970, had not planned a vineyard when he and his wife bought their seventy-three mountainside acres south of Salmon Arm in 1987. While some grapes were grown near this community around 1905, the area was so little regarded for grape-growing that it was not included in the atlas of Okanagan grape-growing sites published by the federal government. Nevrkla was on his own when, at the urging of friends who planted a few vines in his yard almost as a joke, he decided to grow grapes. He experimented with "a row of everything" on his site which, while it has a fine southern exposure, also is at an elevation of two thousand feet. The winery debuted in 1997 with a 1995 vintage Ortega in a style he called "typically big and very full-bodied," with a good cool-climate crispness. Ironically, the cuttings from which Larch Hills developed its four-acre planting came from a vineyard south of Oliver, a hot location ill-suited to a variety that was created for cool-climate winegrowing in Germany's Mosel Valley. There are years when even Ortega is challenged by cool weather; the 1996 vintage was one of those for Larch Hills. Even though the grapes remained on the vines until the

Hans Nevrkla

second week of October, a month later than in 1995, they only ripened enough to produce a light wine with nine percent alcohol. "It's not something I am disappointed with but it was not as good as 1995," Nevrkla says candidly. At the nearby Recline Ridge vineyard, proprietor Michael Smith believes his site can ripen grapes as much as ten days earlier than Larch Hills because it is located in a warm bowl at the confluence of two valleys and at an elevation of thirteen hundred feet.

A good Ortega table wine, when grown in a cool climate, has enough acidity to give the wine a fresh lift on the palate. Because Ortega ripens easily and early, it is possible to make a big wine lacking subtlety. "It's not a forgiving grape if you pick it too early or too late," Loretta Zanatta has learned. "You have to be really careful to avoid over-ripening." Hans Kiltz at Blue Grouse, another Cowichan Valley winery, agrees entirely. "If you pick it too early, it's not good—but if you over-ripen it, it gets bitter. You have only a relatively small window for picking."

Zanatta depends as much on the grape's appearance as on its technical numbers in making the decision when to pick. A mature Ortega grape has a slightly golden, freckled skin. Zanatta also studies the colour of the stalk that attaches each bunch to the vine: the stem should be mostly brown, but with a hint of greenness to indicate that ripening is not fully complete. A totally brown stalk is a sign of grapes heading toward over-ripeness and the point where the natural acidity falls away, leaving grapes that yield alcoholic wine lacking in freshness. "It does not make a good late harvest wine," asserts Wayne Ulrich of Cherry Point Vineyards; that is not only because the acidity drops off with maturity but, as he discovered in 1994, the wasps will swarm onto ripe bunches, suck out the juice and leave hollow shells.

Zanatta maintains that the grape should be handled gently in the winery. She gives the grapes the lightest possible pressing to extract the juice. "I'm trying to avoid a lot of intense flavours," she says. "It is quite an intense grape." As is typical with most white wines, the juice is fermented at cold temperatures. Zanatta uses Champagne yeast, dependable because it does not cause off-flavours. Within nine months of vintage, the wine gets a light filtration and is bottled, to be released for consumption within three months, when the bouquet and the flavours are still quite lively. "I like it with a fruity nose," Zanatta says. "The bouquet is everything at first." In her Ortega, which is finished dry, she finds notes of Muscat and apricot. While she prefers the wine when it is young, Vigneti Zanatta's Ortega has fans who prefer the wine with three years of age when the flavours will have become darker and more intense. While Zanatta agrees that the customer is always right, she warns that she uses sulphur sparingly in her winemaking, with the result that the wines might not always be that long-lived. Nevrkla, who thinks that it is not a wine for aging, finds a note of peaches in Ortega. The fruitiness in a wine that usually is finished dry makes it a flexible candidate for serving both to consumers with a leaning toward a sweeter wine and those who like drier wines. "You can almost convince anybody that this is a wine they will like," Nevrkla says, a mischievous twinkle in his blue eyes.

Notwithstanding Ulrich's opinion, Ortega occasionally can yield a good late harvest wine. Hans Kiltz at Blue Grouse managed to produce a botrytis-affected Ortega in the 1996 vintage because the unusually cool weather that year slowed down the rate of maturity. But several years earlier he had a more typical experience when he left his Ortega grapes on the vines an extra four weeks with the intention of producing a dessert wine. The experiment did not work. The sugar level in the grapes did not rise appreciably in those four weeks while the acidity fell away abruptly. Without a good tart acidity, a dessert wine is just another flabby confection. Perhaps the most consistent success with a dessert-version Ortega has been enjoyed by Domaine de Chaberton, where the unique circumstances of climate have enabled the production of award-winning botrytis-affected Ortega wines since the 1993 vintage. Domaine de Chaberton proprietor Claude Violet, who has between four and five acres of this variety, began producing a late-harvest version in 1992, having found that the grapes on his site retain the essential acidity. The following year botrytis established itself on these grapes, initially to the dismay of the pickers because the grapes appeared to be rotting. Violet recognized that his Ortega had not been struck with ordinary rot but with what is called "noble" rot—because noble dessert wines can be made from the grapes. The fungus dehydrates the grapes without breaking the skins. This concentrates both the piquant, spicy flavours and the natural sugar, with intense aromas at crush attracting dense swarms of bees and wasps, to the dismay of winery employees. "For us," Violet says, shaking his head, "it is the worst moment of the vintage."

PINOT BLANC

WHITE TABLE WINE This reliably crisp and dry table wine is ideal with most seafood and harmonious with many other dishes. It is by far the most successful variety recommended for British Columbia by the late Dr. Helmut Becker, who included it in test plantings in the Okanagan in the late 1970s. In the Becker trials, the variety carried its German name, *Weissburgunder*. The industry avoided what would have been a marketing disaster when all but two settled on Pinot Blanc, the better-known French name. Divino and Vigneti Zanatta, wineries with Italian heritage, opted for *Pinot Bianco*. The grapes mature to good sugar levels. A versatile grape that can yield neutral wine, Pinot Blanc in the hands of a conscientious winemaker can be classically flinty; or show a bouquet of tropical fruit; or be as richly complex as Chardonnay when barrel-fermented.

The Producers

Bighorn Vineyards
Blue Mountain**
Calona
Carriage House
CedarCreek
Cherry Point
Divino
Gersighel Wineberg
Gray Monk
Hainle
(cont'd)

This varietal deserves far more respect that it gets. Calona Vineyards winemaker Howard Soon calls Pinot Blanc an "entry-level" introduction to British Columbia table wines because he finds it an easy wine to like. Winemaker Ross Mirko describes Pinot Blanc as the poor man's Chardonnay. Pinot Blanc usually is lower priced than Chardonnay, which has little to do with the relative quality of the two varietals and everything to do with which wine is more fashionable.

Pinot Blanc has adapted superbly to vineyards from the Okanagan to Vancouver Island. Wayne Ulrich at Cherry Point Vineyards on Vancouver Island even insists that the variety ripens too quickly in hotter parts of the Okanagan. "We get more bright fruit flavours while growers in the Okanagan get more weight and body." Many styles of Pinot Blanc are produced, from flinty to rich and buttery, perhaps to the point where consumers are never quite sure what style will greet them unless they are familiar with an individual winery's approach. The only certainty is that all styles are easily matched with food. "It is our fondue wine here," says Cherie Jones, the winemaker at St. Hubertus, whose proprietors are Swiss and where the Pinot Blanc aims to be "as pure and simple as it comes, grapey and fresh and alive on

* Two or more versions, including barrel-fermented reserve wine.
** Partially barrel-fermented

the palate." At Inniskillin Okanagan, this style may be tweaked somewhat by a minor quantity of barrel-fermented wine in the blend, not to accent the flavour but just to broaden the texture. "But I love Pinot Blanc the way it is now—nice, crisp flavours, a hint of acidity, a nice enough volume. And it lingers just long to tell you, yes, you've had the Pinot Blanc," winemaker Christine Leroux says.

"Pinot Blanc has not found its niche here," maintains Jackson-Triggs winemaker Bruce Nicholson, speaking of British Columbia. "You can find many different styles and nobody has really settled on one. I've tried Pinot Blancs that might be mistaken for a Chardonnay." Indeed, he handles the variety much as he would Chardonnay—a small portion fermented in oak, a major portion in steel, with the final blend aiming for fruit with just a grace note of the oak. "It is very versatile," he says. "I like the variety just for that reason." Tilman Hainle, an exponent of the austere and flinty style, maintains that Pinot Blanc "really responds to being treated well. A lot of people take advantage of Pinot Blanc a little bit. It has a tendency to crop heavily if you let it and still produce decent sugars. Some say, 'great, why not get eight or ten tons from an acre and at 19, 20 percent sugar, make a nice light wine from it?' That's fine as far as it goes but if you do keep the crop down, it really comes through with lots of intensity and honey, caramel apple, spicy characteristics. It comes with the grape. When you get the bin in [at harvest], that's the aroma that wafts out of the bin."

At Hester Creek, winemaker Frank Supernak so admires Pinot Blanc that, in his first vintage at that winery in 1996, he made *four* different Pinot Blanc wines from his grapes, including an icewine. Most of the grapes were dedicated to the winery's estate-bottled release, its bread and butter Pinot Blanc, made from grapes grown primarily in a cooler section of the vineyard—that part with an exposure to the northeast. Fermented cold in stainless steel tanks, this is the mainstream Okanagan style, which Supernak compares to Alsace. "Intense fruit, with peaches and gooseberries, with a crisp, dry finish," he finds, recommending it as "unbelievable" with salmon. Continuing, he describes his barrel-fermented Grand Reserve Pinot Blanc as Burgundian. At the top of his tier of table wine Pinot Blancs is a super-premium wine bottled as a "Signature Release"—essentially a Grand Reserve with additional barrel-aging. The fully-ripened grapes are drawn from the vineyard's sunniest southeast corner, designated by Hester Creek as the vineyard's Grand Reserve block. Supernak recalls the quality of the grapes as they came into the winery that vintage. "From the first day of fermentation, I couldn't believe the fruit that we smelled and tasted." Coolly confident, he assured Hester Creek proprietor Hans-Jorg Lochbichler that a benchmark wine would emerge. "It was cold fermented, about nine degrees, to retain all that fruit and intensity. It was fermented in barrels for about fourteen or fifteen days." The wine then was racked into stainless steel tanks to complete fermentation and to go through malolactic fermentation, a secondary process that softens a wine's acidity and sometimes adds a buttery note to the flavours. The additional months in American oak for the Signature Release version added what some find as a butterscotch richness to the palate, not unlike a Chardonnay with full-blown oak treatment. Supernak so enjoys the variety that it, not Chardonnay, occupies top rank in his personal pecking order.

Blue Mountain's Ian Mavety ranks varieties differently, with Chardonnay in the first tier, followed by Pinot Gris and only then by Pinot Blanc. But the latter gets the same careful winemaking that is accorded the other varietals, beginning with fermenting a high proportion of the wine in barrels. Three- and four-year-old barrels, not new barrels, so that the character is not submerged by oak. "We're trying to blow off some of the fruit character that is in the Pinot Blanc," he explains. "To me, Pinot Blanc tends to be flowery, blossomy and then there is fruit behind it. When I say 'blow off,' that's not a correct term. The barrel fermentation tends to be warmer, so there is less fruit captured in the wine—but it allows the other sides to be built on, like the lees contact which tones the fruit down a little bit." Blue Mountain Pinot Blanc, while retaining the variety's crispness and clean apple flavours, has broadened its texture slightly by its time in the barrel. "When you analyze it, it is actually less daring, I think, to make wine in barrels," Mavety believes. "The barrels work for you." Most winemakers hesitate to give Pinot Blanc the full-blown oak treatment often employed with Chardonnay. "What you don't want to do is make a pseudo-Chardonnay," Calona's Howard Soon contends. "I believe it doesn't have the depth of fruit that Chardonnay does. In British Columbia we still have a mission in life to make sure that things are true to type." For all the interest in barrels for Pinot Blanc, the wines rarely are as boldly oaked as Chardonnay. "I really like using oak minimally," Pinot Reach's Susan Dulik says. "I don't like it to overpower the character of the fruit in the grape because I like the wines to taste like the grapes when you eat them during harvest. And I like them to smell the way they do from the crusher." Her plan is to ferment the variety in barrels that are a year or two old, avoiding the flavours of new oak but achieving wines with fresh fruit but the soft, buttery character of barrel-treated wines. "I prefer a lighter oak style," agrees Hillside's John Fletcher who ferments a portion of his grapes in barrels and the rest in stainless steel, blending the two lots into a finished wine.

Sumac Ridge has been producing Pinot Blanc since 1986 and the style has evolved as vines got older and as the winery has become more daring with the use of barrels. The winery's regular Pinot Blanc, while including some barrel-fermented wine in the blend, comes closest to defining the mainstream British Columbia style: crisp and flinty. But winemaker Mark Wendenburg swings for a home run with the winery's Private Reserve Pinot Blanc. "What we are looking for in a wine style is a *big* wine with an alcohol of 12.5 percent," he says. "We're looking for a malolactic character. We want the oak to show but not dominate. And we want aging potential. We try to get that by choosing vineyards where the grapes get very ripe, such as Black Sage." The reference is to Sumac Ridge's sun-drenched vineyards south of Oliver, the source of much of the winery's fruit. He uses Pinot Blanc from cooler sites for the blend in Sumac's *Stellars Jay* sparkling wine.

Mavety planted Pinot Blanc at the vineyard in the mid-1980s, well before he had decided to create a winery. It was becoming clear that a switch to vinifera grape varieties was beginning and Mavety was in the vanguard. Pinot Blanc was a star performer in the Becker Project (the extensive trials of grape varieties done in the Okanagan between 1977 and 1985) while the viability of Chardonnay had yet to be demonstrated. Because many wineries showed considerable interest in Pinot Blanc, Mavety shrewdly figured it was certain to be in demand. "It was the only variety at that time of which we could plant a commercial lot and be assured of a commercial sale," he says. "We had proven we could grow viniferas but the viniferas that were being marketed were not necessarily food wines," Mavety says, referring chiefly to Riesling and other German varietals made primarily as apéritif wines. "You look around the world," he suggests. "The real demand is for wine to accompany food." And that clearly is Pinot Blanc's strong point: whether made crisply fresh or in a buttery barrel-fermented style, the wine complements a wide number of cuisines and overpowers none. By the harvest of 1997, the 595 tons of Pinot Blanc that growers produced was 14 percent of the total crop of white varieties, ahead of Riesling (504 or 12 percent) but behind Chardonnay (881 tons or 21 percent).

Mission Hill winemaker John Simes had never worked with Pinot Blanc before he arrived in British Columbia in 1992 from New Zealand, where the variety is practically unknown. His New Zealand technique is to make wines that express their fruit vividly. Thus, while Blue Mountain's Mavety avoids skin contact, Simes gives the grapes plenty of skin contact to bring out the fruit flavours. Most of the juice then is fermented in stainless steel tanks to retain those flavours. "Fruit, that's the name of the game with Pinot Blanc," Simes believes. "Tropical flavours come through [in the finished wine]. Sometimes, some sort of earthy flavours come through as well." He agrees that Pinot Blanc also can handle lees contact and malolactic fermentation, both of which fatten the texture, but that is not the style at Mission Hill. In 1994, he did ferment some of his Pinot Blanc in barrels. "It was just wonderful," he admits, "but it was basically a business decision that at the moment, we just do the one style." Evidently, it was a good business decision: Mission Hill's Private Reserve Pinot Blancs, of which eight thousand cases are made each year, sell quickly.

At Calona, which produces about five thousand cases of Pinot Blanc each year, winemaker Howard Soon prefers to press whole clusters of grapes, avoiding any risk of oxidation—a browning of the juice—that might occur when the grapes are crushed before being pressed. The juice is fermented at cool temperatures. "Our tendency has been to do Pinot Blanc in stainless steel," Soon says. He concedes that when the wine is made entirely in steel, there is a risk that flavours can be simple. For the first time in the 1996 vintage, Soon fermented a portion of the juice in American oak barrels, later assembling a blend of the two in a quest for some complexity in the finished wine. But in the end, he is looking for the same fruitiness admired by Simes. "If you lose the fruit in the wine, you know you have done something wrong," Soon maintains. "Barrel fermenting enhances the fruit."

"I really like Alsatian wines as a style," says Tony Vlcek, the winemaker at Andrés, as he explains the crisp style chosen for the winery's first release (from 1996) under its new Bighorn Vineyards label. Since the 1995 vintage, he has been offering two styles under the winery's other premium label, Peller Estates; one is a super-premium barrel-fermented wine and the other offers clean, straightforward fruit. "Pinot blanc has some really unique fruit characters," Vlcek says, noting citrus and apple flavours as typical. "If you tank ferment that, it expresses some really nice clean, crisp fruit. It also does well in barrel-fermented programs but you have to be careful not to mask the fruit with a lot of oak." CedarCreek's Pinot Blanc—as much as four thousand cases are made each year—also has been evolving in style. Ross Mirko has had success by fermenting about three-quarters of the juice in tanks and the rest in barrels to assemble a blend where the complexity of barrel treatment underlies the variety's fruit flavours. "It is geared at being a restaurant, food-style wine— for seafood and light pastas."

PINOT GRIS

WHITE TABLE WINE Believed to be a mutation of Pinot Noir, this variety is grown widely in Europe and under a variety of names (Tokay in Alsace, Ruländer in Germany, Pinot Grigio in Italy). In the vineyards of British Columbia (as in Oregon), Pinot Gris is a winner. "We'd like to see more of it," writes winemaker Tilman Hainle who, with no Pinot Gris in his own vineyard, scrambled to find grapes through four vintages until he was able to settle on a long-term contract with a grower in 1995. It is a versatile food wine, often paired with seafood. "Pinot Gris with baked salmon—that's a natural," says Gray Monk winemaker George Heiss Jr. "Poached salmon," insists Blue Mountain's Ian Mavety. "Not barbecued salmon, not grilled salmon." The wines, while made in various styles, are refreshing whites with remarkable lengths of flavour, including a hint of spice or anise on the finish. Mavety finds a full spectrum of citrus flavours "from orange to tangerine to orange peel."

The Producers

Alderlea

Blue Grouse

Blue Mountain

Burrowing Owl

Calona

Cherry Point

Divino (as Pinot Grigio)

Gehringer

Gray Monk

Hainle

Hester Creek

Hillside

Mission Hill

Nichol Vineyard

Peller Estates

Red Rooster

Tinhorn Creek

Vigneti Zanatta

(as Pinot Grigio)

Pinot Gris (pronounced *pee-no gree*) provides signature wines at several British Columbia wineries but it would take a handwriting expert to find the similarities in the signatures. Winemakers approach the grape differently, a reflection both of personal styles and of the potential delivered to them from the sites where the grapes are grown. The excellent variety is gaining in prestige even though, in the 1997 harvest, Pinot Gris was only 5 percent of British Columbia's white grape production. That volume is certain to rise. "It's an earlier ripening grape and it is another option for some of the cooler vineyards," Mission Hill's John Simes believes. He made his first Pinot Gris in the 1996 vintage, producing a refreshing wine, some of the components of which had been barrel-fermented and allowed to go through malolactic fermentation. "I'm pretty excited about Pinot Gris." Most winemakers are.

The varietal was pioneered in British Columbia by Gray Monk, where the Heiss family, who own the winery, imported this variety, along with several others, from nurseries in Alsace. "Some of the first wines that we made—in carboys in the basement—were Pinot Gris, Auxerrois and Kerner," recalls George Heiss Jr. Pinot Gris also was planted in the Gehringer Brothers vineyard after that family bought the property, then in hybrid grapes, in 1981. Unfortunately, the vines became diseased and were replaced with Müller-Thurgau. The Gehringers came to regret choosing Müller-Thurgau, which makes a somewhat bland wine when grown at a warm site, and decided in 1993 to return to Pinot Gris when an opportunity came along to purchase some grapes. The wisdom of their decision to re-introduce Pinot Gris into their vineyard was confirmed when the winery's 1994 vintage from purchased grapes gained a "Best-of-Show" award for Gehringer at the Los Angeles County Fair. Beginning with the 1995 vintage, Gehringer released its Pinot Gris with a Private Reserve designation, a dry and disciplined wine successfully aimed at restaurant wine lists. The slowness with which other growers adopted the vine may have something to do with its undisciplined behaviour in the vineyard, where it likes to grow in all directions except upwards. "It's more labour intensive to control the green growth," Heiss says. "It's not overly consistent, either." In his experience, the vines produce heavily one year and lightly another year, perhaps because a good crop of grapes will not set in a year when there is rain or cool weather while the vines are in bloom. "Oh well," Heiss shrugs. "Every variety has its own quirks."

The style of the wines made from Pinot Gris at Gray Monk has been consistently fruity. Heiss begins by crushing the grapes—whose skins have a gray-pink blush at maturity—and leaving the juice in contact with the skins for a time, extracting colour and flavour. He ferments cool and in stainless steel tanks only, racking the wine off the yeast lees soon after fermentation, all of which is aimed at capturing fruitiness. He was a bit disturbed that the vintages made in 1995 and 1996 spontaneously went through malolactic fermentation, somewhat muting the fruitiness of the traditional Gray Monk style. It had him doing extensive detective work to determine the source of the malolactic bacteria. They are not uncommon in vineyards and in the wineries and are desirable for certain wine styles. "The wine seems to turn out all right," he says, "but the difference between the 1994 Pinot Gris and the 1995 is unbelievable." The 1994 version, which did not undergo malolactic fermentation, was finished with a hint of residual sugar balancing its somewhat higher acidity while the 1995 was finished bone dry. "I like the fruitier Pinot Gris," Heiss says, which also is a reason why he does not age any in barrel. "I don't find that oak enhances it in any way. I like the flavour the grapes bring in themselves. Oak has a tendency of overpowering that."

At Tinhorn Creek, winemaker Sandra Oldfield admits that she has been "easing into a style" with a variety new to her when she arrived from California. "I am really starting to like Pinot Gris as a grape," she said after her third vintage with the variety. The winery's first vintage of Pinot Gris in 1994 was a conservative and straightforward wine, some of which had been aged in new oak. But starting with the following vintage, Oldfield began exploring the possibilities of the variety, including malolactic fermentation which gives the wine a soft texture she admires. By 1996 she had determined that about half of each vintage should spend time in barrels, no more than three or four months, and those barrels preferably will be three years old by which time the wood flavours have been muted. "If you taste our Pinot Gris now, you would be hard-pressed to find oak," she says. "Unlike the Chardonnay, Pinot Gris is a much more fruity grape to work with and you don't want to lose that." The winery added a cooling system in 1997 for controlled cool fermentation of the white wines, enabling Oldfield to capture even more of the inherent fruitiness of Pinot Gris. "They'll still be dry," she adds. The wines also are white, which is not as odd as it sounds, for this variety's pink skin can colour the juice if skin contact is excessive. The free-run juice—the essentially colourless juice which drains by gravity after the grapes have been crushed—is fermented separately from the juice derived from the first light pressing and the second heavy pressing, both of which are pink. The colour usually drops out during fermentation but Oldfield prefers to avoid the risk of a pink wine, as tasty as it may be, for the sound commercial reason that restaurants demand *white* Pinot Gris. In the 1996 vintage, the press broke as Tinhorn Creek was pressing the juice from its Pinot Gris and it was well into the early hours the next day when a repair was completed. "The press portion was very pink and I was convinced it would never drop out and we were going to be making a certain amount of pink Pinot Gris," she said. "It did drop out, though. But we have a very small amount of red Pinot Gris, just a few litres, and we decided it will have to be our lunch wine here. I have no problem making a pink Pinot Gris; I really love tasting them—but it is just not our style here."

It is the style, famously so, of Nichol Vineyard, where winemaker Alex Nichol is reluctant to waste anything, colour included, that the vineyard delivers him. He was chagrined that the cool 1996 season failed to give him mature, rose-dusted grapes. "This year, for the first time, it's going to be white," he laughed

after the vintage. He always begins by leaving the crushed grapes on the skins a full twenty-four hours, precisely to extract the pink colour and lively flavour. The first several vintages also were fully barrel-fermented; sometimes, the wine will undergo malolactic fermentation to fatten the wine's texture. "I've stuck with my style because I like it, even though it is old-fashioned," he says. "I find initially, in the early months after fermentation, there is a bit of a tannic edge but that falls away with maturity." He has been producing his salmon-pink, but dry, Pinot Gris since the 1992 vintage, a style which the Vintners' Quality Alliance tasting panels initially found so controversial that, in the first two years, Nichol Vineyard was refused the VQA certification. The tasting panel contended (wrongly) that the wine was oxidized. Nichol stuck to his guns. "The 1994 was even darker in colour." Just as the VQA panel finally adjusted to his style, Nichol changed again, maturing only half of his Pinot Gris in oak and the rest in stainless steel, an approach which more successfully showcases the peach and almond flavours of the wine. Admirers of Nichol's stubborn dedication to pink Pinot Gris will not find abundant quantities. Tiny Nichol Vineyard only produces about two hundred cases a year of this varietal.

The winery most closely associated with Pinot Gris's rising star in British Columbia is Blue Mountain at Okanagan Falls, which released its first example from the 1991 vintage and which now produces about twelve hundred cases of the wine each year. Blue Mountain's Ian Mavety planted Pinot Gris after noting that the varietal from others in the Okanagan invariably impressed visiting tasters. "Pinot Gris inherently has this richness or lushness to it and it comes through very well in this valley, even when it is made in the more traditional tank-fermented style and even if it is picked at a younger maturity. It still has this weight to it."

The variety is well suited to the Blue Mountain vineyard, a large site undulating generally toward the south with Vaseaux Lake sparkling in the distance. The southern horizon is defined by McIntyre Bluff and, at certain times of the day, by a blue haze that inspires the vineyard name. Mavety believes that the vineyard, generally recognized as one of the Okanagan's best sites, has a Burgundian climate and that belief guided his decision to concentrate on grapes of the Pinot family. He has found Pinot Gris to be as suitable as Pinot Noir. "It has been a very consistent producer for us."

From the beginning the Blue Mountain style, involving a portion of barrel-fermented wine, explored the complexities of the variety to a greater degree than any other winery did at the time. As in all good winemaking, the use of barrels was driven by the grapes the vineyard delivered. "There were several reasons why we used the barrels," Mavety recalls. "Because of the acid levels in the grapes, we required that a certain portion of the fermentation go through malolactic [fermentation]." He much prefers to do this in barrels, rather than in tanks, because the wine gains more complexity. "We had young vineyards as well," he continues. He has found that vines produce leaner wines when the vineyard is young. "By using a barrel ferment and the additional lees contact, you can round a wine out a little bit. Once we decided on those two aspects, it was a matter of deciding what kind of barrels we were going to use. We didn't want to turn it into a Chardonnay, so we tended to use older barrels. In the beginning it was very simple winemaking: 50 percent tank-fermented, 50 percent barrel-fermented and all the barrel fermentation went through malolactic."

The clean flavours of the wine reflect Mavety's aversion to leaving the juice on the skins. "None of the whites we make get any skin contact whatsoever," he says firmly. "They've had six months of it and that's all they need." He goes a further step to ensure starting out with clean fruit by pressing whole bunches of

Ian Mavety

grapes rather than crushing and then pressing. "Pinot Gris and Pinot Blanc are particularly notorious for the phenols in the skins," Mavety explains. (Phenolics are chemical compounds that include pigments, tannins and flavour elements in the skin of grapes.) "Pinot Blanc, just before you pick it, you can go out and chew on the skins and they are as tannic as red wines. Anytime you crush it or chew it up, you're going to get that into your juice. Sit them on the skins and you will extract even more of it." He admits that winemakers at more northerly vineyards than his need not avoid skin contact rigorously with white varieties. High phenolic content is more likely in riper southern Okanagan grapes. "One of the contributing factors is the heat of the sun," Mavety explains.

As Blue Mountain's Pinot Gris vines have gotten older and begun delivering more fruit flavours and more substance, the winemaking has changed accordingly. Less of each vintage needs either barrel treatment or malolactic fermentation. "The grape is expressing itself much more in terms of weight and mouthfeel," Mavety says in a 1997 interview. "As a vintage now, we would be looking at somewhere between 65 to 70 percent tank-fermented." The reserve or stripped label Pinot Gris, which Blue Mountain began releasing with the 1995 vintage, is blended with even a higher percentage of wine that has never seen a barrel. "More obvious fruit or more obvious barrel does not make a better wine, in our minds," he explains. "It's the balances. The goal is finesse and power. Finesse in the sense that when you smell it and taste it, the wine is very pleasant. And then it is only with time, when you are drinking it, that you realize how much power it has and how long the finish is. Finally, when you are consuming it with a meal, you realize what flavours really are there, although they were subtle in the beginning."

PINOT MEUNIER

RED TABLE WINE Seldom seen as a varietal on its own, this red vinifera in France is used in Champagne blends. In British Columbia, besides serving as a sparkling wine component, it has been launched on its own, pioneered by Lang Vineyards at Naramata. The wines are light- to medium-bodied, often with lively cherry flavours and a hint of pepper in the aroma. The variety sometimes is called Meunier, a French word that means miller. Jancis Robinson in *The Oxford Companion to Wine* suggests that the name was inspired because the underside of the variety's leaves have the appearance of being dusted with flour. The Germans call the grape either Müllerrebe (miller's grape) or Schwarzriesling (black riesling). Some years ago, several Australian wineries made a wine from this grape called Miller's Burgundy.

The Producers

Hawthorne Mountain
Lang
Pinot Reach
St. Hubertus Oak Bay
Tinhorn Creek

Pinot Meunier, an early ripening mutation of Pinot Noir, seldom appears as a varietal wine even though it is widely planted in Champagne and elsewhere for the bright fruit element it gives to a great many sparkling wine blends. It has made a modest bid for varietal status in British Columbia after its chance propagation by Günther Lang, one of the owners of Lang Vineyards, a winery that does not even make sparkling wine. It has become his personal favourite among the reds that he makes.

"I didn't chose it, really," he laughs, recounting how the vines got into his Naramata vineyard in the first place. One November day in 1988 Lang drove to Oyama, north of Kelowna, to a favourite sausage supplier there and, on a back road, came across a vineyardist uprooting vines, including some sixty-five young Pinot Meunier plants. "I asked him if he would sell me the plants," Lang recalls. Told he could have the vines at no cost, Lang sealed the bargain by giving the vineyard owner a couple of bottles of Lang's own homemade wine. (His winery then was two years away from being licensed but Lang had been making vintages in his garage.) He replanted the vines at his own property as soon as he got home, a stroke of luck for the weather turned cold that night and the soil remained frozen for several months. With the vines surviving the move, Lang made a trial lot of Pinot Meunier the following vintage and concluded that "I have a winner." To capitalize on being the first producer of this variety in the Okanagan, Lang quickly expanded his planting by grafting Pinot Meunier cuttings onto some mature Maréchal Foch vines in his vineyard. "In the meantime, we ordered some more Meunier plants from France," he says. About three acres of the variety was planted in the Lang vineyard, correctly on rootstock this time, and once those vines became productive, the grafted Pinot Meunier were cut off so that the Foch could return to producing Foch, a variety also hotly in demand at Lang Vineyards. Since its first commercial release from the 1991 vintage, Pinot Meunier indeed has been a winner for Lang Vineyards. The 1992 Pinot Meunier Reserve received a gold medal at the 1993 Okanagan Wine Festival—the winery's first gold in this competition—and subsequent vintages usually have placed in the medals as well.

Red wine is a big part of the winery's portfolio even though Lang is perceived as a meticulous producer of such white wines as Riesling and Gewürztraminer. "As a wine drinker, I drink more red wines myself," he admits. "My goal is to develop a red wine which I like first. If I don't like it, then I don't like to sell it." As a young man in Germany, he was a management trainee with the maker of the luxurious Mercedes Benz automobile. The conservative habits learned there have carried over into making wines that are clean, straightforward expressions of the fruit which, like the car, never is excessively ornamented. "We have no oak with any of our reds because of our philosophy," Lang insists. "God made no mistake with the grapes. I believe the grape has it all—all the colour, the flavour, the acid to develop a great wine." Pinot Meunier, dry, and medium-bodied, is not quite as seductive a wine as Pinot Noir but, whether made with or without oak, is a satisfying red.

The vine's growing characteristics suggest it might have been planted more widely if growers had tested it earlier. The variety buds late, avoiding spring frosts, and ripens early, which is precisely why it grows extensively in Champagne's cool, challenging climate. "It ripens beautifully here," St. Hubertus winemaker Cherie Jones has discovered. That Kelowna-area winery has more than three acres of this variety, having found that the early-maturing red always gets ripe and, in a good year achieves the ripeness that yields a satisfying table wine. There also is a logistical reason for growing Pinot Meunier—it is convenient to have an early variety when many other vinifera reds grown in the Okanagan have maturities clumped together late in the season. "Only having so many red fermenting tanks, you don't want every red coming in right at the end of the vintage," Jones observes. "You run out of space. It is nice to stagger them throughout the harvest."

At St. Hubertus, the red fermenters are squat stainless steel tanks formerly used in a dairy. There is an advantage to the squatness. The petite Jones, short enough to be lost between two vine rows, only needs an overturned bucket on which to stand when she is punching down the frothing cap of Pinot Meunier in each fermenter, a task she still prefers to do by hand. "They are all managed very gently," she says of the Pinot Meunier grapes. As larger quantities of grapes come from recently expanded plantings, the winery will install larger fermenters and Jones will need climbing equipment more sophisticated than the bucket. But the gentle handling of the grapes will continue, a light touch that follows through in the cellar treatment. Jones has aged the variety in older oak barrels, typically three years old. "It seems to pick up great character from that," she says. "It's very delicate. I suppose I will play with putting it in a newer oak barrel but there does not seem to be much need. Just a hint of oak seems to work wonderfully. I find it similar to Pinot Noir—you have the delicacy, the elegance, the finesse." At Pinot Reach Susan Dulik has explored several styles with Pinot Meunier, obtained from vines planted in 1993. A light version from the 1995 vintage—"a red wine that white-wine-only drinkers liked"—was a great favourite with friends and relatives but did not achieve her goal of a reserve-style wine. "I think it can be a heavier red wine than Pinot Noir," she believes.

Tinhorn Creek winemaker Sandra Oldfield is scarcely taller

than Jones but has more modern equipment in the winery. It has not, however, fired her with enthusiasm for Pinot Meunier as a varietal on its own. Oldfield has to deal with six varietals each vintage and, perhaps with the bias that comes from growing up in California where most wineries are tightly focused, she would prefer to have no more than four. "I know a lot of wineries where I come from that do two wines really well," she observes. Pinot Meunier, a minor planting in the Tinhorn Creek vineyard, is one more than she considers desirable, which is why the variety is destined only to add fruit to the Pinot Noir blends. However, the grape may have something to say about it as well because, as at Lang Vineyards, it insists on being a winner. The 1995 vintage from Tinhorn Creek won the young winery its first gold medal, creating an unsought following for Pinot Meunier. The 1996 vintage had such a powerful aroma of black pepper when still in oak that it had to be bottled on its own for fear of overpowering the more delicate Pinot Noir, had the two been blended. Somewhere in the future the winery's Pinot Noir production will be large enough that the Pinot Meunier can disappear into the wine safely. "It's not in our plans to do Pinot Meunier as a separate varietal," Oldfield says, "but those may be famous last words. What may end up happening in the future is that Sandy ends up making a couple of hundred cases for the tasting room."

PINOT NOIR

RED TABLE WINE Profound mystique surrounds wines made from Pinot Noir because no major red variety so challenges the winemaker. The benchmark wines are the great reds from Burgundy, voluptuously full-bodied wines that, with a few years of maturity, develop a uniquely silken texture. A young Pinot Noir often has aromas of raspberry and spice and an astringent edge. "I would like to bring out the raspberries, strawberries and salmonberries," winemaker Loretta Zanatta says of her Pinot Noir, her descriptors showing what a berry bouquet the grape produces. Susan Dulik has compared some of her Pinot Noirs to Black Forest cake—"a chocolatey-cherry taste." Mature Pinot Noir develops an array of aromas ranging from rose petals and strawberries to plummy flavours and a smoky earthiness sometimes characterized, in what is meant to be a positive reference, as the barnyard or saddle soap aroma. This is a versatile wine. The lighter non-oaked styles, lightly chilled, complement salmon and summer picnics. The medium-bodied and robust styles, almost always matured in oak, complement red meats. "One of the favourite meals I've had with Pinot was duck breast on diced vegetables," says Quails' Gate winemaker Jeff Martin. Summerhill's Alan Marks, son of a chef, likes pairing it with sockeye salmon or tuna steak. Andrea McDonald of Crowsnest Vineyards advocates cooking with Pinot Noir. "I do a lot of stir frying," she says. "I just put a splash of Pinot Noir in and it's wonderful."

The Producers

Light-bodied
Alderlea
Blue Grouse
Cherry Point
Crowsnest
First Estate Cellars
Gersighel Wineberg
Golden Mile Cellars
Gray Monk
Hainle Adelheid's Vineyard
Lake Breeze (Blanc de Noir)
Lang
Larch Hills
LeComte
Scherzinger
Vigneti Zanatta
Wild Goose
(cont'd)

"When it is poorly made, it is the worst red wine in the world," Quails' Gate winemaker Jeff Martin says of Pinot Noir. Unspoken is the flip side of the coin: good Pinot Noirs are among the world's greatest red wines, which is why vintners struggle with this grape like preachers wrestling the devil. The American wine writer Robert M. Parker Jr., in his 1990 book, *Burgundy: A Comprehensive Guide to the Producers, Appellations, and Wines,*[1] calls Pinot Noir "the world's most fickle grape." The Canadian writer Marq de Villiers fittingly titled his 1993 Pinot Noir book *The Heart-*

---

1   Parker, Robert M. Jr.: *Burgundy: A Comprehensive Guide to the Producers, Appellations, and Wines,* Simon and Shuster, New York, 1990.

break Grape[2]. Pinot Noir is a demanding, sensual temptress. "Cabernet Sauvignon appeals to the mind while Pinot Noir appeals to the senses," asserts Inniskillin's Karl Kaiser, once a novice in an Austrian monastery and now a winemaker with three decades of experience in Canada. Tilman Hainle chimes in: "In a Pinot Noir, if it doesn't have that hedonistic factor, if it is not pleasurable, I don't see the point in it. It should have immediate appeal." Susan Dulik named her winery "Pinot Reach" when it opened in 1997 to symbolize a goal of reaching for quality with the Pinot varieties. "It's my favourite red grape variety," she says of Pinot Noir. "Unfortunately, it is one of the most difficult to make."

Almost half the wineries in British Columbia make Pinot Noir, which rivals Merlot as the most widely planted red vinifera. The 1997 harvest of Pinot Noir totaled 484 tons (a quarter of the total harvest of red varieties) compared with 428 tons of Merlot. "The [Okanagan] valley has great potential to make Pinot Noir," Martin believes. "There is some great fruit here." Ian Mavety of Blue Mountain, agreeing strongly, says, "From what I have seen of Pinot Noirs in the new world, if anybody can do it, British Columbia can. The climate is going for you here. That's all Pinot is—climate and vineyard management." Since both the variety and most winemakers are relatively recent arrivals in British Columbia, no one has much experience with a grape that has a long learning curve. Born in Australia in 1957, Martin learned red winemaking skills there, a land renowned for Shiraz and Cabernet but hardly for Pinot Noir. When Mavety, a skilled Okanagan grape grower, began making Pinot Noir in 1992, he wisely engaged a professional French-born California-based consulting winemaker, tacitly recognizing that there is, after all, a little more to the variety than climate and grapegrowing. Tim Watts and Robert Ferguson, the owners of the Kettle Valley winery, are respectively a geologist and an accountant who came to Pinot Noir as amateur winemakers. All have modified their approach to Pinot Noir with each succeeding vintage in the pursuit of excellence. "Pinot Noir is the big learning curve variety that people call the 'especially' grape," winemaker Ross Mirko observes. "For example if you want to play with yeasts and see how they affect wine—well, they especially affect Pinot Noir. [It

---

2   De Villiers, Marq: *The Heartbreak Grape, A Journey in Search of the Perfect Pinot Noir*, HarperCollins Publishers Ltd., Toronto, 1993.

is always] especially this and especially that!"

Pinot Noir is an ancient variety. The Roman historian Pliny in the first century wrote about *Vitis allobrogica,* describing a pinot-like vine that the Romans found being cultivated in what is modern-day Burgundy. It would not have been the only variety grown there. Because Pinot Noir, more than any other classic variety, spontaneously generates clones, the vineyards would have been filled with cousins, including such latter day relatives as Pinot Gris and Pinot Blanc. One widely-grown presumed relative is the Gamay, the Beaujolais variety. In 1395 Philip the Bold, the Duke of Burgundy, ordered that Gamay be replaced with Pinot Noir, judging that the latter variety produced the better red wine, at least in Burgundy. Generations of winegrowers who have confronted this challenging vine since would agree that the Duke's decision was bold. "You have to have growers that are fanatic," Martin says. One such individual is Naramata grower Don Munro, a former professor of forestry at the University of British Columbia who once, as a sideline, raised herb-fed lambs exclusively for one of Vancouver's finest restaurants. When Munro retired to the Okanagan, he decided he would plant grapes on his property, less than four acres in size. Not just any grapes but Pinot Noir. Methodically, he tasted Pinot Noir wines from around the Okanagan before deciding that Kettle Valley made the style of wine he would like to dedicate his grapes to. Then Munro talked Kettle Valley into giving him a contract, paying him by the acre rather than by the ton to ensure he would not be tempted to overcrop.

No doubt, he also appreciated the fanaticism that Kettle Valley's Ferguson and Watts display when, in most vintages, they pick the ripe fruit so selectively that, in the pursuit of 24° Brix grapes, they stretch their Pinot Noir harvest through several weeks. "We net everything," says Tim Watts, explaining how the super mature fruit is saved from the birds. He tries to leave his Pinot Noir on the vines, with minimal watering, well into October, even after some of the grapes have begun to shrivel to raisins. Picking very mature grapes achieves concentrated flavours and strapping alcohols in the wines. For the same reason, the vines usually are more densely grown than other varieties, a practice that reduces each vine's production but increases the flavours of the grapes. The quest for intensity is central to growing Pinot Noir, even when rosés and blush wines are being produced from

The Producers (cont'd)

Robust
Blue Mountain
Kettle Valley
Quails' Gate
Stag's Hollow
Sumac Ridge
Tinhorn Creek

the variety. "I would much rather have a somewhat funky, really expressive Pinot Noir than I would a wimpy, thin wine that is technically sound," says Tilman Hainle.

Unlike Cabernet Sauvignon, Pinot Noir has not adapted easily to vineyards in continents and climates distant from Burgundy. The variety tolerates a narrow range of temperatures and soils and must be cultivated carefully to achieve, when mature, a wine with 13 percent alcohol, the degree at which it is most likely to display its magic silky textures and its complex array of flavours. It is easy to miss that window. "The special character of its wine is lost in hot, dry conditions," writes the authoritative French ampelographer Pierre Galet.[3] "It really doesn't like hot weather," Hainle agrees, "and we've noticed in our own vineyards that ripening stalls until the temperature moderates."[4] In the Okanagan, therefore, most of the premier Pinot Noir vineyards are found north of McIntyre Bluff, the prominent cliff which pinches the valley south of Okanagan Falls. "We are in 'hot' Pinot country," Summerhill winemaker Alan Marks says, meaning, paradoxically, that the Kelowna area winery's own vineyard and other northerly vineyards from which it gets Pinot Noir are prized because they are cooler than the truly hot vineyards south of Oliver. The vineyards south of McIntyre Bluff, which comprise the largest vine growing area in the valley, are planted on Canada's only desert. While Pinot Noir succeeds on the cooler western slope of the valley, the stars here are sunbathers like Cabernet Sauvignon and Merlot.

Until the 1990s none of the classic varieties were widely cultivated in the Okanagan. There were neither knowledgeable growers nor winemakers to champion them. Among the earliest champions of vinifera in British Columbia were Virgil and Eugene Rittich, who grew grapes in the Kelowna area in the 1930s and 1940s and whose out of print 1941 book, *European Grape Growing in Cooler Districts Where Winter Protection is Necessary*, was the first tract on viticulture in the Okanagan. Even the Rittich brothers were hesitant. "We have not planted it [Pinot Noir] yet because of its drawbacks," they wrote, noting that the variety first was planted a year or so before their book by a grower at Vernon.

---

3   Galet, Pierre: *A Practical Ampelography: Grapevine Identification*, Cornell University Press, Ithaca, N.Y., 1979.

4   *Hainle Vineyards Newsletter*, September, 1996, Volume 8, Number 3.

"The *vine is hardy* and would not suffer in our country if covered in Winter." Perhaps their most commercially chilling conclusion was that the variety's yield should be restricted to one and a half tons of grapes per acre. The hybrid red varieties which the growers began planting in the 1950s readily yielded ten tons of fruit an acre and no one needed to bury those vines each winter. Pinot Noir today at $1,500 a ton is one of the highest-priced varieties; but even at that price, a grower is unlikely to break even at less than two tons to the acre.

At Quails' Gate, Pinot Noir was first planted in 1975, with vines from a block in Sunnyside, Washington, that had been fostered there in cooperation with the University of California's Davis campus. By 1997 the Quails' Gate vineyard's Pinot Noir block, located near the central Okanagan community of Westbank, had expanded to ten and a half acres, with seven clones (not counting another twelve clones under trial in the vineyard's test block). The vineyard is on a southeastern-facing slope of a plateau that rises gently toward Boucherie Mountain to the west. The mountain ridge protects the vineyard from the prevailing winds while the slope of the plateau, which ends abruptly in a sharp drop toward Okanagan Lake, provides the air drainage that keeps the vines healthy and protects them from frost in late spring or early autumn. This air circulation is especially important because the Pinot Noir vine produces tightly compact bunches which, in the Okanagan's rare wet autumns, are susceptible to disease. The vintage of 1996 was one with a cool, wet summer; consequently, botrytis, a fungal rot, appeared on the bunches. "Botrytis in red wines is catastrophic," Martin says. "It destroys the colour." The pickers at Quails' Gate were instructed not to pick any botrytized bunches and were paid by the hour rather than by quantity picked (as is the usual custom) to discourage fast but careless picking. "You can deal with a small amount of botrytis, the odd berry, but if you have more than five percent, you have a problem," Martin says. Fortunately, the problem is rare because the Okanagan's average rainfall, already less than fifteen inches a year, seldom occurs during the vintage.

Pinot Noir's riotous clonal diversity is a virtue, one of the reasons why there will be layers of flavour in a wine made from several clones. "We've got probably eight different clones. We have one of the Washington clones that was selected there for cropping level, not necessarily quality, but that particular clone on different vineyard sites is producing a difference," Martin has found. "I already know there are two blocks on Quails' Gate that produce the best fruit. Our best block is right up at the top of the vineyard. The lesser blocks are a hundred yards down the hill." The quality difference is attributed to the added warmth from the radiant heat that reflects from the hillside above the vineyard and the open-textured soil which, with gentle irrigation, affords a disciplined control of the amount of water permitted to the vines. As Quails' Gate added to its Pinot Noir plantings in the 1990s, clones from France were chosen. "The clonal differences are that great that, if you've got a choice and you've got one block to plant, why limit yourself to one dimension of fruit flavours? Why not plant three clones?" Martin says. "Generally when people see a darker colour Pinot Noir, they assume it's a better wine. Generally it does show that the wine has more extract [although] that is not necessarily so. Pinot has to have flesh and mouthfeel, so that colour is not the be-all and end-all. The French clones that were planted are showing very nice flesh and berry characters. One of the distinctive things of Quails' Gate Pinots is that they've all got more dark fruits than the red berries. I think that's due to the Washington clone. It's very important that you try to capitalize on all the clones." Wines from individual blocks are vinified in small separate lots and matured individually in barrels. When the final blends are assembled, Martin thus has a palette of flavours and textures to work with.

With fewer clones to work with, Kettle Valley's Bob Ferguson, who has the main responsibility for winemaking, achieves complexity by combining several processing techniques (such as differing periods of skin contact for various lots of grapes). "Our main concern when we are making Pinot Noirs is that quite often, they are missing something," says his partner, Tim Watts. "They are missing the finish or they have this great nose and the flavour disappoints. We thought by doing different treatments we could avoid having holes in the wine." The most intense Pinot Noir from Hainle Estate Vineyards is that labeled *Elisabeth's Vineyard*, so named because the grapes are grown near Okanagan Falls by Swiss-born Elisabeth Harbeck. The primary Pinot Noir in her vineyard is the Wädenswill Clone (named for a Swiss research station) which produces what Hainle describes as a concentrated fruit character with notes of cinnamon and nutmeg.

It has become fashionable to credit the grower for the quality of a wine. "Great wines are made in the vineyard," Martin agrees, "but grapes don't make wine, people do." It is the art of the winemaker to capture and enhance the quality delivered by the vineyard. As do most winemakers, Martin handles his Pinot Noir grapes gently, so gently that the skins of only half the grapes will be broken as the fruit passes through the crusher and into the fermentation vats. In this way, the seeds are not bruised and cannot release their hard, steeped-tea tannins into the wine. The grapes usually arrive at the winery naturally chilled because the overnight temperatures are crisply cool in the Okanagan in October, when Pinot Noir is being picked. Martin lets the crushed grapes sit without starting fermentation for four or five days, a technique called "cold soak" which begins extracting the all-important colour from the skins. Some Oregon Pinot Noir vintners, because the climate can be warmer, have been known to chill the crushed grapes with dry ice. "You basically end up with a brighter colour, more colour," Martin says. "At the end of the maceration the juice is red whereas when you first crushed, it is salmon pink." Sumac Ridge's Mark Wendenburg, who believes in extended skin contact with this variety, nods in agreement. "It can be tough to colour," he says. "You need the colour but you don't want to bash it too much." Aggressively pumping the juice over the crushed skins might extract colour but at the risk of creating what Wendenburg calls "a big tannic monster" which is precisely what a silky Pinot Noir must not be. Both Tilman Hainle and Larry Gerelus at Stag's Hollow have employed a cold soak of almost three weeks to achieve flavour and colour intensity.

Blue Mountain's Ian Mavety decides on the length of cold soak when he brings in the grapes. If the weather is warm at harvest, he believes it is prudent to get fermentation going promptly rather than take the risk of having the crushed grapes oxidizing at tepid temperatures. In 1994, the Okanagan's legendary hot year, no cold soak was needed. In 1995, when an unexpectedly large harvest slightly reduced colour intensity, he took advantage of cooler harvest weather to give two days of cold soak to the grapes. In 1996, when the vintage was late and frigid, the cold soak was extended safely to a week. "None of this is intentional," Mavety says. "All of this is the season." In cooler vintages when the grapes may be less mature, winemakers may try to improve colour and flavour by a technique called *saignée*, French for "bled." In this procedure, a portion of the free-run juice, typically between 5 and 15 percent of the volume, is bled before fermentation from the tanks in which the crushed grapes have been macerating for a day or two. This pink juice is then handled as a white wine. Many tasty rosés, such as the Jackson-Triggs Blanc de Noir, are the result. The remainder of the Pinot Noir, because the ratio of skin to juice now is greater, should be a darker-coloured, fuller wine. "You have to be careful when you're bleeding," winemaker Bruce Nicholson cautions. "You have to worry about astringency because you have left a different ratio of juice to skins. You may pick up more phenolics [tannins] than you might want."

The juice is now ready to be inoculated with yeast for fermentation. Formerly, Okanagan winemakers contented themselves with employing a robust and fast-acting yeast, typically Champagne yeast, which gets the job done quickly and safely since a wine is not out of spoilage danger until the natural sugars have been converted to alcohol. Unfortunately, that is not the way to make a complex Pinot Noir. Martin uses an array of about ten yeasts (each in a different batch)—slow-acting yeasts to enhance flavour, other strains to enhance colour, even wild yeasts found naturally in wineries and vineyards. Summerhill's Marks says he "tends on purpose to let the wild yeasts do their thing up to five or six days and just watch to make sure there are no off flavours or off-odours." Blue Mountain's Ian Mavety just rolls his eyes in mock horror at the notion of wild yeast. "Maybe someday I will risk a tank and try wild yeast," he says. "I'm less interested in manipulating the vintage once it is inside the winery. I'd much rather keep the winemaking as simple as possible and allow the fruit to talk through it rather than have the winemaker stamp it with his winemaking." However, using wild yeast is traditional Burgundian technique. "With Pinot," Summerhill's Marks says, "I want to strive for something that has lots of complexity and maybe even a little bit of earthiness or, as some people call it, horsiness, talking about Burgundy-style Pinots." To be sure, it is living dangerously, which is why almost all winemakers finish the fermentation with reliable cultured yeasts. "You are always managing risk," Martin shrugs. "I use a number of different yeast strains because you will end up with subtle variations. Some will give you mouthfeel, some will give you colour and some will give you more fruit on the aroma. I think it is crazy that people use one yeast strain."

When fermentation is almost complete, the wine is transferred to barrels, finishing what Martin calls the final fizzing in wood and then aging there for nine to eleven months before being assembled into final blends. It is one of the paradoxes of Pinot Noir that this grape does not care for hot weather in the vineyard but responds well to hot fermentation. "Fermentation temperatures rise to a peak of about 25°C - 27°C, enhancing colour and flavour extraction," Tilman Hainle notes. Some winemakers advocate handling Pinot Noir significantly more gently than other reds. Winemaker Mirko, who admires the delicacy of Oregon Pinot Noir, seldom racks his own Pinot Noir throughout its first year in barrel while he racks Merlot two or three times. "Most of the people who we talk to, who make Pinots that I think are good, don't think that it benefits Pinot to be racked," Mirko says. "A ballsier wine like Merlot benefits in that the oxygenation helps the tannins combine and soften whereas Pinot doesn't have those big tannins anyhow. Incorporating oxygen into the wine acts in a negative way."

Most Pinot Noir is matured in barrels. "You can't make red wine in tanks," Mavety says disdainfully. "You can taste a tank-made wine a mile away." At Tinhorn Creek, winemaker Sandra Oldfield prefers to finish a quarter of each vintage in tanks because that gives her a more fruity fraction to add to the barrel-matured wine when she assembles the final blend. While she works with American oak, the majority of winemakers prefer French barrels. "French oak is made for Pinot Noir," Jackson-Triggs's Bruce Nicholson insists. While being prohibitively expensive, the French barrels offer subtle notes of vanilla and nutmeg that blend with rather than overpower the sweet delicacy of Pinot Noir. At Quails' Gate in the 1996 vintage, Martin had about sixty barrels available, the majority being a year or two old. Three-year-old American oak barrels, whose assertive flavours have been muted by use with other wines, may also be used for some Pinot Noir. Kettle Valley's partners like to put some of their Pinot Noir into American oak barrels which have previously been used for barrel-fermenting Chardonnay. "Say I've got twenty new French barrels allocated to Pinot, I'm looking for the best batch of Pinot to go into that oak," Martin says. "The biggest Pinot, the darkest colour, the biggest wine can handle the most new oak. I'm looking for a reserve wine and it would go into our best barrels. You try to give your best wines your best shot." It also depends on the vintage. For 1994, a hot year that produced big, rich wines, Summerhill's Marks aged almost half his Pinot Noir in new oak while only 10 percent new oak was used for the lighter wines from 1996.

Hainle is more cautious in his use of barrels. "I've never used any new oak," he said in a 1997 interview. "The barrels that I do use are seasoned oak, at least two years old, and I use them for the mellowing effect on the wine and for the concentration, rather than for any flavour that might be imparted." With experience, he has increased the time the wine spends in the barrels from six weeks to six to nine months, but he is determined that the wine should not be dominated by oak. "From a consumer point of view, all too often I find myself sticking my nose into a glass and you get almost hammered by a blast of vanilla and toast and tarry, tobacco characteristics," Hainle says. "Lots of people love that but I know it is technique rather than the grapes speaking. I just have this feeling that if I get into that, then I'm like the mad scientist in the lab with a few drops of this and a little tincture of something else. It doesn't seem right to me. I know that we are swimming against the tide but I don't mind being different." He is not flatly opposed to the use of new oak. He just believes that the few wines than can handle bold oak then need prolonged aging in bottle to become harmonious. "I know for a fact that the average length of time that a wine bottle is aged by the customer is somewhere around ten hours." That being the case, he argues, the thousands of dollars spent on new oak may well be money wasted. A few winemakers shun oak entirely. "God made no mistake with the grape," believes Günther Lang at Lang Vineyards. "I believe the grape has it all. Our idea is to develop the wine by itself, without any other tastes."

Pinot Noir is new to British Columbia but that has not deterred wineries from quickly coming to market with reserve-designated wines. Gehringer Brothers called its debut 1995 Pinot Noir a "Private Reserve" while Nanaimo's Chateau Wolff dubbed its first Pinot Noir a "Grand Reserve." The designations vary from winery to winery—Family Reserve at Quails' Gate while Blue Mountain simply uses a striped label for its top-of-line version—but whatever the designation, these are meant to be the wines with a little more of everything. More body, deeper colour, more aroma and more layers of flavour; and usually, more time in barrels. The reserve wines generally are released several months or even years later than the regular wines and are built to be cellared longer. While the reserve wines will show a brilliant colour, they are likely to deposit a light sediment in the bottles with age. That should be considered a positive sign indicating that the wines are unfiltered. "Premium reds don't have to be filtered," Martin insists, who relies on wines falling clear in barrel.

There is a Pinot Noir for every mood or occasion from British Columbia wineries. "Any end of the spectrum can be good as long as they are balanced and fleshy and have a lot of extract and mouthfeel," Martin believes. Blue Mountain's Mavety defines his ideal of Pinot Noir this way: "On the finesse side of things, you want the typical fruit and the fruit should be bright fruit. It can be anywhere from cherries to cassis. I've even had some Pinots that are strawberry-like. It is not a favourite of mine but it is still typical. But the fruits have to be bright and pure. A jammy Pinot— strawberry jam and prunes—is not one with finesse. What you get on the nose should come through as flavours and with it should come that silky, rich, mid-palate character. Definitely, the hallmark is the power of the finish ... that long, long finish."

"I don't pull my hair out making it," Tinhorn Creek's Sandra Oldfield says, a winemaker with a practical attitude of dealing with what the vineyard will deliver. "If I get a heavy one, great. If I don't, fine. People also expect light-style Pinot Noir." At this, she cracks a warm and charming smile to admit that, surprisingly, Tinhorn Creek's *biggest* red in 1996, the infamous cool vintage, was its Pinot Noir. "It was very strange." The apparent explanation is that much of the fruit was from the winery's Rushmere Vineyard, one of two of its vineyards on sun-drenched Black Sage Road. There, if almost nowhere else in 1996, solidly ripe grapes were harvested and a dark, rich wine followed. "I don't always strive for that," she says. "It has to do with the weather that year." Her experience confirms again what a paradoxical grape Pinot Noir is. "For me, it's not going to be a grape that Sandy tries to figure out," she says, a note of exasperation in her voice. "I've had a look at the Pinot Noir genetically and it is a weird grape. It shouldn't be a grape, genetically. It should be an apple or something. So I feel what I'll probably do with it is just let it go: like, what do you want to be this year? Go ahead and be that way. I can't force it to be the way I want it to be. It's one of those grapes that's going to find its own happy spot somewhere." Well ... she does not leave it entirely to do its own thing. Since the 1995 vintage, Tinhorn Creek has blended some Pinot Meunier into its Pinot Noir, a trick that lifts the fruitiness of the wine.

The lighter styles are best when they are youthful and fresh and are best when slightly—*very slightly*—chilled. "It makes a great rosé," says Tilman Hainle, making virtue of necessity. The Pinot Noir grown on the Hainle Estate vineyard seldom delivers the flavour intensity required for a big red and Hainle, who does make medium to big reds from purchased Pinot Noir, is content to make the rosé that is dictated by his clone (Washington State) and his site. The medium-bodied styles of Pinot Noir are likely to be best within their first five years while most of the reserve wines only begin showing their potential at five years. "I am trying to make wines that will live at least the first decade," Martin says. The great Burgundies last for a generation but it is still too soon to know how long a well-made British Columbia Pinot Noir will live.

This array of styles has not made it easier for consumers just discovering the wine. "Some producers can produce good Pinot Noir and some people produce acid rose water," Martin says. "There's such a variation out there that it stops the wine being accepted as widely as Chardonnay and Cabernet. A lot of people have bought a relatively expensive Pinot Noir in a restaurant and been very disappointed. In the market place, just because it's Pinot, a lot of people will charge a relatively high price." Yet Martin quickly adds: "Pinot is more costly to produce than any other red wine because you have to play with it that much more and you have to basically use good French barrels. The good Burgundies—that's what people are basically trying to make." And even Burgundy is expensive and notoriously inconsistent. "There are three hundred wineries in Burgundy and only twenty are Grand Cru," Martin observes. "Even the French have a tough time doing it."

PINOTAGE

RED TABLE WINE Created in South Africa in 1924, this grape is a cross of Pinot Noir and Cinsault. The latter, a Rhone grape, formerly was called Hermitage in South Africa, which accounts for the name, Pinotage. It was only released as a varietal in 1959 by the Stellenbosch Farmers' Winery. It has been garnering a growing reputation in recent years, so much so that 120 South African growers formed the Pinotage Association in 1995 to further develop the variety which, with the exception of New Zealand, is not widely planted elsewhere. The small plot at Lake Breeze is the first in British Columbia.

The Producer

Lake Breeze Vineyards

In his twenty-five years as a plastics manufacturer in South Africa before immigrating to Canada in 1994, Lake Breeze Vineyards founder Paul Moser knew the wines made from Pinotage, the home-grown South African variety. There, it is grown by more than one hundred producers but only accounts for three percent of all the plantings. The vineyard which Moser purchased at the foot of Sammet Road near Naramata already had been dedicated to other vinifera in the mid-1980s by Barry Irvine, the previous owner. However, Moser sentimentally added Pinotage in a small corner near the winery whose design is an elegant postcard from the Cape wine region in South Africa. It was natural that he take the South African theme a further step with some Pinotage.

He would have preferred to import select vines from South Africa but those plants would have been required to spend two years in Canadian quarantine before being released to the winery. Moser learned that a small plot of Pinotage exists at the University of California at Davis, from which he obtained enough cuttings for an initial planting of forty vines in 1996. The block subsequently has been extended and in time, if the initial wines from Pinotage are successful—the first release will be after the year 2000—Moser intended to import vines directly from the Cape where the Pinotage Association is researching new clones. Moser sold Lake Breeze in 1998, placing the future of this variety in the hands of the new owners, Wayne and Joann Finn, who had previously run a helicopter business on Vancouver Island. Whether any other winery will follow Moser's lead is unknown but, given the proliferation of grape varieties already in the Okanagan, Lake Breeze likely will have this niche to itself for some time.

Credit for creating this variety goes to Dr. Abraham Isak Perold, the first professor of viticulture at the University of Stellenbosch. An influential scientist, he was responsible for the importation of Chardonnay to South Africa, among his many accomplishments. The crossing of Cinsault and Pinot Noir occurred in the spring of 1924. The Pinotage Association recounts that only four seeds were produced by this cross rather than the thousands of seeds usually expected. Perold planted the four next year in the garden of his home at an experimental farm near the university. After Perold moved on to a position with a winery, the professor who succeeded him had the vines re-established at a nursery, planted on disease-resistant rootstock. This nurturing and replication of the original quartet took years and it was not until 1941 that the first experimental lot of Pinotage wine was made. The outcome was good enough that two wineries under the umbrella of the Stellenbosch Farmers' cooperative, Kanonkop and Bellevue, planted commercial vineyards. When Pinotage wines swept the Cape Wine Show in 1959 and again in 1961, the variety began to be adopted by other growers. The political isolation of South Africa during the 1980s no doubt retarded the variety gaining international recognition until Kanonkop's 1989 Pinotage won a major award at a London wine show. As the variety has come to be re-evaluated in the 1990s, vintners have recognized the unusual qualities of Pinotage. The wine can be as approachable as a Beaujolais when young but also can be aged for two or three decades, becoming as soft and complex as a Pinot Noir. The Lake Breeze vineyard will be watched with keen anticipation.

Pinotage should do well in the Okanagan. It is an early ripening variety that achieves good colour and high sugar and usually has a satisfactory level of acidity unless overmature. The vine can crank out tonnage but makes its best wines when the vines have been pruned rigorously to control productivity. The style of the wine depends on the producer. In South Africa, most Pinotage wines are made to be accessible at an early age although vineyards with quality grapes produce richly flavoured oak-aged wines that are complex and long-lived. Garron Elmes, the winemaker at Lake Breeze, believes firmly that good red wines need to be aged in barrels. The winemaker in South Africa with whom he gained experience before joining Lake Breeze in 1995 "swore by American oak for Pinotage," Elmes recounts.

Wine from Pinotage, as one book on South African wines says, has "a unique and recognizable personality of its own."[5] In flavour, the wine tends to owe more to its Cinsault parent, a full-bodied, fruity red, than to the more refined Pinot Noir. One distinctive feature of Pinotage is its aroma. "What a lot of Pinotages have is a kind of turpentinish nose," Elmes says, showing a winemaker's typical talent of reaching for a seemingly negative descriptor when a wine's characteristic perfume is almost incomparable. Elmes is trying to define a faint but not unpleasant chemical aroma caused naturally by an ester in the grape called iso amyl acetate. "That aroma takes a bit of getting used to," Elmes suggests. This elusive aroma moderates and ultimately disappears entirely as Pinotage ages in the bottle. It is only with maturity that Pinotage finally shows the complexity of taste and aroma that comes from its Burgundian heritage. "We'll have to see how the general Canadian public takes to this wine," Elmes says.

---

5   Hands, Phyllis, Hughes, Dave and Kench, John: *South African Wine*, Struik Publishers, Cape Town, 1992.

PROPRIETARY WINES

49 NORTH RED: A Mission Hill blend of red wines, some of which have been matured in oak, to produce an affordable every-day wine.

49 NORTH WHITE: A major Mission Hill brand, this white wine is described as a "Germanic blend." The varieties in the blend—which vary from year to year—include Riesling, Ehrenfelser, Bacchus, Pinot Auxerrois, and sometimes Gewürztraminer, Müller-Thurgau, Kerner and Oraniensteiner. "I am trying to get that Germanic fruitiness," winemaker John Simes says of the wine, which is slightly off-dry. "You can have it on the deck before dinner but it is not too sweet. You can carry it inside and have it with your meal."

ALFRESCO: Nichol Vineyard released a mere 285 cases of this in 1997 from the 1995 Syrah vintage. A light, fruity red to be enjoyed lightly chilled at lunch, the wine was so named because, the winery explains, "it spent its entire life outdoors." The wine was matured outdoors in a stainless steel tank between November 1995 and September 1996, with aquarium heaters keeping the tank above freezing in winter and insulation keeping it cool in summer. New winery buildings allowed winemaker Alex Nichol to move his operations indoors in 1997.

AUTUMN BLUSH: A pink, or blush, wine produced by Wild Goose Vineyards, this is a blend of Pinot Noir, Gewürztraminer and Riesling, sufficiently flavoursome that the winery recommends it even with fruit and salads.

AUTUMN GOLD 1996: Wild Goose Vineyards launched this brand in 1993 as a matter of necessity, after the only white wine they could find to top up a partially-filled tank of Riesling was purchased Vidal. When this fruity blend proved popular, winemaker Adolf Kruger standardized the blend on three vinifera varieties grown in his vineyard. The blend now includes 35 percent Riesling, 35 percent Pinot Blanc and 30 percent Gewürztraminer.

BIBENDUM RED: A Hainle Vineyards release in 1997 from a variety known as Samtrot, which does not get its own entry in this book because not even nonconforming Tilman Hainle would release a varietal label that sounds like an obscure foot ailment. The wine is marketed under a proprietary label, Bibendum Red, which comes from the Latin phrase *Nunc est bibendum,* meaning "now is the time to drink." Coincidentally, the round-bellied Michelin man in the tire company's advertisements also is called Bibendum because the early turn of the century drawings showed the caricature with a stein of beer. That history makes Bibendum an odd fit for the occasionally lean style of Hainle wines—until one considers the challenge of marketing a wine called Samtrot.

Samtrot is a German word which translates as *silky red.* The grape is believed to be a mutation of Pinot Meunier. It is grown for Hainle under contract from plant material brought to Canada by the late Walter Hainle, Tilman's father. "It was a grape that my Dad remembered from the very few producers that have it in Germany. Even in Württemberg, where it is most widely planted, it is unusual to find it." The variety makes a light red in Germany but, when grown in possibly more favourable conditions around Okanagan Falls, the vine yields darker and more structured wines that are aromatic and spicy.

BIBENDUM ROSÉ: A fruity Hainle wine from Pinot Noir.

BIBENDUM WHITE: Hainle Vineyards's blend of Chardonnay, Perle of Csaba and Muscat Ottonel.

BIN 52 BARREL SELECT: A refreshing budget-priced VQA white table wine under Jackson-Triggs's Sawmill Creek label. The cornerstone of the blend is Bacchus, a variety with a fragrantly floral aroma. Other varieties in the blend are Müller-Thurgau, Riesling, Verdelet and Optima. "These are excellent varieties. They are not as popular as Chardonnay but they are grown in the valley here and they grow well," Jackson-Triggs winemaker Bruce Nicholson says, explaining one rationale behind this brand. "Bacchus is a nice variety to work with. It's got a great nose and it makes a nice wine."

CHABERTON BLANC: A budget-priced white wine from Domaine de Chaberton, this wine blends Perle of Zala and Vidal with Madeleine Angevine and Madeleine Sylvaner to produce a crisp, dry wine with Muscat perfume.

CHABERTON ROUGE: A dry oak-matured red from Domaine de Chaberton, this is a blend of Chancellor, Baco Noir and Pinot

Noir. The winery described the 1995 vintage as "light and herbal, with modest plum and red cherry fruit picking up a hint of spice on the finish."

CCW RED: This is a brand released under Andrés Peller Estate label. The letters mean Cool Climate Wine. The first release, from the 1996 vintage, is made entirely from Chancellor grapes. The wine is matured either in oak or in contact with oak chips for several months before being bottled. It is intended to be a straightforward red priced under $10 a bottle.

CCW WHITE: Released under the Andrés Peller Estate label, the name successfully plays on the Okanagan's classification as a region for cool climate winegrowing. The first release was from the 1995 vintage, when Ehrenfelser made up 44 percent of the blend with 36 percent Riesling and the remainder Müller-Thurgau. The brand outsells the winery's Ehrenfelser and winemaker Tony Vlcek believes it has to do with name retention after a test he did with members of his recreational hockey team. He sampled them on both wines and found that CCW was the name they remembered.

COVEY NOIR: Red blend from Quails' Gate which comes from vinifera and red hybrid grapes.

CUVÉE NOIR: The Gehringer Brothers blend this dry but mellow red wine from several vintages and several grape varieties to produce a light and uncomplicated everyday red.

CUVÉE ZERO: One of two sparkling wines released in 1998 by Hainle Vineyards for the winery's tenth anniversay, this is based on Pinot Blanc, Pinot Noir, Chardonnay and Pinot Meunier. It is, winemaker Tilman Hainle quips, "as dry as the humour around here."

DELICE 1996: A dessert wine from Lake Breeze based on Muscat and Pinot Blanc.

DERAILER: This unusual late harvest wine was forced on Kettle Valley during the late 1995 vintage by a combination of catastrophes. Partner Tim Watts explains: "We were picking near the end of October and we were leaving the last batch to hang a little bit longer—and the steering broke on the tractor. And we had a tank coming up from Washington and it fell off the truck on the highway. That put us a little bit behind." So late that the winery was forced to make icewine with Chardonnay and Pinot Noir which had not been harvested before the November cold snap. During one of the pressings of Pinot Noir, the must got slightly warmer than is desirable for icewine and the juice was slightly diluted. When this fermented, the alcohol rose naturally to almost 18 percent and the wine finished nearly dry—an attractive bronze wine not unlike a white Port. The winery gave it a light-hearted name and sold it all from the winery at $15 a half bottle. "If we're going to have a problem, I'd like it to be a problem like that," Watts says.

DESERT SUN: An off-dry white from Gehringer Brothers, made of Riesling and Pinot Auxerrois. The name was inspired by the sunshine and the desert of the south Okanagan, where the winery is located. The winery calls this a wine "for every occasion"— from picnics to light meals.

DUNE: A Port-style red from Andrés, under its Peller Estates label, first released in 1995. It is made with Chancellor grapes in the technique of Port: fermentation is stopped while there is considerable residual sugar remaining and the wine is fortified to 19.5 percent. It is then aged in oak. The blend incorporates both young wine and mature wines from the winery's stock of aged Chancellor.

EBONAGE BLANC: Carriage House developed this lightly oak-aged, slightly off-dry blend of Kerner, Pinot Blanc and Chardonnay in 1996. The name *Ebonage* was inspired by the winery's location on Black (as in ebony) Sage Road south of Oliver. A red blend also is planned. "I enjoy blending," winemaker and co-proprietor Dave Wagner says. "There are a lot of varietal wines [that are] all the same out there. A blend is distinct and different." The Ebonage blends are sold almost exclusively in the Carriage House wine shop. "I think of it as an award for [clients] coming to the store," Wagner says. "There's something a little extra here."

ELEGANCE 1992: A white Muscat dessert wine from Sumac Ridge with gobs of sweetness, 16.5 percent alcohol and an aging potential the winery estimates as long as twenty years.

ESSENCE OF MILLEFIORE: An aromatic dry white wine produced by Venturi-Schulze vineyards, combining Schönburger and Ortega. The name is Italian and means "one thousand flowers."

FATHOM: A Port-style red made by Hainle Vineyards and based on Baco Noir. The winery sponsored a competition among its customers and received 617 different suggestions of names. Hainle Vineyards makes this fruity pink wine from Pinot Noir grown on the winery's own vineyard.

GLENORA FANTASIA: An attractive sparkling wine produced at Vigneti Zanatta, whose Vancouver Island vineyard is near Glenora, a country store and crossroads south of Duncan. The unique wine is made from a grape variety called Cayuga, a hybrid developed in New York State and believed to be grown in British Columbia only by this producer.

GRAND RESERVE BARREL SELECT RED: An oak-aged blend from Mission Hill which incorporates Pinot Noir, Maréchal Foch and Gamay to deliver a harmonious wine that usually sells for less that what one would expect from the grandiloquent name. The winery's notes describe it as a "full, forward wine with ample plum fruit backed up with jam, boysenberry and spice."

GOLDEN HARVEST: A medium-dry white produced by Slamka Cellars. The wine is a blend of five varieties, including Traminer and Auxerrois, varieties which are great favourites of winemaker Peter Slamka. The winery recommends Golden Harvest to be enjoyed as an apéritif or at brunch.

HARVEST MOON: Inspired not by the Neil Young song but by an historic Okanagan label for apples, this brand was launched in 1995 for a white wine from Crowsnest Vineyards, a blend of 85 percent Pinot Auxerrois and 15 percent Riesling and finished off-dry because the winery's customers were asking for an off-dry white.

JACKSON-TRIGGS BLANC DE NOIR: A rosé wine based primarily on Pinot Noir with some Bacchus, a white grape, to provide aromatic highlights. Winemaker Bruce Nicholson describes it as an unassuming and approachable wine for picnics and social occasions. "If you have a porch swing," he says, suggesting a suitably casual venue. "Chill it nicely."

LATITUDE FIFTY: Launched in mid-1991, this was the first proprietary white wine from Gray Monk. An attractive fruity blend primarily of Johannisberg Riesling and Bacchus, the wine accounted for half of Gray Monk's entire sales within three years.

The wine was so named because the 50th parallel of latitude, generally regarded as the practical northern limit for viticulture, actually is a few miles *south* of Gray Monk's vineyard.

LE CLASSIQUE: A blend from Blue Grouse.

LONGITUDE 120: A blend of several red varieties from Gray Monk, released in 1998 to add a partner to the successful Latitude Fifty. Proprietor George Heiss declines to give the blend after several of his competitors produced white wines almost duplicating the blend in Latitude Fifty.

MAXINE'S: Winemaker Alex Nichol of Nichol Vineyard named this white wine for his mother-in-law who, in 1973, gave Nichol, then a professional classical musician, his first lesson in making wine from plums. With *Maxine's*, he produced from the tiny 1996 vintage what he called a poor man's Chardonnay. The main variety in the blend is Ehrenfelser, backed up with Pinot Gris. Due to an extraordinarily small harvest, only twenty-four cases of this tribute wine were made.

NORTHERN SUMMER: Red table wine from St. Hubertus with Chancellor and Baco Noir in the blend.

OKANAGAN BLANC: A soft, off-dry white from Sumac Ridge Estate Winery.

OKANAGAN BLUSH 1996: A brilliantly-hued rosé from Sumac Ridge, this fruity wine is a rarely-seen blend of Pinot Noir and Ehrenfelser. The winery's tasting note advises: "A core of cherry with layers of currants, strawberries and peaches."

OKANAGAN SUMMER: A white from St. Hubertus Estate Winery, this blend formerly was known as *Indian Summer*. The name was changed in 1997 when it was discovered that Cave Spring, an Ontario winery, had already registered *Indian Summer* as one of its brands. *Okanagan Summer* is a blend based on Verdelet and, with the declining acreage of the variety, may evolve to a Bacchus-based blend. It is a wine for sushi and summer-time refreshment.

PIGNOLETTO 1995: Perhaps because Schönburger is hard to market as a varietal name, Venturi-Schulze Vineyards of Vancouver Island created this Italinate name for its dry table wine from the German grape.

PIPE: Sumac Ridge chose this name for a Port-style wine made from Chancellor grapes.

PROPRIETOR'S: CedarCreek, Hester Creek, House of Rose Vineyards and LeComte (Hawthorne Mountain) have used variations on this unadorned name to label blends as Proprietor's Select, Proprietor's Reserve or simply Proprietor's Red or White.

PROPRIETOR'S RESERVE WHITE: CedarCreek blend of Gewürztraminer and Scheurebe, two varieties both noted for vivid aromas and flavours.

PROPRIETOR'S RESERVE RED: This CedarCreek wine blends Baco Noir, Merlot and Pinot Noir. The winery's notes on it speak of spice and herb flavours with the taste of blackberries and cherries in the finish.

RIESLING CUVÉE ZERO: This was one of two bone-dry sparkling wines released in 1998 by Hainle Vineyards for the winery's tenth anniversary. This one and partner Cuvée Zero both spent six years resting on the yeast in the bottle, technically qualifying them to be called "late disgorged." Most sparkling wines are released after eighteen months to three years on the yeast.

SIMILKAMEEN SUPERIOR RED: Historic blend developed in the 1970s by Andrés Wines, based initially on De Chaunac, a variety now all but vanished from British Columbia. The current blend includes Chancellor with imported Cabernet Sauvignon and Malbec. The partner brand, *Similkameen Superior White*, includes white hybrids such as Verdelet and Vidal along with imported wines. The regional place name originates from a small vineyard in the Similkameen Valley once owned by Andrés.

TRILOGY: A pair of Calona Vineyards blended table wines. The white is Bacchus, Gewürztraminer and Riesling. The red, according to winemaker Howard Soon, is "more of 'what have you.' "

VALLEY MIST: White blend launched by Cherry Point Vineyards in 1995, this resulted from a happy error in the winery when Helena Ulrich, one of the winery's proprietors, took over the racking of wines one evening in 1995 when her husband, Wayne, had to present Cherry Point wines at a tasting. In her eagerness to leave nothing for Wayne to do when he returned home about midnight, she consolidated into one tank the whites from two half-filled and unlabeled tanks. One tank contained Müller-

Thurgau—but the other contained Auxerrois. The inadvertent but successful blend (there also are minor quantities of Siegerrebe, Ehrenfelser and Pinot Blanc) is refreshing and tasty. "Perhaps we should have called it *Valley Mistake*," chuckles Helena Ulrich.

VALLEY SUNSET: Red blend from Cherry Point Vineyards.

VIN DE CURÉ: White dessert wine from Gersighel Wineberg. This was an ingenious response to the difficult and late vintage in 1996 when the winery had trouble ripening its grapes. Winemaker Dirk DeGussem picked Pinot Blanc and Gewürztraminer grapes and dried them for six weeks to concentrate the sugars before making the wine. The natural sugars got high enough that the finished wine, a golden beverage with flavours recalling orange peel, achieved an alcohol of just over 14 percent. "It has something like a Cognac taste," DeGussem says.

VINTNER'S CHOICE: This House of Rose label denotes the winery's blended white table wine. The drier version is called, logically enough, *Vintner's Choice Dry*.

VIVA: An oak-aged blend of equal parts of Chardonnay and Müller-Thurgau produced by Chateau Wolff and marketed under the winery's Nanaimo Vineyards label. "It's a blend I stumbled across by accident," winemaker Harry von Wolff admits. "It definitely has the character of a Chardonnay—but a fruity Chardonnay."

WHITE BLEND: Bella Vista employs this label for one of its whites. Winemaker Larry Passmore takes as much pride in blended wines as in varietals.

RIESLING

WHITE TABLE WINE This is the Queen of German vineyards where it is called Johannisburg Riesling for a Rhine castle whose vineyard and cellars are famed for the white wine. While some outside Germany still refer to it as "Jo-burg", much of the wine world has settled simply on calling the variety Riesling. Significant plantings in the Okanagan began during the 1970s, urged on the growers by German-born winemakers at the now-vanished Jordan & Ste-Michelle winery in Surrey. They knew that this grape, while a late ripener, grows vigorously, is exceptionally winter-hardy and is flexible enough to make wines ranging from austerely bone-dry through delicately floral and off-dry; as well as luscious dessert wines and elegant icewines without compare. Young dry Rieslings are crisp, with lime and apple flavours that flatter many foods, even simple lunches. "One of my favourites is dry Riesling and cold cuts," Wild Goose vintner Adolf Kruger says. Peller Estates winemaker Tony Vlcek pairs a dry Riesling with a smoked salmon cream sauce on pasta. Aged Rieslings develop complex flavours and aromas, including honey and even kerosene.

"Riesling has a lot of resonance with us," says Tilman Hainle, whose family winery was launched in 1988 with his singularly dry Riesling from the 1985 vintage. "It's about as close as you can get me to saying that it is my favourite." Günther Lang at Lang Vineyards is firm: "Of the white grapes, Riesling is my favourite. For me it is the Queen or the King of grapes, because of that classical fruity taste in the wines. Whether you have a high sugar or a low sugar, you can always make a good wine. I even like to eat the grapes. For me, the most tasty grape is a Riesling—you should be here in the fall and taste it." At Crowsnest Vineyards, Andrea McDonald describes her Riesling as her favourite and credits Walter Gehringer of Gehringer Brothers for urging Crowsnest to plant the variety in the first place. "He said every vineyard should have Riesling," McDonald recalls. "It was the best advice I ever took." Many winemakers sing the praises of the variety even if many consumers prefer other songs. "Riesling anywhere in the world is a hard sell," admits Australian-born Jeff

Martin, whose Riesling vintages at Quails' Gate prove that one need not be German-born (as are Lang and Hainle and Wild Goose's Adolf Kruger) to appreciate the variety and to have a deft hand at making the wine.

Without question, Riesling had been eclipsed internationally among consumers by Chardonnay and even by Sauvignon Blanc. In annual production, it has dropped to third place among white varieties in British Columbia, after Chardonnay and Pinot Blanc. The softening popularity was becoming evident when the Hainle family planned its winery in the 1980s but the Hainles, seldom tempted to follow the crowd, plunged ahead to make the most austere of all the British Columbia Rieslings. They were encouraged by the 1989 World Vinifera Conference in Seattle whose theme was the (hoped-for) renaissance of Riesling. "We all realized that Riesling makes great wine," Hainle says. "The question was, how do you get people to accept Riesling as a substitute for Chardonnay to go with dinner and how do you get them to believe that a dry Riesling is probably better than most Chardonnays on the market for what they were going to have with dinner." A decade later, the same question can still be debated. Riesling wines run the confusing gamut from dry to sweet to sparkling, leaving the consumer navigating the many currents of Riesling to find the style suiting the palate and the occasion.

When the Okanagan began planting vinifera grapes in the 1970s, Riesling was the natural choice. The Jordan & Ste-Michelle winery (since absorbed into Jackson-Triggs) employed a succession of German winemakers who prodded growers to plant Germany's premier white variety. When Andrés Wines sponsored a trial planting in 1975 at Inkameep Vineyards, it took advice and imported vines (including Riesling) from the Geisenheim Institute, Germany's leading plant breeding station. Geisenheim's Dr. Helmut Becker, who ran the plant breeding program there, influenced many Okanagan growers to favour varieties such as Riesling. The Hainle family itself came from Germany, knew Riesling to be a noble, winter-hardy, cool-climate vine, and obtained German vines to plant their vineyard in 1981. Meanwhile, many of the winemakers in the Okanagan were getting professional training in Germany. Perhaps if the shaping influences had been from France rather than from Germany, another white variety would have grabbed the early dominance in the Okanagan vineyards that Riesling secured and has since lost. "I am very opinionated about

Chardonnay," says Adolf Kruger, in a comment that typifies the viewpoint. "I still believe that Chardonnay is a wine of Australia and southern France and California, even though a number of wineries make it here. This is a cool climate area and I don't think we would ever make the greatest Chardonnays in the world."

Adolf Kruger

The Jordan & Ste-Michelle Rieslings, emulating those from the Moselle and the Rhine, set the style. The wines invariably ended with a touch of natural sweetness, in part to balance the acidity and in part to underline the pretty, floral fruit and aroma of young Riesling. Most of the vineyards planted at the time still are producing. Riesling vines were planted in 1978 at the urging of Jordan & Ste-Michelle in the Kelowna-area vineyards now operated by St. Hubertus and by the Dulik family. Susan Dulik gets the choice grapes in her family's vineyard to make the wines for her Pinot Reach farm winery, which opened in 1997. "I love the fresh and lively fruit characters from this region," says Dulik who makes off-dry Rieslings, balancing the northern Okanagan's piquant acidity with sweet reserve (unfermented grape juice "reserved" for this purpose).

As a general rule, mature vines like those in the Dulik or St. Hubertus vineyards deliver the best grapes for winemaking. "Maybe with a younger vineyard, you would not get that intensity of flavour," speculates winemaker Cherie Jones. A woman with a personality as attractively bright as the wines she makes, the petite New Zealand native arrived at St. Hubertus for the 1995 vintage. While many of the varieties she met in the Okanagan were rarely seen in New Zealand, she had experience with Riesling, but in significantly different growing conditions. The decision to pick in New Zealand's Gisborne viticultural region, where the season is long, was made on physical inspection of the grapes. "We would wait until the grapes had turned amber coloured and until we could taste the aromatics and the intense flavours," she recalls. "Here, we are not given that luxury of leaving the grapes [to] hang that long." The late-ripening variety runs into the limitation of the Okanagan's intense but short season. St. Hubertus harvested its Riesling in 1996—one of the cooler years of the decade—at the very end of October in a valiant effort to achieve as much maturity as possible. At vintage the grapes averaged 19.5° Brix, which translates to about 10.5 percent alcohol in finished wines, comparable perhaps to many German Rieslings. The higher maturities experienced with Riesling in New Zealand might let Jones make the austere Alsace-style Riesling that suits her taste. However, the St. Hubertus vineyard produces fruit with a piquant acidity that needs to be balanced, especially in a year like 1996, with a touch of sweet reserve. "I like some residual sugar in it because the acid is high," Jones says. "You don't actually notice the sweetness. Stylistically, the grapes are leading the wine. I want to make it more a mouthfilling wine with some weight and texture." The same style is exemplified at such exponents of Riesling as Gray Monk, Gehringer Brothers, Lang Vineyards and Wild Goose. "I like Walter Gehringer's Riesling," admits Pinot Reach's Susan Dulik. "I'm striving to make a Riesling that is off-dry. I like the way that sweet reserve balances the high acidity in the Rieslings. With time in the bottle, the two flavours just seem to marry and produce that rich, intensely flavourful classic Riesling." Subsequently, German-trained Walter Gehringer and his brother Gordon weighed in with a clean and delicate dry Riesling as a companion to their "regular" Riesling. Even so, it remains closer to their original style than to the curve that Hainle has thrown.

Hainle came on the market in 1988 with a Riesling that was austerely dry, an abrupt shock to consumers familiar with all the off-dry Rieslings others were making. In one of the first articles about the Hainle winery, one wine writer even implied—as Tilman Hainle recalled a decade later with a rueful smile—that the winery's approach was "pig-headed." Indeed, the winery had difficulty getting both its licence and its financing because of its style. "At that point, no one was making bone-dry wines in the Okanagan," Hainle recounts. "It really raised a lot of eyebrows. When we opened the wineshop here and people came to taste, we expected that people would come in and say that is too dry for me. We didn't have a bunch of investors breathing down our necks. We could afford to stick it out. It wasn't a question for us of whether or not we were going to finish it off-dry or completely dry. That's what we were going to do. Faith drove us that way, that it was going to make a very structured, rich, up-character, nervy food wine."

Hainle was essentially on his own with this style until Summerhill Estate winery opened in 1992, primarily producing sparkling wines based on Riesling. However, the winemaker at the time, Eric von Krosigk, also made a superbly structured dry 1991 Riesling, a wine that became something of a legend among his peers. Von Krosigk subsequently moved to Hawthorne Mountain Vineyards for three vintages where he kept Riesling in the prize-winning repertoire, again including a sparkling Riesling. He also advised Pinot Reach on making sparkling Rieslings, lending support to the bouncy, self-confident proprietor who approaches winemaking with a fearless directness. "I hope I'll end up with a really drinkable Champagne right off the bat," Susan Dulik says of the Pinot Reach sparkling wines. "Don't quote me on Champagne," she laughs. "People will probably say 'What? She's making Champagne? She doesn't even know how to make wine, how could she *possibly* make Champagne?' People go to school for ten years to learn how to do this and here I am just sort of doing it. I don't know. It's working." Like the table wines, the sparkling Rieslings were inspired by the Riesling-based German *Sekt,* clean and fresh bubblies sometimes bottled-fermented like Champagne and sometimes fermented more economically in pressure tanks. The examples from Summerhill, Hawthorne Mountain and Pinot Reach all are bottle-fermented and show the versatility of Riesling. With another silvery chuckle, Dulik admits to another motive for making a sparkling version. "For the year 2000. I want to have Champagne available for that."

Jeff Martin at Quails' Gate, who began making wines there with the 1994 vintage, brought his singular fruit-driven style to the production of that winery's tartly dry Rieslings. Fruit from the best Riesling blocks in the vineyard is selected for this wine, picked when the grapes are ripe enough to yield a wine with 11 percent alcohol. "You don't want too high an alcohol or it will make the style too broad and hot," he believes. The juice, after very limited skin contact, is fermented at cool temperatures, very slowly for at least three weeks in order to preserve nuances of aroma and flavour, as well as enhancing the texture of the wine on the palate. "Good Riesling, when it is fruit-driven, has the characteristic of Granny Smith apples and then if you get honey, floral notes and lime over the top of that, you're doing well."

Martin says. "It should not be thin and steely." At Wild Goose, Adolf Kruger divides his Riesling grapes into two lots, fermenting one of them with a widely used yeast and the other with a yeast strain called Wädenswil (after a Swiss viticulture research station) that contributes intense apple notes to the flavour of the wine. This aromatic version often is blended into several other Wild Goose wines where the flavours are appropriate.

While a young Quails' Gate Riesling shows a floral aroma and a bright citrus flavour, the wine, like any classic example from this grape, develops richer fruit flavours and mineral notes as it ages. Like almost all Riesling producers, Quails' Gate also makes what could be called a more popular style in its lower-priced Proprietor's Select range, a wine with about thirteen grams of residual sugar, enough to create an impression of sweetness. "When you say Riesling, most people expect the wine will be sweet," Martin says. Some wineries, such as Wild Goose, cover the broad range of tastes by making both dry and semi-dry Rieslings each year and, when the grapes get very ripe and have begun to raisin, a late harvest or dessert style. In the 1996 vintage Adolf Kruger also produced a dry Riesling that was aged three months in American oak barrels, achieving an almost Chardonnay-like richness with the wine. The motive was to make a Riesling that would be more attractive to restaurateurs. "Customers also dictate the style of the wine they like," says the realistic Kruger. "Customers that come to the wine shop simply like their wines a touch sweeter." The kiss of sweetness lifts the flavours of the Riesling, especially in a year when maturity of the grapes is low and the resulting wine, if completely dry, would be anemic without some sweetness to anchor the flavour. Nowhere is this more evident than late harvest wines and icewines where the remaining unfermented sugar concentrates the luscious tropical flavours.

There is another way, time consuming but effective, to build substance in what would otherwise be a light, dry Riesling from a very cool year. Andrés winemaker Tony Vlcek pulled off an impressive dry 1996 Riesling for the winery's Peller Estates label by leaving the wine on the lees and stirring up the lees in the tanks once a week for four months. "We did something that was not very typical at all," he says. "We just kept working with that wine. I think we helped give it a little bit more complexity and a little more depth. Normally, after it is finished fermenting, we throw it through a centrifuge because, in a good year, the fruit and the richness is already there." In former times, when all the Rieslings from Andrés were made in the off-dry "patio-sipping" style, sweet reserve juice would have been added to give the wine more substance and overcome the shortcomings of the vintage. Under Vlcek's hand, the Peller Estates Rieslings are made in the dry style of Alsace, a region much admired by the young winemaker. "It's not uncommon to be tasting some great Rieslings that are ten years old there," he has found. "A lot of that comes from the lees aging and some different things they are doing in the tanks." That style demanded unusual winemaking from him in 1996. "In some years, you have to put a little more effort in to bring out the quality of the fruit," he observes. "I'm not looking for a Riesling with a lees character but I want that extra depth and richness." Because Peller Estates produces about three thousand cases of VQA Riesling each year, this shift to the dry, food-wine style has placed a market leader firmly behind the dry category. Tilman Hainle definitely is not alone any more.

Grown mostly in the north and central Okanagan, Riesling is a late-ripening variety (sometimes as late as mid-November), fortunately with tough-skinned grapes on hardy vines. At the Wild Goose vineyard at Okanagan Falls, Adolf Kruger reserved the prime growing site (a southwestern exposure) for Riesling. "I'm not saying we grow the best Riesling in the valley—but one of the best," he says. "We get beautiful values; the acidity seems to be just right." In most vineyards, the fruit hangs until it is fully ripe. Hainle, whose Peachland vineyard is cool and late, almost always gets grapes ripe enough to produce at least 11 percent alcohol (alcohol is important to the structure of a dry wine). In part, this degree of ripeness comes from the low yields—less than two and a half tons an acre—necessary in the organically-grown vineyard. "We have to keep our crops low if we want healthy vines," Hainle believes.

The flavour palate delivered by Riesling is arguably broader than that from any other mainstream variety, perhaps because the variety is so responsive to its site and to how it is grown. "Riesling is a great late harvest wine," insists Günther Lang of Naramata's Lang Vineyards. In years when there is a long autumn, Lang will let some Riesling hang well beyond the usual picking time, as he did in 1995 when he was able to achieve an award-winning, lemon-gold, dry late harvest wine with a robust 13.3 percent alcohol and an exquisite ripe mango aroma. "If you have ripe fruit aromas," Lang explains, "even if you have a dry wine, it does not taste dry." That was a year with such a favourably long, warm autumn that other Riesling bunches were allowed to ripen even further, enabling Lang to make an off-dry wine he called select late harvest. Finally that year, he produced a Riesling icewine. "You still have a clean fruity wine," Lang exclaims as he proudly leads a tasting of these wines to demonstrate the Riesling spectrum from dry to sweet.

At Domaine Combret's superb site on the Golden Mile south of Oliver, the variety easily achieves the maturity that has allowed the winery to make dry Riesling in the muscular style of Alsace. "Powerful," is how Robert Combret describes the winery's Riesling which debuted with the 1993 vintage. "They have, as we say in French, when you drink them, they have *matter*, they have fruit." He closes his eyes and smacks his lips as he reaches for descriptors. "Licorice," he says, recalling one note in the flavours of the 1993 Riesling. "When you drink them, you don't feel like you are drinking alcoholized water. They are strong, powerful. That's agreeable." He sighs: "Unfortunately, the Riesling does not have the same notoriety as the Chardonnay." Never in a hurry to push the wines out the door, Domaine Combret dribbled the 1993 into the market until 1998 and only then released the 1994 vintage. While that may have reflected a tepid consumer interest in Riesling wines, however well made, it certainly gave the wine the opportunity to develop complexity in the bottle. Combret would argue that many wineries release their wines too quickly. "The wineries are following the wish of the consumers instead of trying to educate, a little, the people," Robert Combret says. "I don't mean to force the consumers, of course, no. But they are always expecting the new release, just like the new Chevy model or the new Ford model. For a car, it's good, no doubt—but not for the wine. Not for the wine, except for some types of wine, like a young Gamay." His winemaker son Olivier advises drinking the 1993 Riesling only in the year 2008. "It will be an experience," he promises.

Tilman Hainle also appreciates the qualities of older Rieslings which his Peachland vineyard delivers. "It doesn't take long for our Rieslings to start showing the honey, flinty characteristics and, less overtly, the apricot and appley characteristics that often show up in other Rieslings," Hainle finds. "After about two years after release, you can start getting some of the *diesel* notes that older Rieslings are known for." The 1993 Combret Riesling developed that quality by mid-1997. That hallmark of many (though not all) mature Riesling table wines also is referred to as a kerosene or petrol aroma, a complexing factor much appreciated by Riesling connoisseurs but not well understood by more casual consumers. "The proper term is mineral taste," laughs Adolf Kruger, aware that the wine professional's casual use of words like *kerosene* or *diesel* are as likely to deter consumers as attract them. This is part of Riesling's acceptance challenge: while a young Riesling with a touch of sweetness has an easy, exuberant charm, an old, dry Riesling demands, and deserves, studious attention. It is no longer just a wine; it has become an essay in philosophy.

"The oldest vintage we have is the 1985," Hainle said in 1997. "We still open a couple of bottles a year. Given a well-kept bottle, those vintages are still tasting fresh and are still alive." At Quails' Gate, Martin agrees. "These wines will go for ten years," he says of his dry Limited Release Rieslings. Since the winery only makes about six hundred cases a year, not many bottles remain unconsumed that long. Ross Mirko, whose Rieslings at CedarCreek ran from dry to icewine in style, argues that the wines are consumed far too soon. "People don't give it a chance," he says. "The wines don't take on those gorgeous characters for a couple of years. It is tough to convince people to keep them that long." Vlcek dreams that a consumer will come back to him in five years, after having cellared and then tasted a Peller Riesling, and tell the winemaker: "I tasted one of your Rieslings and the fruit, the complexity, the depth was *phenomenal*."

ROTBERGER

ROSÉ TABLE WINE Like humans, grape vines do not produce offspring that are entirely predictable. On one occasion, the plant breeders at Geisenheim, the German research station, crossed Trollinger and Riesling and came up with Kerner, a white grape. But on another, they crossed the same two varieties and produced Rotberger, a red-skinned grape with white flesh. The elder George Heiss, when planting the vineyard that supports the family's Gray Monk winery, was aware of Kerner's qualities, both in the vineyard and as a wine grape. So he took a chance on its relative as well. As a result, Gray Monk, and only Gray Monk, can produce a fresh, fruity rosé table wine each vintage that is snapped up by consumers. About one thousand cases are made each year. There is no better summer-time wine.

The Producer

Gray Monk

In Germany, Rotberger is virtually unknown to consumers because wineries seldom produce it as a varietal, even when authorities like Jancis Robinson, the British wine writer, writes that it is capable of producing "very good wines." Rotberger's brief moment in the sun every year rests primarily in the hands of George Heiss Jr., the serious-minded winemaker at Gray Monk. George Sr., his father, imported some vines from Germany in the 1970s—six short rows, as George Jr. recalls it. "We knew next to nothing about it," the elder Heiss recalls. "I doubt that at the time we took the vines we had ever tasted the wine ... we went totally blind." The Heiss family subsequently expanded its plantings to six acres, having found that the wine has a loyal following in a niche so small that no competitor has asked for Rotberger cuttings. (One other grower once expressed some interest in cuttings but never followed through.) That should not be taken as a reflection on the wine, a fresh and lively rosé with a colour as vibrant as the gleaming paint on a fast sports car. The challenge of Rotberger is twofold. First, the name is comic to those who do not pronounce it correctly: the first syllable rhymes with *vote* and not with *pot*. Secondly, the rosé market is small in a nation that only has three months of summer, which is the preferred time for drinking fresh pink wines. Neither of these difficulties trouble young George Heiss. He knows how to pronounce German grape names and he makes barely enough Rotberger to satisfy the demand.

Born in 1962 in Canada, Heiss aspired to winemaking after his parents, professional hairdressers in Edmonton, settled in the Okanagan in 1972 to grow grapes. Young George went to Germany when he was eighteen to apprentice as a winemaker and came back in 1984 with a diploma from Weinsberg, a practical school for winemakers in southern Germany. Tall, dark and self-effacing, Heiss promptly settled down to a quiet career of making juicy wines with Gray Monk's grapes. Initially ill at ease in public, the experience of accepting awards for his wines has relaxed him somewhat. Notable for its consistency, Rotberger has been one of those prize winners. Usually, the medals have been bronze or silver rather than gold—perhaps because rosé wines, however pleasing to drink, seldom get the acclaim they deserve.

Straightforward in the vineyard, Rotberger is a mid- to late-season variety, ripening about the same time as Riesling. The large berries of Rotberger, when ripe, are dark purple; all the colour is in the skins while the flesh is colourless. Heiss crushes the grapes and begins fermentation immediately on the skins. The hue of the wine is the colour released in the first day; and there is no point leaving the juice on the skins beyond that because the tone will not deepen and may actually begin to brown. What Heiss wants, and invariably gets, is a lively cranberry shade that is achieved by pressing the must after that first day of fermentation and completing the process in stainless steel. "I try to keep it cool," he says. "If it gets too hot, it can lose too much fruitiness."

Fruitiness is the essence of this wine which, when fermentation ends, has no more than 10 or 11 percent alcohol and retains a touch of residual sweetness. "Rotberger has the Riesling acidity," he notes. "The acidity would be too strong to finish it off in a dry style. I find that extra little bit of sweetness brings out the fruitiness as well." The wines usually are ready to be released nine months after harvest. They should be enjoyed when they are fresh and are not designed for long cellaring.

Heiss says simply that it is a wine "for light occasions." He likes it with turkey because he finds a hint of cranberry in the flavour of the wine as well as in the colour. He also has enjoyed it with such dishes as shrimp in pesto sauce. "I was quite amazed at how those two worked together," he recalls. Some wine writers have described Rotberger as a picnic wine. Heiss also accepts that. "It's light and refreshing," he says.

ROUGEON

RED TABLE WINE This French hybrid originally was known only as Seibel 5898—the name of the plant breeder and the number assigned to the cross. The name Rougeon was assigned to it in the 1960s by growers in New York State; and was adopted in Ontario. Wineries in both jurisdictions wanted a commercially viable name under which to release a varietal. The name presumably was inspired by the dark red colour of the grape. The wine is medium- to full-bodied with berry notes. An uncomplicated wine, this is a robust barbecue partner. Calona winemaker Howard Soon says "nothing too fancy" but in the same breath suggests Rougeon with venison and other game.

The Producer

Calona

The Rougeon was one of those sturdy red French hybrid grape varieties brought to British Columbia in the 1960s and 1970s when a young wine industry wanted to notch up the quality of table wines in response to a growing demand for European-style wines. Most of the hybrids ended up in blends of proprietary brands and Rougeon was no exception. The first Rougeon varietal is believed to have been the 1977 vintage from the Claremont estate winery. Since that winery opened in 1978 as Chateau Jonn de Trepanier, its owner at the time, Marion Jonn, would have made that wine. However, former Calona winemaker Bob Claremont, who bought Jonn's winery in 1979, had acquired considerable experience with the variety because Calona and its competitors all blended it into rustic jug wines. "In those days, they did not think that vinifera grapes could make it through the winters and they looked to French hybrids," says Howard Soon, Calona's current winemaker. For more than twenty-five years, Calona purchased Rougeon (and other varieties) from the large vineyards on Black Sage Road, south of Oliver, the source today of quality vinifera grapes. The hybrids from that area, Soon believes, also were among the best grapes then coming into the winery.

Rougeon did not become a familiar varietal at the time for several reasons, including the massive swing of consumers from red to white wines in the 1980s. Calona (and several other wineries) were forced to distill the surplus of reds early in the 1980s, only to see that surplus rebuild because the grape growers could not convert vineyards to white varieties as quickly as consumer preferences switched. By 1988 the winery had more than fifty thousand gallons of Rougeon (among other hybrid varieties) from the vintages of 1986, 1987 and 1988 stored in its vast thirteen-thousand-gallon American oak tanks. After that harvest, Rougeon was one of those varieties that was almost eradicated from the Okanagan in the vine pull that paved the way for the conversion to premium European varieties.

A strange thing happened with Rougeon. Calona released some as a vintage-dated varietal and the wine, having benefited from its extended storage in oak, began to win awards at wine competitions and acclaim from consumers with a taste for robust reds. Then the medical and the general press began trumpeting the claimed coronary benefit of drinking red and consumers swiftly returned to red wines. Calona's Rougeon now became the largest selling VQA red. "It drove our competitors crazy," Soon chuckles. A franchise had developed for the wine—but the franchise was supported only by the diminishing stocks in Calona's tanks.

The large vineyards on Black Sage Road south of Oliver all had been replanted by new owners after the 1988 vine pull and Rougeon was not in anyone's plans. One of the new Black Sage properties was the twenty-five-acre Mistral Vineyards, developed since 1993 as a vigorous retirement project by Robert and Jenny White. At the urging of Calona's Soon, the Whites agreed to dedicate five acres of their property to Rougeon, propagating the vines with cuttings from a handful of old Rougeon vines that had survived the 1988 eradication on their site. "We can always use it, no matter what," Soon told the Whites, who planted vinifera on the rest of their vineyard. The Mistral Vineyards grapes did not come quite soon enough to prevent Calona from running out of Rougeon in 1993 but the winery was able to return to the market with one thousand cases of 1995 vintage. It sold out in three months, proof that the franchise remains.

"We're getting really dark, inky grapes," says Soon, in a note of vindication for having encouraged the novice Whites to plant the variety. They are growing better grapes than he was used to seeing in the 1980s, attributable to viticultural practices similar to the disciplined manner in which vinifera are grown. "In the old days, I think the growers used to fertilize too much," Soon believes. Mistral Vineyards produces between four and five tonnes of fruit from each acre of vines. "In the old days the yield was probably eight to ten tonnes an acre." Soon's winemaking with Rougeon is entirely straightforward. The wine now does not go into oak, not just because the big oak vats have been dismantled at the winery in favour of stainless steel tanks, but because Soon's aim is to produce an appealingly fruity wine. "It's not a subtle wine, like Pinot Noir," he says. "Ideally, it is dark and inky, with a violet aroma, a good sturdy wine, easy to like. It is best drunk young."

Having re-introduced Rougeon, Soon is certain to move the wine up the quality ladder now that the variety has been rescued from oblivion. He has given thought to barrel-aging and he has begun to apply techniques, such as leaving some bunches whole for fermentation, to finesse even more fruit flavours from the grapes. "If you use these winemaking techniques, you can actually get somewhere with it," he insists. "If you just make it like ordinary red wine, a person might not be as happy with it because it would show hybrid characteristics."

Soon, who teaches wine appreciation courses for novices, believes this is a good "cross-over" wine—"for people who say 'I hear red wine is good to drink but I don't know if I like one.' If I were going to start people on a red wine, I might want to start them on something like Rougeon and then progressively move to something else. It is easy to like up front, being soft, with a nice colour—all of the nice things about red wine that we like."

SAUVIGNON BLANC

WHITE TABLE WINE Even though the variety has shown itself the classic cool climate grape, Sauvignon Blanc has not been grown in British Columbia until recently, much to the disappointment of wine lovers. In France where the variety may have originated, it is the author of Sancerre and Pouilly-Fumé, distinguished and zesty white wines. It is, along with Sémillon, the variety employed for nearly all the white wines of Bordeaux. In the New World, fine Sauvignon Blancs have emerged from Chile and South Africa; while the most brilliant examples have been the highly individual white wines from New Zealand. The hallmark of the variety is a pungent aroma that some compare with gooseberry and a lively bouquet of citrus and melon flavours. Cool climate versions show a piquant acidity. These can be powerful wines, best in their first three years but capable of aging well.

The Producers

Calona

Sumac Ridge

Hillside (first release expected 2001 or 2002)

One of the earliest plantings of Sauvignon Blanc in the Okanagan was in the vineyard high above Peachland that operated for many years as the Claremont estate winery, which opened in 1978 as Chateau Jonn de Trepanier and was purchased the following year by Bob Claremont. It is not clear whether he or the initial owner, Marion Jonn, planted the Sauvignon Blanc. It may well have been Jonn who imported a considerable selection of vinifera vines from Washington State in the late 1970s, including Merlot, Pinot Noir, Riesling and Gewürztraminer. Claremont entered the 1983 Okanagan Wine Festival with what the entry list identified as a 1982 Sauvignon (Fumé) Blanc. That vintage failed to score but in the following year's competition, Claremont won his first gold medal with his 1983 Sauvignon (Fumé) Blanc. That was the last heard from Claremont on this variety. The vines did not survive the subsequent neglect of the vineyard when Claremont and then the successor winery both skidded into virtual bankruptcy.

The variety fell into such oblivion that Sumac Ridge, in releasing its first vintage in 1995, believed that it was pioneering the variety in the Okanagan. With vines purchased from a French nursery, Sumac Ridge planted seven acres of this acclaimed cultivar in its Black Sage vineyard south of Oliver, in part because vineyard manager Richard Cleave is a booster of Sauvignon Blanc. The debut release in 1995 was lively and crisp with a bouquet of tropical fruit flavours, recalling the New Zealand style. The 1996 vintage, with bolder oak flavours, was dry and flinty, recalling a French white Graves. At the same time, Sumac Ridge also began producing White Meritage (a blend of Sauvignon Blanc and Sémillon), beginning with the 1995 vintage. All of these attractive wines—frequent winners of awards—must surely have made Sumac Ridge's competitors regret their neglect of Sauvignon Blanc. It will be several years before another winery is expected to release this variety. In the spring of 1998, Hillside Cellars included Sauvignon Blanc among the forty thousand French grape plants that were ordered for the winery's new vineyard just south of Penticton, a twenty-three-hectare southeastern facing site that had been a pioneer apricot orchard but had lain fallow for almost ten years. Hillside also planted Sémillon, a frequent companion variety to Sauvignon Blanc.

"You may recall that Sémillon has been grown in the valley for quite a while," notes Gary Strachan, the manager of First Estate Vineyards, the current owner of the former Claremont winery and vineyard. "My understanding is that Sémillon is slightly more winter hardy than Sauvignon Blanc, and since the two varieties have a similar vegetal character, Sémillon was the variety of choice for that style of wine. Our understanding of the factors affecting winter hardiness has increased so much during the past fifteen years that the time has probably arrived to re-examine a lot of things that we take for granted. For example, I think we could probably grow Zinfandel. There are some things that have to be handled very carefully to be successful. If Bob Claremont had enough time to play with it a bit longer, he might have been able to grow Sauvignon Blanc indefinitely … who knows?"

There may be another reason as well why the variety, which was introduced into Washington State as early as 1941, was largely ignored when Okanagan growers in the 1970s began thinking about replanting with classic European varieties. Sauvignon Blanc is a French variety while the modern-day advocate of European vinifera here was a German, the late Dr. Helmut Becker. That might explain why obscure varieties like Oraniensteiner rather than an old mainstream variety like Sauvignon Blanc were propagated from the Becker test plots. Ampelographer Pierre Galet describes it as a vigorous variety with early maturity. It is likely that the variety failed in Claremont's cool Peachland vineyard because Sauvignon Blanc does not go easily into dormancy in the fall, making it vulnerable to early frost. In the longer frost-free season at the Black Sage vineyard, the vine is more certain to shut down for the winter before the first frost. The vine's vigour also makes it capable of growing so abundantly that the grapes do not mature properly and the resulting wines can be unattractively vegetal. However, that challenge is hardly beyond today's grape grower who has learned to restrict vine productivity in order to ripen vinifera properly. The diseases which trouble the vine, notably powdery mildew and black rot, usually are not major concerns in the dry Okanagan. There should be more Sauvignon Blanc in the Okanagan.

It is evident from elsewhere in the world that the variety is versatile. Those who eschew oak or cannot afford barrels are able to produce pleasant Sauvignon Blancs with uncomplicated fruit flavours. Those with barrels, such as the fine houses in Bordeaux, are able to make long-lived whites that begin life lean and hard and mellows over perhaps a decade. The use of barrels may also explain why Bob Claremont called his wine a Fumé, borrowing a successful marketing term from California. The term Fumé Blanc for a particular style of Sauvignon Blanc was coined in the 1960s by the Robert Mondavi winery in California to distinguish its oak-aged wine from other, sweeter-styled California Sauvignon Blancs. The idea likely came from the Loire where various Sauvignon Blanc wines are called either Pouilly-Fumé or Fumé Blanc, supposedly because the grape on those soils yields wines with a hint of smokiness in the aroma. In North America, a wine released as Fumé Blanc usually is oak-aged and drier than one called Sauvignon Blanc. There is no firm rule about this. The wine from Sumac Ridge, while called Sauvignon Blanc, is dry and oak-aged.

On occasion, Fumé Blanc wines also include Sémillon in the blend. On that score, Sumac Ridge's Meritage could also be identified as Fumé Blanc for the blend includes about 30 percent Sémillon. "In this wine, I believe in oak and fruit," winemaker Mark Wendenburg says, going on to describes some of the characteristic flavours of the two varieties. "The green bean, the asparagus, the herbaceousness has to come through with the oak undertones. There is supposed to be a balance." The grapes—

and this is true both of Sauvignon Blanc and Sémillon—receive a variety of treatments to give Wendenburg a full palette of flavours for the final blend: some lots are fermented only in stainless steel, other lots are fermented in oak, of which a portion is allowed to go through malolactic fermentation. He achieves a degree of complexity that will ensure the wines continue to be interesting after the drama of the first taste; Sauvignon Blanc's vivid flavours can wear out the wine's welcome if they are overly aggressive.

"I've talked to winemakers in California and they just seem to be tired of it," he says, shaking his head. "It's not high on their list. But it is for me. I think it is a super wine for this area." On the Black Sage site, the Sauvignon Blanc ripens easily. "We believe in getting the Sauvignon Blanc very ripe," he says. "I mean 23.5° Brix." The grape develops lush, intense flavours as it matures. In the winery, the juice is left in contact with the crushed skins for at least twenty-four hours, a technique that extracts additional flavour and the renowned fresh aroma that recalls newly cut grass. It is seldom a shy wine. The maturity achieved by Black Sage translated into a 1996 Sauvignon Blanc from Sumac Ridge with a strapping 13.5 percent alcohol and a 1996 Meritage, in which the Naramata-grown Sémillon portion was slightly less ripe, at 13 percent. The alcohol, he believes, is important for the power of the wine. "It's a bit of a fine line, not to let the alcohol get too high," Wendenburg says. "We can do a lot of things in the cellar, but getting rid of excess alcohol is one of the hardest things to do. Aside from blending, it is almost impossible to do." This problem is hypothetical because the vineyard managers generally deliver grapes that need no extraordinary manipulation in the winery.

Wendenburg gained his initial experience with Sauvignon Blanc while apprenticing at Nobilo winery in New Zealand. "What I really liked was the Fumé Blanc," he says, recalling the interplay of oak and fruit in that style. Now there are hints of that same style in the glass of Sumac Ridge Sauvignon Blanc that he savours with guests at the winery. The wine, fresh and aromatic, dances in the glass with silvery-green glints of its youthfulness. "For me," he says, "it's a bright light. I just like it as a new flavour. It's completely different from anything else that is made in the Okanagan and I think it's a winner."

SCHÖNBURGER

The Producers

Gehringer Brothers
Venturi-Schulze

WHITE TABLE WINE   Created at Geisenheim in Germany in 1979, this is an early-ripening variety and, for that reason, has found its way to vineyards in the Okanagan and Vancouver Island, one of the many varieties urged on growers here by the late Dr. Helmut Becker, the long-time director of plant breeding at Geisenheim. The parents in the crossing include Pinot Noir, Chasselas Doré and Muscat Hamburg. The result is a pink-skinned grape that produces wines with the floral notes of the Muscat heritage. It was initially called Rose Muscat before being dubbed Schönburger, yet another Geisenheim variety romantically christened by Becker to commemorate castle ruins along the Rhine. Schönburg means "beautiful fortress." The vines with their rose-coloured grapes are strikingly attractive at maturity.

Walter Gehringer confesses to what he calls a "prejudice" for his alma mater, the Geisenheim viticultural college on the Rhine, when he explains why Schönburger remains in the Gehringer Brothers portfolio. At another Okanagan Valley winery, the variety simply disappears into the Gewürztraminer tank while Venturi-Schulze has such a minuscule quantity of Schönburger that the wine is almost as rare as that winery's famed balsamic vinegar—and in fact is sold under the nom de plume, Pignoletto. For Walter Gehringer the variety forms part of his emotional link to Geisenheim, where he was the first Canadian-born winemaking graduate and subsequently the most ardent proselytizer of Geisenheim-created grapes in British Columbia.

Aptly named, Schönburger begins to sell itself by being beautiful in the vineyard and carries through to deliver a wine that is pretty when a young damsel but also has a surprising ability to age well. "I just enjoy it as a fresh fruit," Gehringer says. "It's a great table grape if you don't mind seeds. And I enjoy the wine. It is similar to Gewürztraminer. In fact, it has maybe a little more distinctiveness through that subtle Muscat character that comes through." When the variety was added to the Gehringer vineyard, marketing considerations were secondary. "I don't think we were so marketing-oriented as to ask who is going to know what this wine is," he admits. "Yes, it is a marketing challenge. And yet I still believe that, since we are not a winery that wants to grow in leaps and bounds, you *can* establish a market—and that market is not going to be easily taken away from you, once you have a following." The winery produces between

250 and 300 cases of Schönburger each year, selling most of it at the winery but releasing a small quantity twice a year to select liquor stores. "It is a novelty," Gehringer says. If you believe Giordano Venturi, the wine only appeals to part of the market. "That's a woman's wine," he says of Schönburger. "Men don't like it."

In the vineyard, Schönburger suffers from not being hardy in winter. Freezing temperatures have reduced the acreage devoted to it by Gehringer Brothers; even in the Cowichan Valley on Van-

Walter Gehringer

couver Island, where winters are not as frigid as in the Okanagan, Venturi-Schulze has found the variety a challenge to grow. But if the vines make it through winter, they usually deliver mature fruit in mid-season. The sugar content at ripeness has a potential of 11 percent alcohol, at most, while the acidity will already have begun to fall. "I don't get too concerned about that in determining the picking date," Gehringer says. "What I am really looking for is flavour development in the spice and Muscat characteristics and that goes together with colour. It is a very pink-coloured grape." While the colour signals that the grape's flavours are ripe, the hue does not carry through into the finished white wine, even if the juice is allowed to remain on the skins.

Like many Muscat heritage grapes, Schönburger offers a subtle challenge to winemakers. "Most of the Muscats show peak intensity of flavour in the fresh fruit," Gehringer believes. "The fermentation, whether it is ice cold or what, takes something away. The biggest unanswered winemaking question is how can I translate all those spice flavours into my finished wine without losing it." Indeed, the variety has the mischievous ability to turn its charm on and off during winemaking. "Sometimes, as you are going through fermentation, the intensity of flavour is just great," Gehringer recounts. "Then when you finish fermentation and clarification, you say, it's all gone, there's nothing left." Flavour re-emerges about Christmas, only to go mute again for several months. "It keeps you guessing," Gehringer admits. "It takes until May or June for the flavours to unfold." After more than a decade of making wine with the variety, Gehringer has learned to live with the grape's mood swings. "But to have a larger volume or a major brand built on it would be a little bit awkward," he concedes.

The Gehringer Brothers Schönburger, cold-fermented, is finished with about eighteen grams of residual sugar per litre (which equates to a number two rating on liquor store shelves). The trace of sweetness fully brings out inherent tropical flavours of papaya and passion fruit. "It is a wine that is quite distinct in its bouquet and flavours," Gehringer asserts. Yet it is another of those Schönburger paradoxes that this should be so, for the acidity almost invariably is low, making the wine soft. But that is deceptive. Gehringer finds that the first taste impression is of a wine with a short finish while the second impression is of a wine which then rallies flavour compounds that actually carry the wine to a finish. "A second wind of flavour," Gehringer chuckles.

Even more surprising is the ability of Schönburger to age, an unexpected quality, given the modest alcohol and the softness of the wine. Walter Gehringer and his brother Gordon were still enjoying the 1985 vintage a dozen years later. The wine had developed a satisfying richness in texture and flavour to compensate for having lost the freshness of youth. "It comes across as a buttery, nutty Chardonnay, you'd almost think," marvels Walter Gehringer. "The development of flavours that you pick up with age is just off on a tangent, full and rich and positive." But an old Schönburger really is a winemaker's conceit, unlikely to be found anywhere but in the winery's cellar. Most consumers drink the wine soon after purchase when, after all, it tastes most like the fresh pink grapes that Gehringer likes to eat from the vine.

"It's a wine to be enjoyed on its own," he advises. "Being as distinctive as it is, it engenders a lot of discussion. It is a nice wine to pour for an icebreaker to a social event. It also goes well with cheeses and fruits. It would go, I guess, with certain Oriental dishes but it is not as if it is so pungent that you have to be careful about what you pair it with. It is still elegant enough to leave the palate clean at the end."

ST. LAURENT

RED TABLE WINE This grape was formerly grown in Alsace where the deep red juice was useful for adding colour to the anemic local Pinot Noir. It once was believed to be another of the many mutations of Pinot Noir but Pierre Galet, the notable French ampelographer, has dismissed that notion. The variety has almost disappeared from Alsace but now has modest rising importance in Austria in the production of solid oak-aged red wines. The tiny Nichol Vineyard plot at Naramata may be the only one in existence in British Columbia and certainly the only one from which a varietal has been made. The wine is sold exclusively to one restaurant.

The Producer

Nichol Vineyard

Perhaps no one has made a greater variety of interesting wines on a shoestring budget than Alex Nichol. When he and his equally frugal wife, Kathleen, first developed their compact Naramata vineyard in 1989, they scavenged trellis wires from other vineyards that had been pulled out after the previous vintage, a creative bit of scrounging that stretched scarce dollars. Because the Nichols happily agreed to another opportunistic bit of salvaging, their vineyard includes seventy-four vines of St. Laurent. "Serendipity," Alex Nichol laughs, recalling the day when John Vielvoye, formerly the British Columbia government's grape specialist, drove up with some St. Laurent vines that were free for the taking, provided that Nichol was prepared to let other interested growers, if any, have cuttings in subsequent years. The vine, a European vinifera that makes good sturdy reds in Austria, was among many varieties under test in the Okanagan in the late 1980s. Nichol readily agreed to Vielvoye's conditions. As it turns out, there has been little interest in cuttings as growers have opted for better known reds, such as Merlot and Pinot Noir, with which consumers already are familiar.

Initially, Nichol believed the variety would be useful primarily for bolstering colour in other reds. "It comes across as Pinot Noir wearing hiking boots," Nichol jokes about the big, dark and softly textured wine that St. Laurent produces. When his vines began producing enough fruit in the big 1994 vintage, his other reds, Syrah and Cabernet Franc, needed no help to deepen their colour in that super mature year. So the St. Laurent, after a year in French oak, was bottled on its own.

Depending on the year, the Nichol vines produce only enough to make between fifteen and thirty cases of wine annually. Nichol's note on the 1994 described the wine as "full-bodied, brimful of cherry, chocolate, and vanilla flavours." He added: "This wine is built to last and will only improve over time." However, collectors who want it for their own cellars may have a difficult time finding Canada's only St. Laurent. The entire vintage is sold to The Grand Okanagan Resort in Kelowna for patrons in the restaurant there.

SÉMILLON

WHITE TABLE WINE This grape is of major importance in France as a component in Bordeaux white wines and as the grape that produces Sauternes. In British Columbia, Sémillon has a small but promising toehold for the production of dry white wines. Here, the *terroir*—that French phrase that sums up soil and climate—seems to bring out lively grapefruit flavours. The ultimate style of the variety in British Columbia remains to be determined, for most plantings are recent and the winemakers still are refining approaches to Sémillon. Some, like Mission Hill, are blending it with Chardonnay, an approach often found in Australian winemaking.

The Producers

Calona
Hillside
Lake Breeze
Mission Hill

This is a grape with such a vivid personality in the Okanagan that Calona winemaker Howard Soon, who has the most experience with it of any Okanagan winemaker, speaks often of "taming" the variety. "It is reminiscent of New Zealand Sauvignon Blanc," he says of Sémillon, a classic French variety that, perhaps because it is a relatively late-ripening vine, has not been widely planted in British Columbia. CedarCreek formerly produced a Sémillon from grapes produced by Summerland grower Hanna Kirschmann until she removed those vines in 1995 to focus entirely on earlier-ripening Gewürztraminer.

There also is the fact that the variety, although widely grown elsewhere, is not familiar to most North Americans. "It is not a known grape," Soon says of Sémillon. "It is not as common as Chardonnay." That very herbaceousness that reminds Soon of New Zealand requires a modest adjustment from some consumers on first encountering the variety. That alone has made wineries reluctant to have much planted. Whether the variety is released on its own or in blends with Sauvignon Blanc (as in Bordeaux) or with Chardonnay (as in Australia), it is a useful variety that merits more attention. Soon has made what he considers a more interesting wine by blending 10 to 15 percent Sauvignon Blanc into Sémillon; and he also has reversed those portions to add complexity to Sauvignon Blanc. For the 1996 vintage, Mission Hill produced a Private Reserve Chardonnay/Sémillon. The 57 percent Chardonnay in the blend was partially barrel-fermented and went through malolactic fermentation to achieve weight and richness. The 38 percent Sémillon, obtained from vineyards near Osoyoos at the very southern end of the Okanagan, was fermented entirely in stainless steel because winemaker John Simes wanted this portion to retain its untamed fruitiness and acidity, bringing crispness and life to the final blend.

Howard Soon

Calona Vineyards has released two styles of Sémillon, each reflecting a different vineyard. What Soon calls the cool-climate Sémillon comes from an Okanagan Falls vineyard whose rock-strewn gravel soil recalls vineyards in the Graves appellation of Bordeaux, the home of flinty white wines. The descriptors that Soon offers for this wine include lemony and grassy, flavour notes that are carefully preserved by fermenting the grapes in stainless steel. Similarly, Lake Breeze gets its grapes from the winery's Naramata vineyard which would also be considered cool compared with the very south of the Okanagan. The Lake Breeze Sémillon also exhibits the fresh and exuberant fruitiness that some describe as herbaceous or grassy. The vivid charm of this style appeals to many, but Soon, concerned that others might find this sensory wake-up call too daring, has considered some techniques to tame the grassiness. He prefers not to leave the juice in contact with the skins, primarily because this would extract grassiness. He has honed a creative technique for adding a note of palate richness: he allows the Sémillon to remain a month or two in the tank which contains Chardonnay lees.

The other Calona style is a barrel-fermented reserve Sémillon from grapes grown at the Burrowing Owl vineyard on Black Sage Road, south of Oliver. This vineyard is no more than a thirty minute drive from Okanagan Falls but both the soil and the climate are significantly different. "When we talk about ripeness in the south, we're talking high numbers," Soon says as he consults his harvest records. "High alcohols, high brix. Sémillon was 13 percent alcohol in 1996, and that was a cool year." The defining feature of the south Okanagan is McIntyre Bluff, the cliff that pinches the valley just north of Oliver. South of the bluff is Canada's only desert, with deep, sandy soil. On this soil, Sémillon's natural vigour is tamed; the vine does not grow an overabundant canopy of leaves and the berries thus receive good exposure to the sun. The resulting fruit, Soon says, has flavours of melon, "like a green honeydew, with just a hint of grassiness." The added ripeness of southern Sémillon not only subdues the vegetal notes but yields a broader array of fruit flavours. Richer-flavoured Sémillon is well suited to be fermented in French oak barrels, as Soon has done in several vintages. "If I had my druthers and lots of money, I would probably always get new French oak," he says. Among the virtues of barrel-finishing the wine is that this tames the herbaceousness.

The two styles of Sémillon suggest different cuisine choices. Soon recommends the fresh, zesty version with grilled seafood or oysters in the half shell. "It's very much akin to squeezing a lemon over fish." The barrel-finished Sémillon is better suited to dishes like veal with cream sauce—what Soon calls "high-end fancy foods." For its blend, Mission Hill maintains the wine, while easy to drink on its own, pairs well with chicken, seafood, soft cheeses and light pasta dishes.

SIEGERREBE

WHITE TABLE WINE   This German white variety was developed in 1916, a cross of Gewürztraminer and Madeleine Angevine, in a quest for a grape that would ripen early and still achieve a high degree of natural sugar. The scientists succeeded. The grape not only packs a lot of sugar into every berry and but also ripe flavours and aromas. An aromatic wine on its own, the variety also is useful in bolstering the tropical fruit notes in blends. Because the ripe grape is so luscious, the fruit attracts swarms of wasps which suck the juice and leave behind hollow, disease-prone bunches of grapes. When a winery succeeds getting it into a bottle, it is a seductive wine before or after dinner.

Trudy Heiss, one of the proprietors at Gray Monk, declares that the rich and fragrant Siegerrebe is her favourite among the wines made at Gray Monk. "If I were to quit making it," her husband George quips, "I can move out!" On Vancouver Island, Giordano Venturi and Marilyn Schulze also are devoted fans of the variety, one of the major components in a wine they call *Millefiori*, Italian for one thousand flowers, aptly interpreting the aromatic charm of Siegerrebe.

Developed by German plant breeders in the Rhineland, Siegerrebe can achieve such high sugars and intense flavours that wine writer Jancis Robinson once suggested the grape is grown by the sort of "exhibitionists" who might otherwise grow giant vegetables. It is so exceptionally powerful that as little as 10 percent in a blend with Riesling will overwhelm the latter. It should be an obvious candidate for dessert wines but for a failing it inherited from its Gewürztraminer parent: as it gets ripe, it loses its acidity.

At Gray Monk, the Heiss family has about 350 Siegerrebe vines, propagated from plant material the winery secured originally from a test plot at the research station at Summerland. The object, George Heiss says, was to use the variety to add a bit of punch to Riesling wines. But once the winery began releasing it as a varietal on its own, Riesling has come to the aid of Siegerrebe. The latter variety's acidity drops so abruptly when it matures that five to seven percent of slightly unripe Riesling grapes (or unripe Auxerrois on occasion) are added to the crush, ensuring that the resulting wine has the necessary life and balance. Dessert wines without good acidity are simple and cloying.

Curiously, a child of Siegerrebe—the Ortega grape, created by crossing Siegerrebe and Müller-Thurgau—does manage to ripen while still retaining sufficient acidity. Giordano Venturi's *Millefiori* is a blend of Ortega and Siegerrebe, with the former bringing the lively acidity that was missing when Venturi first released Siegerrebe from the 1993 vintage as a varietal on its own. That wine "lacked the full palate and the long finish that one would expect from such powerful aromas," the winery explained in its April 1995 newsletter. The problem was overcome in the 1994 *Millefiore*, a totally dry table wine blended from the two varieties to yield what the winery described as "a heavenly blend of aromas, a full palate and a lingering finish."

Michael Smith and Susan Smith

George Heiss has found it is not a complicated variety to grow in the Okanagan. It is another story on Vancouver Island. The vines are susceptible to mildew and require fastidious spraying with sulphur to get them through the problem. "But the wasps are by far their worst enemy," Venturi-Schulze complained in one newsletter. The wasps "seem totally obsessed by their flavour and can readily pierce their thin skins, leaving a beautiful, empty shell within minutes. From 1991 to 1994, we lost between 40 percent and 70 percent of these grapes to wasps." The grapes usually ripen in late August or early September, right in the peak of the wasp season. Heiss, who also has struggled with wasps in the Gray Monk vineyard, has seen bunches of grapes reduced to the semblance of hollow baby rattles after the insects have gorged on the juice.

The variety suffers the additional drawback of being somewhat difficult for non-Germans to pronounce. It is pronounced "seeger-ray-be" or, if one insists on entirely precise German, *"zee-*

ger-ray-be." George Heiss, who speaks German, notes that "sieger" means winner while "rebe" means vine. To its fans this seductive wine is a winner. "We have customers who are definitely Siegerrebe drinkers," Heiss says. One can see why after reading a breathless Venturi-Schulze paean to Siegerrebe: "The wine it produces can be heavenly, with intense aromas and flavours of apricots and ripe peaches, and if picked early enough, it can display exotic, spicy tones, quite rare in a grape grown in such cool climates."

SOVEREIGN OPAL

WHITE TABLE WINE Technically known as Summerland Selection 166, this variety was developed at the Summerland Research Station and provided to growers for trial in 1976. A grape with a dusty pink skin when mature, it is a cross of Golden Muscat and Maréchal Foch. Calona, the only producer, began releasing a varietal Sovereign Opal with the 1987 vintage. The wine has a fresh floral Muscat character and is best when young. Calona winemaker Howard Soon compares the floral spice to Gewürztraminer and Riesling. Summerland's grape program in the early 1970s generated a number of new varieties with the common Sovereign prefix: Sovereign Gold, Sovereign Tiara, Sovereign Noir, Sovereign Royale and Sovereign Sceptre. Only Opal made it to the consumer as a wine varietal.

The Producer

Calona Vineyards

Nobody but Calona makes this wine. "It's nice to be unique and have the only one," grins Howard Soon, Calona's winemaker. He should know something about being unique: he is the only winemaker in British Columbia who is ethnically Chinese. But having said that, the Soon family has been in Canada a lot longer than Sovereign Opal or, for that matter, a lot of other grape varieties. His grandfather, a shopkeeper, emigrated from southern China in the 1880s. Born in 1952, Howard Soon grew up in Vancouver and graduated in biochemistry from the University of British Columbia in 1974, two years before Sovereign Opal emerged from the research station at Summerland. He spent five years in a Winnipeg brewery before the winters drove him back to British Columbia where he chanced to drop off his résumé at Calona Wines just when Calona needed someone in quality control. He had the best part of a decade of experience in the winery before he met Sovereign Opal.

It was once conventional wisdom that the classic European grape varieties could not flourish in British Columbia. As a result, the Summerland Research Station during the 1970s strove to breed the winter-hardy, early-ripening varieties thought to be suitable. Only Sovereign Opal made it into commercial production. This homegrown variety hangs on in the 1990s because

Kelowna grower August Casorso still is prepared to grow it and Calona still is prepared to make the wine.

"It is not necessarily the ideal grape," Soon admits. The variety in fact is challenging to grow. But once into stainless steel tanks in the winery, Sovereign Opal is transformed into a full-flavoured, fruity white wine. Perhaps because his office is a cluttered mezzanine bunker in British Columbia's most cavernous winery, it takes no prompting at all before Soon leads a visitor out amid the towering tanks to taste the current vintage of Sovereign Opal, direct from one of those tanks. "The 1996 is one of the best we've made," he says proudly, swirling the floral-scented wine in a chimney-shaped tasting glass whose design amplifies the perfumed aroma. That a unique wine like Sovereign Opal has not been abandoned in favour of larger volume varietals and brands is a credit to Calona and to winemaker

August Casorso

Soon. "It's a very attractive wine," he insists. "If people like the taste of Sovereign Opal—it's a sort of Gewürz-Riesling taste—they tend to go back to it. Particularly in British Columbia where some people are not all that comfortable with trying all these different strange [varietal] names. Once they latch onto a wine that they like, they will stick with it. Sovereign Opal generally does not let them down."

The variety is vigorous, perhaps because the research scientists and the growers shared the same 1970s attitude that more is better, even with grapes. At maturity, the thin-skinned pinkish berries have the unfortunate tendency of "shattering"—a term that describes berries dropping from the bunch at the slightest shake. Soon has been in the vineyard when frustrated pickers have rolled wheelbarrows or placed buckets under the vines to catch the cascading berries. Because of its thin skin, Sovereign Opal must be handled promptly in the winery because the berries will begin to weep and the juice will oxidize. Soon presses whole clusters of berries without first crushing them so that the vivid Muscat flavours are not overly accentuated by prolonged skin contact. The juice is fermented in tanks, slowly and at cool temperatures, and the wine is usually released during the summer following the vintage.

Because the variety has high acidity, Soon invariably finishes the wine in an off-dry style. "It has to be," he says. "But because of the acidity, it will swallow up quite a bit of sweetness before you would notice it." As that suggests, the wine's balance is such that the residual sugar is not so apparent and the wine can be enjoyed with meals. Soon recommends Sovereign Opal with picnics and luncheons. "It is fairly strong-flavoured—you can get away with some pretty strong-flavoured foods."

Each year Calona produces about fifteen hundred cases of Sovereign Opal. Clearly, the variety—which has won a number of awards—has a loyal following who agree with Soon that "it is nice to be unique and have the only one."

Thanks to aggressive litigation by France during the past forty years, sparkling wines made elsewhere in the world generally cannot be called *Champagne*. The term is reserved for the prestigious bubblies made only in the Champagne region of France. The producers there, quite reasonably, are protecting a name they have made synonymous with high quality. Sparkling wines made elsewhere by the same basic method of production usually carry different names: *Cava* in Spain, *Sekt* in Germany and *Spumante* in Italy. In North America, the terms used include *Méthode Traditionelle* or variants of that phrase. It means the wines are made by time-honoured techniques of Champagne and, given good grapes and attentive winemaking, also are of high quality. It is the custom to drink these wines at festive occasions but too seldom with food, even though sparkling wines surpass most others in versatility with a wide range of cuisine.

There are days when Sumac Ridge winemaker Mark Wendenburg is only able to shake hands gingerly, if at all. It is not that he is rude; far from it. There are few Okanagan winemakers as amiable as Wendenburg, a large-framed, soft-spoken man with reddish-blond hair and laughter in his eyes. The reason he may keep his big right hand to himself is that he makes the sparkling wine at Sumac Ridge. On occasion, a bottle will explode as it is being handled. Wendenburg has the scars to prove it. Bottles with imperceptible flaws in the glass are vulnerable to being blown apart as the pressure builds during the second fermentation in each bottle that creates the fine and expensive bubbles in Champagne-method wines. Usually it happens when no one is around during the many months when the bottles are stacked in the dark and cool winery cellar. Then, the only evidence of a blown bottle is spilled wine, glass fragments and a void in the bottle stack. Bottles rarely explode, however, which is why Wendenburg and other sparkling winemakers continue in their occasionally hazardous art.

To understand why bottles explode in winery cellars and not at home requires an explanation of how sparkling wines are made. There is no reason for consumers to fear that any of the growing number of fine British Columbia sparkling wines are bombs waiting to go off. The only thing that will go off is the bouquet of flavours after the wines are poured. Any grape, red or white, can be used to produce a sparkling wine, but most such wines are made from one of the following varieties, either together or individually: Chardonnay, Pinot Blanc, Pinot Noir and Riesling. All of these grow well in British Columbia vineyards. Occasionally, an unusual variety is turned into a bubbly, one example being Vigneti Zanatta's Glenora Fantasia which is produced from Cayuga, a white hybrid grape developed at an experimental station in Geneva, New York. The grape's exotic spiciness lends the wine a charm of its own.

Grapes for sparkling wine ideally are picked at slightly lower maturity levels (19 to 20° Brix) than grapes for table wines, for two reasons. First, a higher level of acidity is required in sparkling wines, both to lend crispness to the finish and to keep the wine fresh and lively through the lengthy production cycle. Secondly, the grapes going into the blend, or cuvée, for a sparkling wine must start with a lower potential alcohol so that the finished wine, after the second fermentation, does not have an alcohol level significantly over 12 percent, which would unbalance the wine.

The first step in sparkling wine is fermenting the grapes (almost always in stainless steel) in the same way that any table wine would be fermented. When fermentation ends and the wine is clear, it is ready for the second fermentation which may take place in a large pressure tank but more traditionally, and with nearly all British Columbia sparkling wines, happens in individual bottles. Most wineries here make sparkling wines in such limited quantity—only two hundred cases of Zanatta's Glenora Fantasia are made each year—that large pressure tanks are not required. Sugar and yeast are added starting a new fermentation in each bottle. At this stage, the bottles are sealed with crown caps (like beer bottles) and stacked in a cool dark room. Because the bottles are sealed, the carbon dioxide bubbles generated by fermentation cannot escape and the gas, under pressure, binds with the wine. During this fermentation, the pressure in each bottle can reach six or seven times atmospheric pressure. At this point, the few bottles with manufacturing weaknesses are liable to explode. Once fermentation is complete, the wine rests in the bottle eighteen months to three years in contact with the spent yeast cells where it picks up classic "bread" flavours. Indeed, this time spent on the lees—or *en tirage*, as this period is called—may even be longer. The Summerhill winery, a specialist in bubblies, only released in 1998 a Chardonnay-based sparkling wine that was put *en tirage* after the 1991 vintage, achieving a wine with a creamy texture and toasty, nutty flavours supporting the fruit. The longer the wine spends resting on the lees, the more costly it is to make. This wine, Cipes Gabriel 1991, was priced at $100 a bottle when released.

When the *en tirage* period is finished, the sparkling wine must be "riddled." This is when the winemaker's hands are most at risk. The bottles are put horizontally into individual holes in A-frame racks and, daily for three to four weeks, the winemaker or an assistant gives each bottle a sharp twist by hand, rotating it an eighth to a quarter turn. At the same time, the bottles are gradually moved into neck-down position. Riddling moves the spent yeast cells into the neck of each bottle. (In some very large European and California wineries, mechanical devices do the riddling.) When the yeast cells all have been shaken into the neck, it is immersed briefly into a solution that freezes this residue into a solid plug. Then the crown seal is removed and the pressure in the bottle expels the plug. Coincidentally, this also reduces the pressure in each bottle so that none will explode in the consumer's hands. Each bottle is quickly topped up with wine similar to that in the bottle and then sealed with the familiar mushroom-shaped Champagne cork. Crown caps would be practical but not traditional for prestige wines. Once the wine has rested a few months, it is ready to be enjoyed.

Using a pressure tank to make sparkling wine is called the *Charmat* process, named for the French technologist who invented the method early in the twentieth century. Both the now-vanished Casabello winery in Penticton and Calona had Charmat tanks in the 1970s. Just before leaving Calona in 1979, winemaker Bob Claremont even made a dry red sparkling wine which was released under the overblown label, *Maisonneuve Mousseux Rouge*. Sparkling red wines, which currently have become popular in Australia, seldom have gained a consumer following elsewhere and this one, perhaps years ahead of the market, also failed to win a franchise. At the time the market was infatuated with *Baby Duck* and its many imitators, inexpensive products which, like soft drinks, get their bubbles through carbonation, not fermentation. The Charmat process is a reliable and economic way of achieving bubbles through fermentation but the wines usually lack the complexity or the fine, long-lasting bubbles of bottle-fermented sparkling wines that spent a long period *en tirage*. Nor are Charmat wines meant to. Their role is to provide the sparkling wine experience for consumers on a budget.

Sumac Ridge was among the first of the current generation of British Columbia wineries to commit itself to making traditional sparkling wines, taking part in winemaking trials during the 1980s at the Summerland Research Station. These trials helped Sumac Ridge to settle on a blend or cuvée for its first commercial release, 534 cases, in 1991. Named after the British Columbia provincial bird, the wine is *Stellar's Jay Cuvée*, made from a blend of Pinot Blanc, Pinot Noir and Chardonnay. "Pinot Noir usually gives structure, mouthfeel, creaminess," Wendenburg says. "Chardonnay gives smoothness, flavour, acid. The Chardonnay can often lend a malolactic note. The Pinot Blanc adds more of citrus notes. With the three of them, we are looking for complexity and balance." This wine is finished with a barely perceptible hint of sweetness. Sumac Ridge's other drier sparkling wine, *Blanc de Noirs*, is totally Pinot Noir and typically is a little fuller in texture than *Stellar's Jay*, in part because its time *en tirage,* forty-two months, is a bit longer.

Sparkling Rieslings, in the tradition of German Sekt, were made first by the Summerhill winery for a brand called Cipes Brut, named for Summerhill owner Stephen Cipes. In the late 1980s, Cipes took part in a venture to make sparkling wines in British Columbia in cooperation with Schramsberg, a capable California sparkling wine producer. After the Californians pulled out, doubting enough grapes were available for large-scale production, both Cipes and another participant, Blue Mountain's Ian Mavety, went ahead on their own. Blue Mountain retained a French-trained consulting winemaker to make elegant sparkling wines based on cuvées of Chardonnay and Pinot Noir; sometimes Pinot Gris also is added. Cipes initially settled on a sparkling wine based on Riesling because that variety was abundant in the Summerhill vineyard and because Eric von Krosigk, Summerhill's first winemaker, had just returned from six years of study in Germany, some of it with a Sekt producer. Von Krosigk knew how to handle sparkling Riesling. When he became the winemaker at Hawthorne Mountain in 1994, he promptly launched a sparkling Riesling there as well. Three years later, as a consultant, he guided Pinot Reach and Hillside Cellars to make sparkling wine.

The *Cipes Brut* is Summerhill's flagship wine. "It empha-sizes the great Riesling that is grown here without too strong a varietal character," asserts winemaker Alan Marks, who succeeded von Krosigk at Summerhill. "Of course, we pick a little bit ear-lier for varietal sparklings and you don't develop the stronger varietal characters of Riesling—but we don't want that for spar-kling wine. If it was too fruity, it would not be balanced." Most of this wine is consumed soon after being released but cellaring the wine for a few years will hardly disappoint. "A little bit of the aged character does develop," Marks says, referring to Riesling's penchant to take on what is called a "petrol" note in the nose and flavour after several years. "A lot of people really just love it," Marks finds. "I wouldn't say it is petrol but it has a definite aged character to the wine. It is just different." However, most spar-kling Rieslings preserve the crisp freshness of the grape. *Cipes Brut* spends only about twelve months *en tirage*, rather than the three to five years common with other bubblies. "Riesling doesn't seem to benefit by leaving it three, four years on the lees," Marks believes. "You don't seem to gain much by doing that."

From the very start, however, Summerhill also laid down cuvées, or blends, of sparkling wine based on what the French would consider traditional varieties. In 1997 the winery released *Cipes Aurora* 1992, based on a blend of Chardonnay and Pinot Blanc, followed by the 1991 *Cipes Gabriel*. Marks has put aside similar cuvées to the Aurora in subsequent years, typically as-sembled with 60 percent Chardonnay, 30 percent Pinot Noir and 10 percent Pinot Meunier, a classic Champagne formula. "It is nice to be able to do that every year and leave those on the yeast for three, four, even five years and get something very nice and rich and creamy in, for want of a better word, the true Cham-pagne style," he says. "Some people like that style and others don't, which is why we will always keep the Cipes line which emphasizes the fruit and the freshness." One of the more original sparkling wines produced at Summerhill is *Cipes Demi Sec*, a wine deliberately sweetened with icewine—not to the point of being obviously sweet but enough to give the wine a weight and a fresh, fruity aroma.

Summerhill also produces a pink sparkling wine, a Pinot Noir Brut. "That's very popular," Marks says, adding, "In a lot of Champagne houses, the Brut Rosés are a prestige product. A lot

of the houses are proud of their rosé sparklers—and we are, too."
The clones of Pinot Noir at the Summerhill vineyard are Champagne clones, well suited for making such sparkling wines. "I'd like to make it all into sparkling," Marks confesses, "but red wine demand is so high that I cannot ignore red wine production." The cuvée for the Pinot Noir Brut spends six to eighteen months on the yeast lees, with careful monitoring. "You want the raspberry and the berry fruit of the Pinot to come out," Marks says. "You don't want to overshadow that too much."

The mystique of making bubblies has captured the imagination of other winemakers as well. "I want to do a lot of different sparkling wines," confesses Loretta Zanatta, whose graduate degree in enology from an Italian university included practical experience making sparkling wine at a firm owned by a relative in northern Italy. When Vigneti Zanatta opened in 1992 near Duncan on Vancouver Island, the debut wines were a dry white table wine from the Ortega grape and the sparkling wine made from Cayuga and called *Glenora Fantasia*, Glenora being the name of the rural community in which the Zanatta vineyard and winery are located. The small planting of Cayuga—less than an acre—is believed to be the only significant planting of this variety in British Columbia. It is an American hybrid released in 1973 by the Geneva experimental station in New York State and draws its name from the nearby Cayuga Lake in the state's Finger Lakes winegrowing district. In the Zanatta vineyard it produces the desired combination of flavour and crisp acidity to yield a fresh-tasting sparkling wine so admired by its fans that much of it is pre-ordered each year by them.

Zanatta has been experimenting with cuvées of Pinot Noir since 1992, working toward a complex sparkler with a full five years resting on its lees. In 1996 she made five hundred litres which, it if develops as expected, will be released in 2001. "I don't want to release it too early," she says. "Especially Pinot Noir. It is a traditional grape for the traditional method." She also has conducted sparkling wine trials with Muscat and with two less traditional reds, Castel and Cabernet Franc. "I really like Cabernet as a sparkler," she says, noting that the variety also is used to make sparkling wine in northern Italy and is popular. "But you have to like bubbles a lot—and a lot of people don't," she adds, a little surprised that this should be so. "It looks very nice when you pour it into a glass. I like it a lot."

SYRAH

RED TABLE WINE This variety, best known as the author of full-bodied, satisfying red wines, sometimes also is called Shiraz. That was the capital of ancient Persia. It has been suggested that the variety originated there and cuttings were brought back to Europe by the Crusaders. A more plausible theory is that the vine is indigenous to the south of France. Imported to Australia in 1832, the variety has been extraordinarily successful there in the production of everything from sparking reds to fortified Port-style wines. It has been a fast-rising star with wine lovers everywhere in the 1990s who savour Syrah's rich fruit, its often early accessibility and, in some styles, its cellaring potential. "It's definitely a red meat wine," vintner Alex Nichol says, recommending ostrich steaks.

Long before they planted grapes, Alex and Kathleen Nichol, the proprietors of tiny Nichol Vineyard at Naramata, were fans of Syrah-based wines from the northern Rhone and of the richly dark Shiraz wines for which Australia is famed. However, they did not think that the variety would be viable in their four and a half-acre vineyard, even with the rock face at the north end that soaks in the sun all day and radiates it back over the vines at night. Thinking cool-climate, the Nichols ordered early-maturing Pinot Meunier from an Oregon nursery. Except for a handful of vines, the order never was filled because the nursery was frozen out. After the Oregon supplier abandoned the grape business for fruit trees, the Nichols scrambled for an alternative. John Vielvoye, then active as the grape specialist for the British Columbia government, suggested Syrah from Morisson-Couderc, a French supplier from the Rhone that Vielvoye introduced to many growers in the Okanagan. Nichol planted a quarter of his vineyard to Syrah and, since the 1993 vintage, has had the domestic Syrah market all to himself. But far from protecting his monopoly, Nichol provided cuttings to a grower supplying Hillside Cellars, for a plot on a steep slope just southeast of Penticton.

While Syrah is not a cool-climate grape, it is not entirely happy with very high temperatures either, Nichol has learned.

"You can expect a half dozen days where it goes up into the mid-40s," he says of his site. "And that is just too hot. Those plants in July, a lot of them are shut down from late morning until later in the day. It really takes an Indian summer on this site to give us the optimum results." In the vineyard Syrah is tender in winter and a challenge during the season. Its vigorous and floppy habits can cause tangled and shaded growth. Training the undisciplined vines so that the grapes get proper exposure to the sun demands hard and constant toil. Nichol has found that the late-ripening variety responds dramatically to the season. In the 1993 vintage, a relatively cool year, he produced two wines, a light but peppery wine released as *Vin de Nuits* and a barrel-aged red of moderate intensity. That was followed by a blockbuster wine from the very warm and long 1994 vintage, classically rich and expansive with the soft tannins that made the wine accessible by its second birthday, by which time much of the limited production had found its way onto wine lists at a few exclusive restaurants. "That's a mighty hard act to follow," Nichol said later. "Those kinds of vintages don't happen every year." The excellent growing conditions of 1995, when there was a fine Indian summer, enabled him again to make both a dark, barrel-aged red and another peppery light red in the fruity style of Beaujolais. In part because the varietal character was not intense, the fruity wine was released under a cheery proprietary name, *alfresco*. He then suffered a major setback in the winter of 1995-1996 when cold weather froze about 80 percent of the buds. The vines recovered but the quantity produced in the 1996 vintage was less than half of the previous year. "It was a stinking hot July and we didn't get our Indian summer," he recalls. To spread out the limited Syrah inventory, Nichol did not release the barrel-aged version until March 1998, after the *alfresco* had been sold.

And so it is that Nichol has found himself making two distinct styles of Syrah wines. "It's really just in response to the vintage," he says. "What are we going to do?" In cool years Nichol has noted significant differences in maturity on the Syrah rows closer to the rock face and those farther away. In fact, there even are differences between bunches on the east side of the row of vines and the west side. "The side of the row that gets the morning light is riper than the west side," he has observed. "The style of a wine is determined by the growing season. You don't try to create a style different from what the season dictates—otherwise, you are fighting a losing battle."

As a winemaker, Nichol is self-taught but exceptionally well read, having completed a major part of the tough British Master of Wine course in London. He has an eye for detail and a memory that retains what the eye sees. "They talk about Syrah as something you want to be gentle with," he says, drawing on that stored knowledge. "You don't want to beat it up too much." He crushes the grapes minimally so that there are many whole berries in the fermentation tank, a technique to enhance the fruitiness. Until the winery could afford a gentle pump in 1996, the crushed grapes simply were loaded into the fermenting tank by bucket to avoid transferring them by an efficient but bruising pump that had served Nichol through initial vintages at his winery. "We kind of make our wines the way the Egyptians built their pyramids—if there is a labour intensive way of doing it, we'll do it," Nichol laughs. The preferred brisk fermentation is preceded by a cold soak of up to two weeks and is followed by a week to ten days of further maceration on the skins. "More is better," believes Nichol, who aims for robust, full-bodied reds when the vintage lets him. His initial barrel-aged Syrahs were aged as much as sixteen months on oak, mostly used French oak barrels with some American oak. Since 1994, barrel-aging periods have been re-duced as he decided that, sometimes, more is not always better.

For all its challenge, Nichol opted to plant more Syrah in 1997 when he decided to replace the 380 Ehrenfelser vines in his vineyard. He likes the white variety but his customers prefer Syrah. Consequently, he had Syrah cuttings grafted to the Ehrenfelser vines, a viticultural shortcut to convert vines quickly while losing only one year of adequate productivity rather than three or four under conventional replanting. His customers can hardly wait for more of this hard-to-find red.

TRAMINER

WHITE TABLE WINE This ancient grape variety, pronounced "tra-MEEN-er, is thought to be a predecessor of the now widely grown Gewürztraminer. The vine takes its name from the town of Tramin in northern Italy, but even in Italy the variety appears to have been eclipsed by Gewürztraminer, which the Italians call Traminer Aromatico because it is the more aromatic of the two. Winemaker Tilman Hainle says that wines from Traminer are similar to those from its evolutionary mate although Traminer "is usually more subtle, and a little earthier in its aromas." Only Hainle and Slamka Cellars are known to grow it in British Columbia.

The Producers

Hainle Estate Vineyards
Slamka Cellars

Traminer was planted by chance in the Hainle Estate vineyard at Peachland. The Hainle family had ordered Gewürztraminer from Washington State and only discovered a few years later, when the vines were producing, that the nursery had erred and had shipped Traminer instead. The error seems to have turned out for the best. "It's quite a fortunate match-up because this variety suits itself more to our winemaking style," says Hainle, noted for his boldly-flavoured dry table wines. At the Slamka Cellars vineyard on the shoulder of Boucherie Mountain near Westbank, the small patch of Traminer has been propagated from ten plants that Peter Slamka's grandmother brought from Austria late in the 1970s. The circumstances surrounding that informal importation have been forgotten. "They were from certified stock," assures Slamka, who still has winegrowing relatives in Europe. His block of Traminer is the backbone of the winery's popular Golden Harvest blend. "I wouldn't mind making Traminer [as a varietal]," says Slamka, who is expanding his small block.

Perhaps Traminer has lost out to Gewürztraminer because the vine is vulnerable to freezing temperatures, notably on a site as cool as the high elevation Hainle vineyard. In 1990 Hainle harvested over two tons of grapes from his Traminer block. It was then hit hard by the succeeding winter's cold, which killed not only most of the buds but also canes and even trunks of the vines. In 1991 Hainle's Traminer harvest was an insignificant three buckets. Fortunately the wines, which are growing on their own roots, regenerated from the ground up. "They are resilient," a relieved Hainle sighs.

In notes for his 1994 release, Hainle recalls that Traminer is "a very old variety (reputed to originate in the town of Tramin in the north of Italy) which is now quite rare, as it has been replaced by its more aromatic offspring, Gewürztraminer. Traminer shares a similar fruitiness and spiciness with Gewürztraminer, but is usually more subtle, and a little earthier in its aromas." In the vineyard, it is a mid- to late-season ripener but one that always achieves good sugar levels; like its cousin and like other varieties in what is loosely called the Muscat family, Traminer will lose its acidity if it becomes too ripe. In the hot vintage of 1994, Hainle, who always challenges the standard parameters, made what he later called his *tour de force*. The grapes were harvested on October 19 and 20, late enough for the wine to qualify as a late harvest wine, when the grapes were so ripe that the wine achieved an awesome 13.8 percent alcohol when fermented fully dry. Hainle built the personality of the wine further by leaving it for nine months on the lees in stainless steel tanks before bottling. It was then bottled in half-litre bottles, a sensible choice for this powerful wine. "I would accept the criticism that it was a little too soft in acid," he admitted later. However, the alcohol and the concentration of flavours gave the wine considerable staying power. "As this variety ages, beautifully rich nut character develops and the texture becomes more honeyed and oily on the palate," Hainle said, recommending that this vintage could be cellared up to its tenth birthday. Since only 134 cases of the wine were made, it is doubtful that anyone but the Hainle family will still have some resting in cellars in the new millennium.

In a more average year than 1994, the alcohol will be lower but the Hainle style otherwise will be much the same. Hainle leaves the juice in contact with the pink-hued skins of the mature grapes a full twenty-four hours after the grapes are crushed, a technique that extracts flavour and elements which give the wine its structure. "I'm not afraid to let the fermentation temperatures go to $24C° -25C°$," he says. "I want a vigorous and complete fermentation." While some other vintners opt for cooler temperatures and slower fermentations, Hainle, having based the winery's style on fully dry wines except for icewines, wants to avoid the risk of so-called stuck fermentations. (When that happens, the yeast stops converting sugar to alcohol before all of the sugar is consumed.) Before being bottled, the wine is left on the yeast lees for as long as ten months, a technique that fattens the texture of this and other white wines and, because the lees are anti-oxidants, protects the wine against oxidizing. "It helps the overall health of the wine," Hainle has found.

Bone dry does not necessarily mean austere. Because Hainle sets out to use only fully ripe grapes, he relies on the rich and extractive flavours that come from ripeness to take the place of natural sugar in giving weight and length to the finished wine. "The wine has aromas suggesting tropical or soft fruit, with hints of nut," according to the winery's tasting guide for its Traminer. These characters carry through into the flavours.

Traminer calls for ingenious food pairing. "We've had lots of success with sweet vegetables, root vegetables and squash," Hainle says, remembering a butternut squash ravioli inventively created by his wife, Sandra Hainle, that he describes as "just made for Traminer." An imaginative chef despite having practiced law previously, Sandra Hainle has crafted many dishes to show off her husband's wines. "There's another recipe I used often with Traminer, a carrot timbale—a small custard baked in a ramekin," she says. This is made of puréed carrots with cream; the ramekin is lined with toasted hazelnuts, giving the finished product a hazelnut crust, the flavours of which complement the nuttiness of Traminer. "It can take some light curries and Asian spices," Tilman Hainle adds, warning against overdoing the spices in the food. "Traminer is often surprisingly delicate in the aromas."

TREBBIANO

The Producer

Hester Creek

WHITE TABLE WINE This is one of Europe's most widely-grown white vinifera grapes. In France it is called Ugni Blanc and is the primary grape for distillation into Cognac. It also is grown for brandy-making in California and Argentina. Trebbiano's popularity rests in its ability to produce high yields with good acidity, although many table wines made from it are blandly neutral. A late-maturing vine, it is not really suited to the Okanagan but the one vineyard growing it manages nonetheless to produce wines of considerable interest.

The vineyard now owned by Hester Creek was planted initially by Joe Busnardo who, in an effort to discover what would grow successfully, showered a vast array of grape varieties on the site. As an immigrant from northern Italy, he naturally included Trebbiano, Italy's most widely-grown variety. The two and a half acres of Trebbiano at Hester Creek, immediately in front of the winery, is the only such plot in British Columbia and very likely in Canada. The vines are distinctive, bearing large cylindrical bunches of grapes which, when ripe, are the bright golden colour of banana skins. After Hester Creek acquired the property in 1996 from Busnardo (who had operated it as the Divino Estate winery), plans were laid for a significant redevelopment of the undisciplined vineyard. But the Trebbiano stayed and Hester Creek winemaker Frank Supernak decided to double the planting on the existing area, propagating the plants with cuttings from the existing mature vines. The intention is to produce Trebbiano in two styles in most years: a crisply dry white as is commonly encountered in northern Italy and a late harvest wine. "Trebbiano to Italians is like Chardonnay to everyone else," Supernak says. "It is by far their largest cultivar. The wines are very steely, with green apple." He stops himself and chuckles: "I guess I'm describing a Pacific Northwest Chardonnay done without oak."

Supernak and Hans-Jorg Lochbichler, the Hester Creek proprietors, took over the sixty-eight-acre vineyard and winery in June 1996. In what was a difficult year for them viticulturally and commercially, they did not have a great deal of time to think about dealing with the tiny Trebbiano patch. A late-ripening variety, the vine hardly advanced its own cause either that season. "The sugars weren't quite ready," Supernak recalls. "Fortunately, Mother Nature decided what we were going to do with it." The

grapes were still on the vines when winter set in. As planned, Supernak had an adjoining block of Pinot Blanc picked for icewine on November 20, 1996, at -11°C, just about the perfect amount of freezing for icewine. "We forgot all about the Trebbiano," he says. The weather still was cold the next day, but only -5°C, not cold enough for icewine. So the Trebbiano was picked for a late harvest wine which need not, in fact, should not, be as thick and sweet as an icewine. In the cool Hester Creek cellar, the juice fermented very slowly, finishing fermenting on January 8, 1997. "Because of that, we retained a lot of the nice, fruity characters.

Frank Supernak

We had huge honey and tropical fruit notes in the wine," Supernak found. With crisp acidity to balance the inherent sweetness, the wine is immediately appealing. In the Hester Creek tasting room, Supernak has been known to down a glass of it in one swallow and ask for a second glass. "It's a wonderful sipping wine," he says, admiring his own craftsmanship.

There were not too many opportunities for him or anyone else, for that matter, to quaff much of the Trebbiano, for the winery only produced 2,500 half-bottles of the 1996 vintage. Soon after being released in July 1997, the wine won a gold medal for Hester Creek in 1997 at the Indiana State Fair, only accelerating the sales of the wine. It also confirmed Supernak's decision to continue making this unusual dessert wine. "I prefer a late harvest to an icewine," he admits. "For one thing, I don't like getting up in the middle of the night picking icewine grapes. And I don't like pressing it for a day and a half. Late harvest wines are less finicky to make and they turn out, in my opinion, as fruity, as rich, but not as cloying."

The dessert wine serves as an intriguing counterpoint to the dry Trebbiano. For this version, the winemaking is straightforward, with the juice being fermented quite cool in stainless steel. "It's an excellent seafood wine and an excellent pasta wine," Supernak believes.

VERDELET

WHITE TABLE WINE Despite its melodious French pronunciation—"vair-de-lay"—this is a vanishing variety. A French hybrid, it was known originally as Seibel 9110. Formerly, it was one of the most widely planted of the white French hybrids in Ontario. That explains why Okanagan growers also turned to this grape as one of the vines of choice in the 1960s. That and the vine's amiable productivity. In 1993, a generally bountiful year, one small grower delivered an astonishing 120 tonnes of Verdelet grapes from a six-acre vineyard. The resulting wine, of course, was an empty beverage. At best, Verdelet wines range from neutral to fruity, but lack the finesse that the producers can achieve with better white vinifera varieties, provided those varieties are not cropped excessively.

The Producers

Gehringer
House of Rose
Sumac Ridge

This variety is history. Sumac Ridge made its last vintage in 1994, sadly noting in the back label that it was time to say good-bye to an "old friend," a grape from which the winery produced some of its first varietals in the 1980s. The last grower contracted to Sumac Ridge who even had Verdelet in his vineyard was Summerland grower Gerard Moore who, before his death in 1996, had converted most of his vineyard to vinifera. In 1995, the St. Hubertus Estate Winery pulled out a twenty-seven-year-old planting of Verdelet, one of the most mature such plantings in the Okanagan, and replaced it with classic vinifera varieties. Long since dropped as a varietal by that winery, Verdelet had been reduced to a supporting role in a proprietary blend, with the winery turning to purchased grapes once its own vineyard was gone. Another former grower of Verdelet, Paradise Vineyards at Naramata, converted those vines in 1995 by grafting them over to vinifera. The Gehringer Brothers vineyard at Oliver has been a supplier of Verdelet to several wineries but, as the focus has switched to vinifera, portions of that acreage also have been converted.

In its time, Verdelet enjoyed some popularity because it produced generally inoffensive wines clearly more palatable than those made from labrusca-based hybrids which as Diamond and Elvira and arguably more pleasant than Okanagan Riesling, formerly the dominant white variety in British Columbia. The only other French hybrids to rival Verdelet were Seyval Blanc (originally known as Seyve-Villard 5276) and Vidal, both of which are still found in vineyards elsewhere in North America. Seyval Blanc never was planted in any significant quantity in British Columbia while Vidal, despite its suitability for icewines, also has largely been displaced by vinifera grapes.

The most spirited defense of Verdelet comes from Walter Gehringer, one of the most capable producers of white wine in British Columbia who has had Verdelet in the Gehringer Brothers portfolio since the winery opened in 1986. The Verdelet planting, which was about seven and a half acres in 1997, was already in place in 1981 when the Gehringer family bought the property, then entirely planted to hybrids, for their future winery. The Gehringers quickly removed Okanagan Riesling, Rosette and Rougeon but retained the Verdelet. It was a reasonable decision at the time: both Andrés winemaker Ron Taylor, with whom Walter Gehringer worked, and Dr. Helmut Becker of Geisenheim, where Gehringer had studied, offered words of praise for the quality of the fruit from that vineyard. "It's quite easy to grow," Gehringer has found. The variety also is easily overcropped although the price of producing a huge crop in one year is that the vines, needing rest, will produce sparingly the following year. The Gehringers would never let the vines churn out twenty tonnes an acre. However, it is a question how long they are likely to continue growing the variety at all. As the demand for the grapes declines, they have begun to look carefully at replacing the vines with varieties such as Ehrenfelser, Sauvignon Blanc and Gewürztraminer.

"We wrestle with whether we should keep Verdelet or not," Walter Gehringer admitted in a 1997 interview. "This might even be its last year this year." He added a little sadly, "I think the problem is that we are a bit racist as professional people. We don't like its genetic background. As a hybrid, it is considered a second-class citizen amongst the professional public." Even some wine consumers had begun to ask why the variety remained in the Gehringer portfolio. "It is the most intensive, distinctive-flavoured wine that we produce and therefore [engenders] a love-hate situation. If you like those flavours, you'll really love the wine. If you don't like the flavours, then you're really going to hate the wine because it is overpowering. It's just like tarragon or curry—either you like those flavours or you don't." His Verdelet, he says, almost always shows a distinctive hint of banana, especially on the bouquet, with sharp citric acidity.

"It is just an ideal glass of wine to ice right down," Gehringer recommends. "It does not lose a whole world of flavour and because of its crisp acidity, it is a refreshing glass of wine on a hot day on the patio."

VIDAL BLANC

WHITE TABLE WINE This variety arguably makes better wine than any other white hybrid. Even so, it clings to a precarious toehold in British Columbia because the grape yields lusciously expressive icewine. Only one winery releases it as a dry table wine. Whether made dry or as icewine, Vidal's flavours and aromas of peaches and lichees are seductive. Numerous wineries in Ontario and the eastern United States produce Vidal. Even there, the variety struggles for recognition in the face of a consumer bias against nearly all wines from hybrid varieties. Like many hybrids, Vidal deserves some appreciation.

Vidal was one of two varieties (Chasselas was the other) that was being grown in the seven-acre Okanagan Falls vineyard that Larry Gerelus and his wife, Linda Pruegger, purchased in 1992. By the time they launched their Stag's Hollow winery in 1996, all of the Chasselas and three-quarters of the Vidal had been grafted over to Chardonnay, Merlot or Pinot Noir. But with the remaining Vidal, retained primarily for the production of dessert wine, Stag's Hollow carved out a tiny niche for a grape that was never widely planted in British Columbia and now has almost disappeared.

Vidal (the Blanc half of the name generally is not used since the colour of the wine is obvious) has vinifera blood in its veins. One parent is Ugni Blanc, a widely planted white grape in France where most of it is turned into Cognac and other brandies. In Italy, believed to be the variety's ancestral home, the grape is called Trebbiano and the white wines made from it often are light and rather neutral. The other parent in the cross is Seyval Blanc, a French hybrid now grown mostly in Ontario and the eastern United States, usually producing crisp white wines. Curiously, neither of Vidal's parents demonstrates its tendency toward intense tropical flavours.

A late-ripening variety, Vidal is the vineyard's foot-long hot-dog. It produces large pendulous bunches of medium-sized berries so thick-skinned that even the birds pass them by. "That's a real big bonus," laughs Gerelus, whose vineyard is in an area so populated with birds that many of his neighbours net their vines each summer. The thick skin also is one reason why Vidal often is dedicated to icewine. The grapes can be left on the vines very late in the season without deteriorating. Gerelus, in fact, usually does not pick the grapes until the leaves have fallen off the vines, something that happens after there has been a touch of frost. "I haven't experienced it developing nice flavours until it *has* frozen and thawed," he says.

Vidal also is a vigorous vine, capable of producing a prodigious ten tonnes of grapes from an acre of vines, as happened at Stag's Hollow in 1993. Gerelus attributes that yield to the previous owner's liberal use of nitrogen fertilizer on a vine that is naturally eager to grow, given half a chance. "We took the vineyard over on June 12, 1992," he remembers. "I could not walk between the rows, it was so overgrown. I needed a machete to make my way through the vines." Gerelus

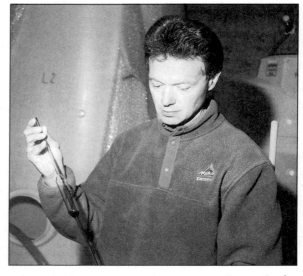

Larry Gerelus

subsequently reduced the use of fertilizer and irrigation water, limiting the cropping levels to perhaps a third of the 1993 output. He aims to achieve more concentrated flavours, especially for the dessert wines that he once intended to make exclusively with his Vidal. He only made a dry table wine when the abundant 1995 vintage delivered grapes with ideal sugar and acidity for such wine. Processing these grapes is straightforward: Gerelus presses the juice from the crushed skins immediately and, after a twenty-four hour period of settling, ferments the clear juice slowly and at cool temperatures. The wine is ready to be bottled and released within nine months and, with its crisp acidity, readily retains its freshness for three or four years. In the 1996 vintage Gerelus blended 30 percent Ehrenfelser into his Vidal. The blend started out as a matter of necessity—he did not have enough Ehrenfelser to justify making a separate wine. "They complemented each other very well," he discovered.

There never will be major quantities of Vidal available from Stag's Hollow or from any other British Columbia vineyard for a sound commercial reason. The bias against most hybrid wines makes Vidal difficult to sell in commercial channels. When Gerelus began sampling restaurateurs, his Vidal always drew compliments but seldom orders. The familiar whites, like Chardonnay, sell themselves from restaurant lists while every bottle of Vidal would need to be talked up by the wine waiter before most consumers would order it; not many restaurants bother listing hard-sell wines. In the winery, however, Gerelus and Pruegger have the time and the knowledge to proselytize their Vidal. In that environment, the wine actually has outsold Chardonnay two to one—and both have been award-winning wines. Will consumers discovered Vidal one day? "I'm hoping, in time ..." Gerelus says, wistfully. "Look what's happening with Foch—people love it!"

Not a subtle wine, Vidal appeals because of its explosive flavours. "Definitely an intense lichee nut character is one of the first major components of [the flavour]," Gerelus says. "There's apricot, citrus; an appley component—and that's the initial flavour profile," he finds. "What happens after you start to taste it is that it becomes a little more herbaceous and even spicy in the finish. There is clove, anise and even a peppery component."

It is a wine that Gerelus and Pruegger have matched with a wide range of foods, including prawns in a Thai curry broth and pork tenderloins with apple chutney. "It's got enough of the spicy herbaceousness in it to hold up to spicier foods. Anything that has a lemon/lime/citrus component to it ... anything that has a bit of sweetness to it like apple chutney. And it works well with most seafood, depending on the sauces." The winery's 1995 Vidal Reserve, while only slightly sweeter, was pressed into service as a dessert wine, in part because Gerelus intends to explore the grape's ability to make several styles.

"I've hedged my bets in the vineyard," Gerelus admits. "I've cropped half the Vidal to a very low level to achieve the late harvest style and left the other portion at a more normal cropping level." He is not inclined to join the icewine sweepstakes, if only because so many already are on the market. "From a consumer's perspective, what I am really going to try to do is create a very intense late harvest Vidal and hopefully keep the price point significantly lower [than icewine]. That's my objective. Whether it is possible, only time will tell. Otherwise, I will make an icewine because Vidal makes beautiful icewine."